The War Correspondent

Greg McLaughlin

Pluto Press

LONDON • STERLING, VIRGINIA

First published 2002 by Pluto Press
345 Archway Road, London N6 5AA
and 22883 Quicksilver Drive,
Sterling, VA 20166–2012, USA

www.plutobooks.com

British Library Cataloguing in Publication Data
A catalogue record for this book is available from the British Library

ISBN 0 7453 1449 X hardback
ISBN 0 7453 1444 9 paperback

Library of Congress Cataloging in Publication Data
McLaughlin, Greg.
  The war correspondent / Greg McLaughlin.
    p. cm.
  Includes bibliographical references.
  ISBN 0–7453–1449–X — ISBN 0–7453–1444–9 (pbk.)
  1. War—Press coverage. 2. War correspondents—Interviews. I.
Title.
  PN4784.W37 M39 2002
  070.4'333—dc21
                                                    2001005062

10   9   8   7   6   5   4   3   2

Designed and produced for Pluto Press by
Chase Publishing Services, Fortescue, Sidmouth EX10 9QG
Typeset from disk by Stanford DTP Services, Towcester
Printed in the European Union by Antony Rowe, Chippenham, England

Contents

To my mother, Maureen,
and in memory of my father, Louis

Acknowledgements

First and foremost, thanks must go to Roger van Zwanenberg and his colleagues at Pluto Press for their unstinting support, encouragement and patience throughout the research and writing of this book. The moral and practical support of all my colleagues in Media Studies and in the Research Office at the University of Ulster was crucially important and greatly appreciated, as was the award of a small research support grant from the Arts and Humanities Research Board.

I interviewed a range of leading foreign and war correspondents for this book and wish to thank all of them for their valuable time and fascinating contributions: CNN's special correspondent Christiane Amanpour, who was on leave but kindly responded to my email questions; former BBC correspondent Martin Bell; Victoria Brittain, deputy Foreign Desk Editor for the *Guardian*; Robert Fisk, Middle East correspondent for the *Independent*; Nik Gowing, Diplomatic Editor, BBC World; Mark Laity, former Defence Correspondent for the BBC and now Assistant Press Secretary, NATO; Jacques Leslie, former correspondent for the *Los Angeles Times* in Vietnam; Jake Lynch, correspondent for *Sky News*; Mike Nicholson, foreign correspondent for ITN; Maggie O'Kane, foreign correspondent for the *Guardian*; independent journalist and documentary film-maker John Pilger; John Simpson, BBC World Affairs editor; Alex Thomson, correspondent and news anchor for *Channel Four News*; and Mark Urban, Diplomatic Editor, BBC2 *Newsnight*. Jamie Shea, NATO's press secretary in Brussels, also gave generously of his time. Thanks also to Steve Bell of the *Guardian* for permission to reproduce a sample of his *If* cartoon strip featuring Kosovo war correspondent Lucan Hardnose.

Finally, writing is sometimes characterised as the loneliness of the long-distance runner. In my case it felt like a marathon twice over, at once painful and exhilarating but made possible and bearable with the constant love, support and patience of family and friends; especially Margery, whose role will always be treasured.

Part I

The War Correspondent in History

1   Introduction

We were called thrill freaks, death-wishers, wound-seekers, war-lovers, hero-worshippers, closet queens, dope addicts, low-grade alcoholics, ghouls, communists, seditionists, more nasty things than I can remember.

Michael Herr, Dispatches, 1978

One of the most abiding images of the war correspondent is of the loner, the existential 'war junkie' who bunkers down at the local Hilton and sends the expense account and the blood pressure of his editor soaring into orbit. As with all stereotypes there is an element of truth in this. William Prochnau (1995) describes the American press corps in Saigon during the Vietnam War and how young, driven journalists like David Halberstam and Neil Sheehan would clash with their newspapers as much over day to day administration issues as over their reporting. Sheehan, especially, came under considerable pressure to account for his day to day expenses but he was too interested in doing the job he was sent to do, which was to describe and explain a complex conflict in which his country was deeply involved. Life in Saigon was too short for paperwork. Whatever their political instincts or ideological position, journalists such as Sheehan place themselves at the very centre of crises and conflicts around the world. Some, like Martha Gellhorn or James Cameron, have passed from us but at their very best they not only provided us with facts and information but more especially what great American sociologist C. Wright Mills refers to as 'orienting values', those 'suitable ways of feeling and styles of emotion and vocabularies of motive' that transform our understanding of a complex conflict into something meaningful, something to which we can relate our everyday existence; styles and vocabularies and qualities that inform 'the sociological imagination'. Yet for Mills, writing in 1959, contemporary American culture – art, literature and journalism – was failing to make sense of the social, political and economic upheavals of the times. 'It does not matter whether or not these qualities are to be found [in culture]', he writes, 'what matters is that [we] do not often find them there'(1959, p.17). This is perhaps too pessimistic even for today. In the midst of mass propaganda in wartime, much of it reproduced uncritically by certain sections of the news media, it must matter a great deal that those currents flow at all, making us see things a different way, making us think about a conflict in terms of history, context and the human cost.

There are moments when we see such potential realised. Polish journalist Ryszard Kapuscinski sees his job chronicling wars, revolutions and coups around the world as not an end in itself: 'For me, events in, say, Iran or Ethiopia, are just disguises behind which I can examine certain universal models.'[1] We look around the world today at the many conflicts and humanitarian crises and we ask how and why and we talk sometimes about our powerlessness, our inability to understand, our inability to take the time to think and relate the horror we see to the circumstances of our own lives. The diagnosis we often hear, from those who want us to believe we do not care, is 'compassion fatigue'. This, says John Pilger, is nonsense. He has great faith in people to respond in even the smallest ways to the extreme situations in which others find themselves around the world, in Iraq or Indonesia or Burma.[2] We need journalists whose writing possesses the vision and sensibility not just to present us with the human picture of war but to confront us with it, to force us to rethink our attitude to it rather than merely react to it, a mode of writing imbued with the sociological imagination. Anne Sebba argues that '[a] good reporter must know how to stand back from the events to be described while a novelist must be able to thrust forward into the heart of his or her character and think for them. Imagination is the prerequisite for one and an encumbrance for the other, but the experience of reporting may provide the stimulus to unlock [our] imagination' (1995, p.6).

In most other significant respects, Mills' indictment of contemporary culture still holds. There are many external and internal forces corroding what imaginative potential might exist in mainstream journalism to make sense of war. The rapid changes in both military and media technologies, the development of sophisticated military public relations, the cult of celebrity journalism: these have all contributed to a crisis in the role and function of the war reporter in the 1990s; these all put into question the ability or willingness of the journalist to be imaginative, to say something meaningful about the nature of modern warfare.

William Howard Russell is known as 'the first war correspondent' but he called himself the 'miserable parent of a luckless tribe'. This book examines what it means to be part of the luckless tribe today. It begins by looking at how correspondents see themselves in terms of tradition and motivation, and then sets their ideas and aspirations, chapter by chapter, against the contemporary realities of modern war zones: the commercial and technological pressures of an intensely concentrated, competitive news media environment, and the seductive power of military 'public relations'. A special case study in military–media relations during NATO's propaganda operation during the 1999 bombing of Yugoslavia and Kosovo suggests that in spite of the criticisms of widespread passivity among the correspondents who attended the daily NATO briefings, some sections of the news media asked the hard questions of NATO strategy and policy. But the book draws on a wider concept of war than just the highly organised and controlled mode favoured by today's global and regional economic powers. Journalists face different pressures and dilemmas when they report civil conflicts such as Bosnia and Kosovo or when they find themselves confronted with genocide in Rwanda. The pressure to put their personal ethics of honesty and conscience above their professional ethic of objectivity and impartiality, to make a clear moral choice between reporting the facts or taking sides or pleading a cause, is one some reporters can withstand and others cannot.

The book draws from case study analysis of war reporting including the Persian Gulf War in 1991, the American bombing of Iraq in 1998, and post-Cold War conflicts such as Bosnia, Somalia and Kosovo. The analysis also draws from interviews with prominent war and foreign correspondents who took time out to give me some fascinating insights into their job and the many contemporary debates that surround it. Since this is first and foremost a book about the war correspondents themselves, it begins by looking at what motivates them to report from one war zone to another all over the world and take the sort of risks that would unsettle even the most hardened insurers. Is it all glamour and excitement? Or is there a deeper sense of history and tradition, of doing something more than simply telling the story of war?

2   The War Correspondent

William Howard Russell is widely regarded as one of the first war correspondents to write for a commercial daily newspaper in Britain. He became famous for his dispatches from the Crimean War for *The Times* and he seemed to appreciate that he was blazing a trail for a new breed of reporter, calling himself the 'miserable parent of a luckless tribe'. Charles Page, an American contemporary of Russell, also seemed to see the miserable side of the job. In an article called *An Invalid's Whims...The Miseries of Correspondents*, he compared himself and his colleagues to invalids, 'proverbially querulous and unreasonable.They may fret and scold, abuse their toast and their friends, scatter their maledictions and their furniture' (1898, p.143). The war correspondent, he warned, 'will inevitably write things that will offend somebody. Somebody will say harsh things of you, and perhaps seek you out to destroy you. Never mind. Such is a part of the misery of correspondents' (ibid, p.146). During the Anglo-Zulu war of 1879, a 'Special Correspondent' for the *Natal Witness* (19 June) complained that '[To] enthusiastic persons, the position of War Correspondent may be a very pretty one...but a little practical experience of such work will rub off a great deal of its gloss' (Laband and Knight, 1996, p.v).

MOTIVATION

So what sort of man or woman becomes part of this tribe? What motivates them to take and accept these obvious risks? Like all journalists, war or foreign correspondents profess a variety of different motivations for doing their job. At a very basic level, the job may satisfy the 'terrible show-off' in a journalist.[1] Some reporters talk about war reporting as 'something in our background, in our childhood, in our upbringing, which makes us feel slightly deficient somewhere, and makes us want to do something where we get noticed' and that requires one 'to be tenacious, tenacious, tenacious to the point of being insufferable, being obsequious, being an absolute bastard' in order to get the story ahead of the competition.[2] For many reporters, most of them men, modern warfare provides the ultimate media spectacle and may even fulfil their dearest *Boy's Own* fantasies. A BBC defence correspondent remembers always being 'a complete fanatic about aircraft, military aircraft in particular'.[3] Richard Dowden of the *Independent* confesses to fascination as well as fear and revulsion: 'Half of me never wants to do anything like that ever again, and another part of me says, "Where's the next one? That was great!".' Tony Clifton, editor of *Newsweek*, compares the Gulf War with sex: it was 'a hell of a lot of foreplay and one final orgasm that lasted eight and a half seconds'. And on a slightly more psychadelic plane, Robert Fox of the *Daily Telegraph*, 'a kid of the sixties...brought up on Camus and the existentialists', admits to 'a mad, depersonalised' sense of excitement, 'the lunatic on the edge...the moment when things come together'.[4] Alex Thomson of *Channel Four News* talks of 'an enormous drive and an enormous excitement and an enormous addiction' to the job. It was the excitement and glamour that first caught his attention when watching the news as a child:

> I watched people do it on TV and I thought, 'Jesus! That looks quite fun!' I mean really if I'm honest with you that is part of the motivation...I think that anyone who doesn't say that being a war correspondent is a glamourous way of making a living is bullshit-ting you because it is and I'm no different from the person out there. You travel to interesting, different places. You are there at moments of history. You are there when...the Cruise missiles come over Baghdad, the Scuds in Dhahran, when the Marines come up the beach in Somalia, when the peace treaty is signed at the end of the Gulf War, when the Marines come into Port-au-Prince, you know, it is a fantastic opportunity, purely selfishly, leaving the job aside, to be at, to be present where things are happening.[5]

Mike Nicholson reported up to 16 wars in his career as a corres-pondent for Independent Television News (ITN). He says that 'the motivation is not that you like going to war, though I do; it's the promise of excitement and...the knowledge and the certainty of getting all the big stories'. For him, the excitement and glamour are central:

> Obviously, travel is the main attraction or was the main attraction...I used to sit there [as a cub reporter] and see these guys going off to Africa or Australia, going off to all these wars and felt very jealous about it as every young blood did and probably still

does. So that was the motivation. I wanted to do all the exciting things I was watching other people do and eventually, and by luck really, it's usually luck, I was given the chance to [report] the Nigerian civil war. And once it's in the blood it's very hard to get rid of...If a company spends a lot of money sending you to foreign places a long way away you can be guaranteed it's going to get pretty prominent place in the running order. So it's also that. You're going to get high-profile. There's that glamour attached to being a foreign correspondent, a roving correspondent, or a fireman war correspondent.[6]

The abiding attraction, however, is a fascination with war:

I like going to war and you have to be very honest about it...which makes you sound rather inhuman; in fact you *do* sound inhuman. And I quite shamelessly remind people of that scene in [the movie] *Patton*,...with George C. Scott, and he goes on top of the hill and after a big tank battle and looks across at the smouldering tanks and he looks up to heaven and says. 'God forgive me but I love it!' And you have to be honest. No use me saying, 'Well, I like to go to these places so that people know what's going on in the world, so that they can stop wars happening, so that the suffering of people can be transmitted to those who can do something to ease the suffering.' All that's part and parcel of the job. Of course it is. But in a way it's incidental. The motivation is that I did get quite a thrill from being under fire, being with soldiers, watching the fighting. It's a very exciting, exhilarating existence and I'd be dishonest if I didn't admit it.[7]

By its very nature, war reporting is also a very hazardous occupation. Writing in 1939, the journalist Wilfred Hindle mused, 'It is not perhaps generally realised that bombs, arrests, and attempted murder are also the things a foreign correspondent may have to face' (p.2). Andrew Lambert has referred to it more recently as a 'fellowship of danger' (1987, p.13) and the risks are all too real. On 24 May 2000, Reuters correspondent Kurt Schork and his colleague Miguel Moreno, a cameraman with Associated Press, were shot dead in Sierra Leone by a band of RUF rebels. Among the outpouring of tributes to Schork, journalists Peter Beaumont and John Sweeney called him 'Brother Number One' among 'brother correspondents'; journalists who stayed behind to report the most dangerous war zones when the celebrity correspondents have long gone.[8] One also thinks of journalists such as Martin Bell who incurred serious injury reporting from Bosnia or Russian journalist Andrei Babitsky who was mysteriously abducted while reporting in Chechnya.[9] Luckily they survived to tell their tale. Others were not so fortunate. St Bride's Chapel in the City of London houses a permanent memorial to journalists who have lost their lives reporting various wars and conflicts around the world. There is a similar memorial in Arlington, Virginia, erected by the Freedom Forum; it has over 900 names of reporters killed doing their job but most striking is the large amount of empty space left for names to be added (Teichner, 1996). These tributes highlight the considerable risks and sacrifices some journalists are prepared to accept when doing their job. Between 1982 and 1987, a total of 273 of them died reporting conflicts around the world (Sussman, 1991, p.195). Bring those statistics up to date and the picture does not get any better. According to journalists' lobby organisations such as the International Press Institute (IPI) in Vienna and the Committee to Protect Journalists (CPJ) in New York, over 700 journalists and media workers have been killed doing their job in the period 1987–2001, the majority of them reporting wars or conflicts of some description. Of these, 60 died in Algeria reporting the civil war there from 1992, most of them local correspondents. Taoufiq Derradji, an exiled Algerian journalist, writes that:

> In Algeria the life of a journalist has become an anonymous fugitive existence. Your day begins with a journey to the newsroom and if you take a taxi, as many journalists do, you change cabs during your trip to confuse anyone who may be following you. You exit the taxi far from the newsroom, so that no one will know that you work at a newspaper or a broadcasting studio. You spend the day at your desk, avoiding public exposure. As the day ends, the pressure of your deadline fades into the anxiety of your trip home and one more circuitous taxi ride. Once you are home you stay indoors. Banks, shops and restaurants are dangerous places: You remember Said Mekbel, editor in chief of the daily *Le Matin*, shot down in an Algiers restaurant. Your entire existence is defined by your home, your newsroom, and the taxi ride between them. (1996)

Journalists in Algeria became, as Derradji says, 'caught between two fires': between the Islamist FIS (Front Islamique de Salut) that regarded them as traitors for approving the suspension of democratic elections and the ruling FLN (Front Liberation Nationale) government that accused the media of giving the FIS undue publicity, thus encouragement to continue with their terrorist campaign. It was a clear choice: 'murder or the muzzle', death or self-censorship (ibid).

Twenty-six reporters and media workers were killed reporting the war in Bosnia, while more journalists lost their lives reporting the crisis in Kosovo than NATO personnel did dealing with it.[10] The IPI estimates that 1999, the year of the bombing of Serbia/Kosovo, was one of the worst years in recent times: 86 reporters died and many more were seriously injured while working in the Balkans, Sierra Leone and Colombia amongst other places. Indeed, the most dangerous place for journalists today is no longer Algeria but Colombia where 24 journalists have been murdered since 1999, mostly in connection with the 'drugs war' and/or political violence.[11] Over 60 journalists have been 'wounded, beaten, arrested [or] harassed' in the Intifada el-Aksa since its outbreak in October 2000 (Bushinsky, 2001). The IPI noted in conclusion that: 'Despite much talk of ethical principles and human rights, the struggle for press freedom still remains a lofty ambition in many parts of the world...There is a fear that we are slipping back into the dark days of the early 1990s when the killing of journalists became almost a routine business for crooks and terror gangs.'[12] Some news managers see it in more pragmatic terms. Jay's Bushinsky's boss at the *Chicago Daily News* reprimanded him for taking unncessary risks in his reporting of the Six Day War in the Middle East, in 1967: 'A dead correspondent is a useless correspondent' (Bushinsky, 2001).

It should be noted, however, that among the journalists and media personnel killed in 1999, 16 of them died in NATO's bomb attack on the Serb TV station in April that year. The IPI noted that the 'misguided and reckless decision of NATO...did not solve the problem of propaganda nor did it prevent the imposition of new legal and political pressures on journalists'.[13] However, when interviewed nearly a year after the event, NATO spokesman, Jamie Shea, claimed that the station was not hit because of its propaganda output, which was considerable if somewhat crude, but because it doubled as a military communications facility.[14] However, the widely shared view at the time was that as a propaganada outlet it was a legitmate military target. Opinion among most journalists was rather muted. Robert Fisk expressed it most strongly when he wrote in the *Independent*: 'Once you kill people because you don't like what they say, you have changed the rules of war.'[15] But Maggie O'Kane, of the *Guardian,* took a bullish, unsentimental view of it:

> People were holding it up as an attack on freedom of speech, on the institutions of the press; it was therefore an attack on democracy. I don't accept that argument because I don't think it was an institution of democracy, I think it was an institution for evil. I think it was one of the main kinds of weapons used by Milosevic, I know it was. So in that context I wouldn't see it as an attack on democracy or journalists and I wouldn't as a journalist feel I should show solidarity with them, although as a human being I'm sorry that people were killed.[16]

News Editor-in-Chief of ITN Richard Tait thinks the 'profession has become unacceptably dangerous' but wants to avoid sending 'a message to the teams on the frontline that we are no longer committed to enterprising, courageous and original journalism' (2001). In response to these concerns, ITN has joined with BBC, CNN, Reuters and APTN to set up a safety group and draw up guidelines on 'assignment, training, protective equipment, post traumatic counselling and insurance' (ibid; see Appendix 1). There are already training courses on offer to journalists in the UK and the US for reporting in dangerous or hostile regions. A company in Britain, AKE, offers a course of between one and five days in length for up to US$1400. According to the IPI, which stops just short of explicitly endorsing the course, around 500 journalists have already attended. Instructed by former Special Air Service (SAS) personnel, participants are trained in the awareness, anticipation, and avoidance of danger; they are also 'team building' and medical training, and coping in extremes of 'weather, disease and war' (see Appendix 2 for the full syllabus). Most reporters, says Lindsey Hilsum, have little time or patience for this:

> We're all supposed to be in danger all the time and we're all supposed to be traumatised and in need of psychotherapy because of all the dangerous things that we do...I mean it's bollocks! We choose to do this and it is sometimes dangerous but so are lots of other jobs. Nobody forces me to do this.[17]

One suspects that all this has as much to do with liable news organisations and their nervous insurers as corrrespondents clamouring for instant-fix training and risk reduction. Most correspondents accept the risks: some celebrate them and others rationalise them in philosophical terms. 'I think I shall take chances all my life', wrote the French reporter Victor Franco, 'it's part of my trade' (1963, p.2). Mike Nicholson talks of 'that fatalism in the people who do the job that I do...the certainty that you're never going to get clobbered. It's never crossed my mind that I'd ever get hurt or killed or wounded in any way...I really do believe in a kind of immortality...otherwise I'd never want to do it again.'[18] Maggie O'Kane reported on the second war in Chechnya for the *Guardian*. Her determination to get behind Chechen rebel lines in the country took her to neighbouring Georgia. There, she spent time making contact with the rebels and persuading them to allow her to accompany their supply run on a hazardous route over the Caucasus mountains, which form the natural border between the two countries, and down on to the open road to the capital, Grozny:

> In order to travel from the border with Georgia in towards Grozny where I was trying to go, you had to travel at night and there was only one road and the road was bombed all the time from the air. So the people I was travelling with who were rebel soldiers, who did the run for supplies, guns as well as medicine, could time when the bombing runs would take place and seemed to know places to hide. There's something very vulnerable about driving along a road or across a field in an open plain and having aircraft above you who are trying to kill you. So that's why I was frightened because I felt that there was nowhere to hide. Sarajevo was very gentle really compared to Chechnya, and that's a hard thing to say when over 10,000 people died there, but you know the attacks were from mortars whereas these planes were dropping 1000 lb bombs. If you're in a field and they happen to drop it near you there wasn't anything you could do whereas in Sarajevo you could get into a cellar and hide...The fear I had in Chechnya was there was nothing that was a target, the whole country was a target, therefore you were completely vulnerable.[19]

There is no doubt that news organisations are thinking twice before committing correspondents to what they see as the most dangerous war zones but such inhibition encourages undue selectivity of stories on the foreign news agenda and distorts the picture of the world we receive. When ABC producer David Kaplan was shot dead in Sarajevo in 1992, his colleague Sam Donaldson talked about rethinking the need to cover conflicts in which American troops were not directly involved. It did not seem worth the risk.[20] Alex Thomson, however, thinks the attraction to the risks and danger of war reporting is crucial if other important but more inaccessible conflicts are to be reported:

> You see, the business of war coverage is that you're always pitting your wits first and foremost against people who don't want you to do your job. And the most difficult thing about war coverage is actually getting to the place were the fighting is happening. And that is becoming more and more and more difficult despite – and this is the paradox – despite the fact that wars are less and less based on a battlefield. If you want to see a good old-fashioned frontal war happening now, probably the only place you'll see it is Eritrea, Ethiopia and nobody covers that. More and more it's happening in towns, in villages, Chechnya for example, and largely against civilian populations and yet the difficulty of getting there is enormous, witnessed by the fact that Chechnya is effectively a secret war.[21]

This is not to argue that all foreign or war correspondents are thrill-seekers, 'parachutists' or 'ambulance chasers' after the quick scoop and then off to the next one. Talk to them at length and they reveal the conflicts and dilemmas that constantly haunt their efforts to 'get the story' more than their more conventional colleagues on purely political or diplomatic beats. Scratch those surface values of excitement, glamour, even danger, and one reveals deeper instincts that seem to almost embarrass the correspondents interviewed for this book. As well as 'curiosity and the desire to tell a story', Christiane Amanpour of CNN talks of being 'further motivated by a deep conviction that the stories I cover are important and absolutely need to be told...stories such as the genocide in Bosnia and Rwanda'.[22] The BBC World Affairs editor John Simpson concedes the importance of a 'serious moral purpose' in one's work as a journalist but insists that he does not see himself 'as being on any kind of crusade to change the world'. The ultimate litmus test for him is telling the story and getting behind the news to look at 'what is really going on...the sort of underside of the whole thing...the submerged realities'. He does not so much go for the breaking news as for 'the sort of grander, broader stories and also to be the sweeper-up who tells you what's happened in places that you might think have dropped out of public attention'.[23]

Maggie O'Kane's sees more to her job than dodging 1000 lb bombs on the Grozny road and living to tell the tale. 'I think in the beginning', she says, 'it was an exciting way to make a living and a very adventurous way to make a living [but] I suppose as I got more into it I began to believe and still believe that you can make a difference'.[24] The desire to 'make a difference', however, is sometimes tempered by a certain battle weariness, especially among more experienced correspondents. Anthony Lawrence (1972) reflects with some disillusionment on what the job of 'foreign correspon-dent' really added up to in the end: 'The rewards are elusive and related to memories. You had a chance to travel to strange places and sometimes have a seat booked in the spectator stands of great events...Then you remember fragments of talk in the small hours...long, deceitful news conferences, the baking concrete of innumerable airports, enormous bedrooms in old hotels; the jungle' (p.9). Reflecting on his reporting of the atom bomb tests on Bikini Atoll in 1947, James Cameron writes of how: 'One had tried; one had travelled 22,000 miles, one had stewed and steamed, one had fought for the words against the clock. But one was only a reporter, not a historian; one had suffered while from the occupational delusion of importance. At home nobody gave a damn' (1967, p.67). Mike Nicholson looks back on his long career and measures the ideals of his job against its potential to change things:

> I actually believe that we are one of the four cornerstones of democracy. It stands to reason. If we weren't here making public some of the misdemeanours of government...and all the other rot-tennesses in society, who would know about it?...One begins one's career as a young man really in a kind of cavalier fashion but underlying all that is a belief that your pen, camera,...your writing can help change the way the world is. By making it public, by showing suffering, by showing war, by showing corruption, by showing misdemeanour,...you're going to help change it. But when the time comes to hang up your boots as I'm just about doing you realise that you've done very little to change the world. All you've really done is to advertise its ills. It's a very sad epitaph.[25]

A few correspondents profess utter confidence in their own convictions. Mark Urban, Diplomatic Editor on BBC *Newsnight* professes to be guided in his work by 'Truth, the belief in the power of truth', even if that means perhaps complicating a delicate political process like the peace process in Northern Ireland or the Middle East.[26]

John Pilger and Robert Fisk have long been thought of as dissenting voices when the flags run full mast at wartime. There is no greater motivation for them than to pursue the truth in their own very different, very individual styles. Pilger applies two principles when reporting wars: 'to report them from the ground up, from the point of view of both civilian and combatants because most wars now are against civilians directly or indirectly', and to reveal the hidden agendas of war:

> It's a wider principle of do you report from the side of the powerful or do you report from the side of people? I think it's a choice many have to face...But I think it's essential to be with those who are either fighting the war, struggling for their lives in the war, or are victims of the war. I think the other motivation is to attempt to explain the war, to deconstruct it, to find out what the real agendas of the war are...The hidden agendas, which are really the truth of the wars, have only emerged later. That is true of all those wars. We've only just found out that the Gulf War was not a war at all, it was a slaughter, and that the reporters were only playing theatrical bit parts in the slaughter, standing on top of hotel buildings, admiring the technology, or being captive members of press conferences, military people showed them video games of people being blown up on bridges...I mention all that because [revealing] that agenda...is the most important aspect of war reporting.[27]

Many of the journalists I spoke to talked about history or, as Martin Bell puts it, getting 'a front row seat in the making of history. There's nothing quite like the buzz of being there when important events are taking place.'[28] Robert Fisk of the Independent sees it as 'a job where we are uniquely witnesses to history' although for him history is something that should also inform the craft of reporting: 'One of the things I always say to some of my younger colleagues when they're going off on a story is take a history book. Don't just go there and report it as if it's a crime story. Take a history book.' When he arrived in Beirut in the 1970s to report the Middle East conflict he did so armed with a good working knowledge of the history of the area and the significance of the conflict that helped explain the reactions and responses and reflexes of the various protagonists:

> I was very conscious from the very start it was not just a story about Arabs and Israelis and conflict over one piece of real estate in particular, Palestine/Israel. It was also about the Jewish Holocaust in the Second World War. It was about the results of the Armenian genocide by the Turks, it was about the carving-up of the Middle East by the victorious Allied powers at the end of the First World War in which my father fought, therefore had a direct connection to Sarajevo. Therefore I was aware when I went to Beirut, for example, that most of the countries which were invented or whose borders were created in the two years after the First World War, ended up with serious internal conflicts: Lebanon, Syria, Palestine, Yugoslavia, Northern Ireland and the Free State. All these borders we drew at the same time had been covered in blood. So when I started in Beirut, even though it was the height of the civil war, which was of course dramatic and so on...I knew at the start I was covering something with enormous historical perspective to it. It wasn't for me something to dip into for a few years and then go on somewhere else.[29]

A perspective such as this brings us closer to a sense of foreign and conflict reporting as part of something more idealistic and serious. Fisk talks of it as journalism as 'a vocation' and describes himself as a foreign correspondent, not a war reporter'. He eschews generalism and careerism in journalism for a lifetime of specialism. 'There's a problem', he says:

> When a journalist starts to rise and he starts writing the truth, he's told that he can't see the wood for the trees. When he's long enough to understand it, he's gone native.Well, I think both of those are rubbish. If you read up properly and start carefully you can be very good from the beginning and you can keep going. And as long as you don't ally yourself with one side or another – and my story's far too risky for any sane person to do that – I think you should stay there. I mean, it's an investment for the paper. I have contacts I would never have if I started anywhere else. I understand the region, the culture and so on...I think in general

it's time that correspondents thought more in terms of career in a particular location and becoming a specialist.[30]

Victoria Brittain's fascination with the Vietnam War was not just its currency as 'the big foreign policy issue' of the times but also because of 'the broader issues [such as] the balance of power between third world countries...and the big powerful Western countries'. This became the abiding specialism underpinning the rest of her reporting career. She based herself in Algiers in the 1970s 'which at the time...was very much the centre of the third world movement – more economic equality and so on. Intellectually, it was a very important influence on the rest of the Third World.' She was able to stop and look with some breadth and depth at 'the whole question of what South Africa was doing to the continent...and more interested in the other countries affected by that'. Brittain returned every year to look and see what was happening in the various countries across the continent. She was astonished at how African countries were under-reported and misreported by the western news media but she found them 'so fascinating I just wanted to know more and I wanted to write more so I kind of got stuck into that'. She agrees with Robert Fisk that in some respects the whole idea of the grounded specialist correspondent in newspaper terms has been compromised by media economics or at least by the pretext that media organisations can no longer afford to commit area specialists to places like Johannesburg and Jakarta. But she also points to 'a kind of a cultural shift', a generation gap in terms of aspirations and ambitions. Young journalists these days 'don't want to take the risk of going off and trying to hack it in some obscure place'. Instead, 'they are so aware that big careers in media now are either made in television or [writing] flashy columns about themselves because that's thought to be a very successful thing to do. I think for my generation what could possibly be duller?'[31]

The idea of the specialist correspondent sits uncomfortably with many news media who see the commercial realities of journalism impinging more and more on their ability to provide and maintain credible foreign news coverage. Alex Thomson thinks that in this respect newspapers have an advantage over television news:

Some newspapers for instance may send their...specialist[s] to those conflicts – he or she will speak the language and be very well versed in the politics and the history traditions of the place. But of course no television company except possibly the BBC can afford that. So I think in terms of the heavy broadsheet newspaper, there is a pool of resources there for indepth coverage and they undoubtedly have more time. They're like me, they've got the luxury of only one deadline a day.[32]

But as Nik Gowing points out, sending the best roving correspondent on a temporary assignment somewhere on the other side of the world 'happens less and less in some ways because more information is coming in more quickly from more parts of the world than ever before from people who are based in the region and therefore you've got to work out where the value added is [in] sending a correspondent and that's a cold calculation that only editors can take'.[33] Yet a foreign desk editor such as Victoria Brittain would also assume a 'facilitator' role – standing by their correspondents, fighting their corner in the newsroom and taking the chill off the 'cold calculations' editors make about budgets and resources:

> I love the correspondents. The best part of my day is talking to the correspondents and trying to work out with them what stories they want to do, how best we can place them in the paper, whether we should be concentrating more on this, more on that and so on...But of course above me is a whole layer of editors who are only interested as you say in budgets and what it's going to cost and do we really need a man in Harare, those sort of preoccupations...It's a very lonely business being a foreign correspondent and unless you're incredibly self-sufficient you need a friendly, understanding presence back at base to help you do those things and I hope that's what I do for a lot of people. It's certainly what I try to do.[34]

The importance of a good relationship between editor and war correspondent recalls the excellent friendship between William Howard Russell and John Delane, his editor at *The Times*. Throughout the Crimean War, Delane supported Russell and protected him from political and military pressures to have him recalled. It was a solid relationship of mutual trust in a powerful institution. Robert Fisk talks of his good working relationship with his editor at the Independent and how important it is to have his friendship and trust: 'Mine's is my friend. I go to see him, I talk to him on the phone, I write to him...The editor must trust you. Don't fight your editor...We also have a lot of readers unprompted who write to the editor saying they want to read Bob Fisk. That helps too. It's very important.' He thinks that is why readers matter, too, but the commercial pressures which the *Independent* has faced throughout its short existence, including take overs and revamps, provides a salutory lesson that the best newspapers with the best specialist correspondents and columnists cannot take reader loyalty for granted:

> When Murdoch deliberately [lowered] the price of *The Times* using money from elsewhere in his conglomerate, his attempt was to put us out of business. We were selling at 50p so he went down to 30 or 20. And we believed that our readers were loyal. Great readers of the *Independent*! And in one week we lost 20 per cent of them. Our loyal readers decided they wanted to pay 20p and not 50p. Big problem. And you can say we got this right and we got that right, and we tell the truth and we don't go along with the NATO briefings. They left and we still haven't got most of them back because they want a cheaper paper.[35]

Commercial realities such as these rather put into perspective the glamour and excitement of war reporting and perhaps herald a news future in which, instead of sending their best writers and reporters halfway round the world to East Timor or Sierra Leone, organisations simply graze on various inflows of information, from the news agencies and the satellite feeds. Is it possible that we are seeing the end of a tradition of war reporting, a sense and sensibility among some correspondents today that they are part of a line going back to William Howard Russell, Archibald Forbes or Richard Harding Davis?

TRADITION

Walter Cronkite writes that 'nothing in the field of journalism is more glamorous than being a war correspondent' and recalls 'the model of the newspaper reporter dashing from one scene of action to the next, press badge tucked into his hatband, notebook in hand. His mandatory costume reeks of wartime experience – the trenchcoat with its vestigial epaulets' (Stenbuck, 1995, p.viii). This is a rather stereotypical model of the war correspondent, far removed from reality and it is a very male image at a time when some of the highest paid, highest profile war correspondents are women such as Christiane Amanpour (CNN), Kate Adie (BBC) or Maggie O'Kane

(*Guardian*). So when war reporter John Burrowes (1984) dedicates his memoirs 'To reporters everywhere – and the women who have to suffer them', he rather misses the point. There is no doubting that the glamour and excitement of the job have attracted many to the ranks of the 'luckless tribe', regardless of sex or the perceived risks. Yet, among some older, more experienced war correspondents, there is a palpable sense also of being part of the luckless tribe with a tradition and a history going back almost 150 years to their 'miserable parent', William Howard Russell.

It is remarkable to hear 'the luckless tribe' pay homage to the 'miserable parent' 150 years after his groundbreaking dispatches from Crimea. William Howard Russell is still today the reference point for war reporters and foreign correspondents of different backgrounds, motivations and even political outlooks. His reputation is certainly formidable. Alan Hankinson refers to 'the sharpness of his observation, an appraising intelligence which enabled him to find the truth in a welter of conflicting evidence, his broad historical sense of the struggle and the political implications of the events he had witnessed, the courage with which he set down his impressions and judgements' (1982, p.269). Unlike many of his journalist colleagues of the day, Russell was 'serious, not superficial...an observer of events, not a participant'. Opinionated but not prejudiced, '[his] judgements sprang from two strong and complimentary qualities: a realistic view, based on his reading of history and his maturing experience, of the way men and armies and nations behave in moments of stress; and high standards of what constituted decent, civilised, humane conduct' (ibid). This was the tradition many feel Russell set down, 'the uncompromising quest for the truth, and the belief that society can only hope to be just and healthy if it is blessed with an independent and critical and courageous press' (ibid, p.270).

John Simpson is the ultimate public service news journalist and John Pilger the radical independent yet both place themselves in the shadow and tradition of Russell and they do so with considerable admiration. Pilger boasts as a 'prize possession' a first edition copy of Russell's *War Diaries*. Russell was for Pilger and many others the war correspondent, one who 'stuck to his principles of reporting the blunders and the disasters, everything he saw and everything he knew to be true, without fear or favour'.[36] Simpson looks at Russell's reporting in the Crimea 'as being about the ultimate that you can do to cut through the...mystification that any government then or now tends to try to build up around its activities and tell what's really going on. He cut through all the 'gallantry of war' aspect of it, the idea that because the British government was doing something it must be [getting] done in a sensible and rational and good way, and he showed people what the reality was. I don't think there's anything better than that.'[37]

In a study of the 'warcos', the war correspondents who reported on the Second World War, Collier mentions that even then reporters clung to an abiding image of the war correspondent as 'intrepid individualist, long on courage and short on introspection', an image very much inspired by correspondents like Russell and Richard Harding Davis: 'Such shining examples, along with hazy adolescent memories of Tennyson's Charge of the Light Brigade and Kipling's Barrack Room Ballads, had forged the war correspondent of 1939' (Collier, 1989, p.20).

But there are other sources of journalistic tradition that inspire correspondents. For Mark Laity, it is British public service broadcast journalism – 'the style, the careful authoritative style, unsensational, concerned,...just getting it right and eschewing bells and whistles'. Significantly for him, its origins lie in the reporting of the Second World War; all the BBC's war reporters inspired him in his work as the corporation's defence correspondent in the 1990s.[38] Martin Bell looks first to George Orwell whose journalism was characterised 'by plain speaking, by eye-witness and not being blinded by preconceptions' but he also speaks of his admiration for James Cameron.[39] Lindsey Hilsum believes that most reporters like her 'would want to be in the same tradition as James Cameron and Martha Gellhorn...because those are journalists who are honourable, those are journalists who wrote incredibly well and were able to convey things' not normally conveyed by journalist in the war zone.[40] Cameron's name occurred almost as often as Russell in my interviews for this book, a reporter who was controversial only for doing the job he was supposed to do. John Pilger refers back to Cameron's attempts to report the Vietnam War from the North, funding the assignment from his own pocket only to meet with opposition not from the frontline censors but from within the BBC who refused to use his material. In the way he went about getting that footage and struggling to have it aired, Cameron demonstrated 'all the initiative and curiosity and passion and all those things that make up a good maverick reporter'. It is this determination that inspires Pilger and reminds him when he watches journalists regurgitate the propaganda line from Downing Street or the White House that 'it needn't be like this'.[41]

Other journalists are rather more reticent when talking about a specific tradition of war reporting and hesitate to single out particular journalists who have inspired them. They prefer to talk in terms of simply reporting and explaining the story and hoping, like John Simpson and Victoria Brittain, that as a result people will know more about the war in Afghanistan or Sierra Leone. Brittain stresses a 'tradition in which the reporter is of absolutely no importance [where] you certainly wouldn't use the word "I" or anything like that; you're kind of a transmission vehicle'. Nowadays, she thinks, 'there's a kind of a thing about reporters as stars and I'm not that, I'm not that tradition'.[42] Maggie O'Kane confesses some ambivalence about the idea of working within a tradition 'because in a way I think a lot of the journalism...was very inhumane. A lot of the war correspondents were very much part of a particular class and a particular sex and were introduced to the war through positions within the army and military rank. So the accessibility to the story and the way that they did it was something I certainly didn't aspire to emulate because it didn't sound very exciting really.'[43]

There is a possible generation gap here that might even mark the end of tradition in war reporting in the face of new political and commercial realities in journalism. Alex Thomson talks not of some abstract notion of tradition but 'a deep-seated belief [that] any government that is talking to you is likely to be lying to you and that the establishment, the received view, is likely to be a bigger lie. And I think that is true in terms of war as in terms of many other things. Politics, I know, is all we've got but I certainly know that...politicians are not to be trusted, least of all when they're getting involved in the business of killing people.'[44] Mike Nicholson wishes he could look to the work of Richard Dimbleby and James Cameron and say he was part of that tradition but he cannot because unlike newspaper reporting, television, the medium in which he has always reported, has developed beyond tradition in terms of technology and professional practice:

We have to do things that newspaper reporters aren't often called upon to do. They don't need to be at the front line. Because we stand alongside a camera, we always have to be where it's happening, or at least we have to try to be where it's happening, whereas newspaper reporters can actually sit in a bar can't they and pick up gossip, they can go to the AP line, they can talk to us; there's so much the newspaper man can do that we can't do. We simply have to be there with our lens.[45]

Nik Gowing agrees with much of this and warns that the old-style newspaper reporting of James Cameron is impossible for the broadcast journalist today because the technology and the immediacy makes the reporter instantly accountable: 'What you say is heard by people, seen by people, and in a transparent environment they know very quickly if you're not telling the truth, if you're being too florid in your language, you know, embellishing it because it sounds good.'[46]

CONCLUDING REMARKS

War correspondents talk readily and easily about the motives and impulses that drive them to take so many obvious risks to report from the world's war zones, about what fascinates and excites them about what they see as a job or even a vocation. As we have seen, few if any of the correspondents interviewed for this book spoke about it as a 'career'. There seems to be less certainty about the notion of following in tradition, especially among younger journalists and certainly among young television journalists. Correspondents now in their thirties see war reporting like any other type of journalism. It is simply about 'reporting the facts' and 'telling the story' as best and as honestly as they can. The modern war zone is a high-octane, high-risk space in which reporters are susceptible not just to a host of physical risks but also to a range of military, political, technological and economic pressures – the pressure to be selective with the facts, to be more circumspect in comment and analysis, to censor themselves, to accept restrictions on their movements, to submit to the tyranny of the satellite uplink and the demands of the 24-hour 'real-time' news agenda.

3 From Telegraph to Satellite: The Impact of Media Technology on War Reporting

One of the features of conflicts in the post-Cold War era has been their liveness, their status as instant news. CNN, Cable Network News, became famous for its habit of being on the spot at the latest global crisis to report events live as they happen: the Tiananmen Square massacre in Beijing, the East European revolutions, the Gulf War, the August coup in the Soviet Union. And it is this liveness that concentrates the minds of policy-makers, analysts, military and media professionals alike. They have identified something called the 'CNN effect' (Neuman, 1995) or as Martin Bell prefers to call it, the 'BBC effect' (1997, pp.13ff), by which live instant news appears to lead to instant decision-making, instant diplomacy, by the world's most powerful countries. Historical precedent, however, should temper the hyperbole. News of the Crimean War in 1854 reached Britain days, even weeks after the recorded event actually took place because the telegraph was still in its infancy and not yet commercially viable. Yet, nearly one hundred and thirty years later, with the telegraph rendered obsolete by a 'communications revolution', news of Britain's war with Argentina in the Falklands in 1982 reached home days, even weeks after the recorded event actually took place. The Royal Navy had almost absolute control over the movement of journalists and over access to the only effective means of communication, the radio and satellite communications aboard ship.

It is not a simple case, then, of there being a direct line of technological advance from the mid-nineteenth century to the end of the twentieth century but even a brief history of the technologies of war reporting throws up some surprising parallels with today. We look at three technologies in particular. The telegraph is a medium that in today's so-called post-industrial age is barely thought about yet it revolutionised communication in the nineteenth century. Photography and the moving image have had a major role in reporting and visually representing the great conflicts of the twentieth century. The idea that 'the camera never lies' has long been contested but it was held as a central truth when photography and film were first used on a commercial basis as tools of reporting in the Boer War of 1899. Radio was a medium that came into its own in the Second World War and for the first time allowed people to hear the sounds of battle, to experience something of war at first hand. Even today, in the era of digital sound recording, the magnetic sound recordings from the BBC's coverage of the First World War still hold a certain excitement and fascination as authentic records of 'history in the making'. The telegraph, the camera, the radio all had their day on the battle front and each in its own way appeared to bring new qualities of immediacy and authenticity to the reporting of war.

THE TELEGRAPH

The telegraph was invented in 1843 and was initially greeted with some scepticism and resistance among politicians and the press. In 1889, the *London Spectator* lamented the impact of the telegraph on diplomacy and journalism. The editorial complained that 'The world is for purpose of intelligence reduced to a village. All men are compelled to think of all things, at the same time, on imperfect information, and with too little interval for reflection.' The telegraph, it went on, encouraged rumour and speculation and emotionalism in the conduct of international relations: 'The constant diffusion of statements in snippets, the constant excitements of feeling unjustified by fact, the constant formation of hasty or erroneous opinions, must in the end, one would think, deteriorate the intelligence of all to whom the telegraph appeals' (Neuman, 1995, p.19). The armies of the great European powers, on the other hand, viewed it as a communications technology they could deploy to considerable tactical advantage. Diplomats saw the advantages, too, although they were concerned that it was too instantaneous, that it would cut valuable negotiating time and rob them of their power and their sense of indispensability (ibid, p.30).

The status of the American Civil War as the first major conflict to receive comprehensive press coverage was helped by the telegraph. Its use coincided with other developments in transport and technology that speeded up the time it took a dispatch to reach the newsroom from the front line onto the front page. It lent immediacy to reports and therefore made them more valuable in the eyes of newspapers and their readers alike. The importance proprietors attached to coverage was underlined by the level of investment they put in to ensure their reporters were at the front to describe the major battles and strategic developments. About 500 correspondents reported on the war on the Union side alone (Knightley, 1982, p.20). The Confederate states were less well served – their press was much poorer in terms of resources and about thirty years behind the North in terms of technology. This situation was worsened as the South lost ground to the advancing Union armies. Only a few Southern newspapers, such as the *Memphis Appeal* and the *Chattanooga Rebel*, were able to up sticks and retreat with Confederate forces. Some were closed and dissolved by the North but most were forced into increasingly desperate measures to publish; the *Pictorial Democrat* and the *Stars and Stripes* were reduced to publishing on the blank side of wallpaper (ibid, p.25). Yet as Knightley, Neuman and many others note, all this new technology had little effect in improving the quality of what journalists reported. In the American Civil War, Wilbur F. Storey, editor of the *Chicago Times*, ordered his reporter at the front to 'telegraph fully all news you can get and when there is no news, send rumours' (ibid, p.23).

Neuman shows how the telegraph's use during the Civil War gave rise to two famous bylines in the history of the press. The first was 'By telegraph', signalling immediacy and freshness, if not accuracy. (It had the same impact on readers as today's bylines 'Live via satellite'.) The other was the personal byline, 'from our own correspondent', which meant that the correspondent and the newspaper had to take direct responsibility for the story in matters of libel, slander and inaccuracy. As a result, journalists at the front became much more cautious and less direct in their reporting and that to a certain extent suited the military. William Russell found reporting the Civil War for *The Times* a bitter experience and part of his problem was an inability to adapt to this new technology that speeded up communication from the front but shortened reporting deadlines, that put more pressure on the journalist to write concise copy and write it at speed. The new technology therefore encouraged the development of a new style of journalism that did not suit Russell and his elaborate narrative style. As press coverage of the American Civil war showed, there was little room in the telegraph age for detailed analysis of military strategy, descriptions of military technology, or careful blow by blow accounts of the major battles.

Alan Hankinson (1982) shows that even when Russell went to report the Franco-Prussian war in 1870, he was still as detailed as ever even though he was being scooped by rival correspondents, especially those that came over from America in numbers. Thanks to the transatlantic cable an account of the battle of Metz on 19 August appeared only two days later in the *New York Tribune*. Such a commitment cost the *Tribune* some US$5000 but it was a sound investment: it boosted circulation and thus profits in an era of intense competition to be first with the news. The London press was quick to learn these lessons. The new style of commercial reporting was cut to suit the demands of the telegraph and the pressures of time and space (ibid p.216). It was an affront to everything Russell had stood for. To the new breed of journalist, 'reporting was a job and a glorious game rather than a vocation'. Accuracy and information were secondary on their scale of news values to being first and being entertaining. They bragged about their 'courage and cunning' and would think nothing of cheating to get the scoop (ibid, p.217).

The instantaneous nature of telegraph communication sometimes meant that the press could scoop governments on news of a particular battle or war. In 1847, the US went to war with Mexico over the disputed territories of New Mexico and California. The fall of the key Mexican stronghold of Vera Cruz was a critical moment in the war but the first President Polk heard about it, says Neuman, not through the War Department, as was the convention, but via telegram from the *Baltimore Sun* – and only then after the newspaper published the story (1995, p.36).This probably exalts the role of the telegraph and the press somewhat. Information-wise, the Polk administration was prone to excessive leakiness and details of peace feelers and draft treaties were already in public circulation (Blanchard, 1992, pp.7ff). The Spanish–American War of 1898 was a conflict that saw the worst excesses of the popular yellow press – the coverage was sensationalised and inaccurate and reporters had an inflated sense of self-importance, of their influence on policy and power. Most controversial, for example, was the role of William Randolph Hearst, owner of the *New York Journal* and immortalised by Orson Welles in the movie *Citizen Kane*. Much like Rupert Murdoch in the 1980s, Hearst attempted to monopolise the available technologies of telegraph and industrial printing for competitive advantage; truth and accuracy seldom got in the way. For example, Hearst sent his chief illustrator to Havana to capture some of the action with dramatic images. Days later, he received a telegraph saying: 'Everything is quiet. There is no trouble here. There will be no war. I wish to return.' Hearst telegraphed back: 'Please remain. You furnish the pictures. I'll furnish the war.' At one stage in the war, the *Journal* appeared on the streets with the front page emblazoned with the headline, 'How Do You Like the Journal's War?' (Neuman, 1995, p.43). The war transformed the *Journal's* reputation and circulation figures. In 1896, the paper sold 150,000 copies per day; by the time the Spanish–American War began in 1898, it sold 800,000 copies (ibid, p.45).

The growth and speed of communication via telegraph, and the expansion of the press in Europe and America, were fuelled by the growth in mass literacy and a huge demand for newspapers. War correspondents gained eminence because they provided sellable copy – reports of battles and heroism, most of the time inflated or invented, were immensely popular (Knightley, 1982, p.42). The Franco-Prussian war of 1870 saw the first organised use of the telegraph by journalists to report action from the front. At the instigation of George Smalley, of the *New York Tribune*, they formed a news pool in which they shared the right to use each other's dispatches and helped each other circulate them to the widest possible readership. The scheme worked very well and enabled dispatches to be telegraphed to the US and published within a day or two of the reported event, a tremendous advance on the previous standard of a week (ibid, p.46).

The Spanish–American War also became known as 'the journalist's war'. The conditions enjoyed by reporters were comparable to those prevailing in the Vietnam War – with journalists enjoying tremendous freedom of movement, even in the midst of naval battles. The writing style which had emerged out of coverage of the American Civil War had continued to change and develop in a way that, as Neuman puts it, 'made metaphors of facts and heroes of correspondents' (Neuman, 1995, p.52). There was in its aftermath a sense of unease that the press had exerted an undue influence over the course of the war and even the swashbuckling Richard Harding Davis worried about the speed and seductive power of the new technology. 'The fall of the war correspondent', he said, 'came about through the ease and quickness with which today's news leaps from one end of the earth to the other' via the rapidly expanding telegraph network (ibid, p.53). In the Crimean War, the reporter's dispatches took much longer to reach the front page, usually long after any information it contained could be of benefit to the enemy.

In the Spanish–American War, the speed of the telegraph ended all that and threatened military security.The military responded by tightening censorship. Dispatches from Havana to New York, for example, were in some cases relayed to Madrid, ostensibly for military clearance, but actually as an effective delaying tactic. Harding Davis saw these techniques and devices developed and perfected by the time he went to Europe to report on the First World War in 1914 to such an extent that he declared the end of the war correspondent (ibid).

The telegraph, then, speeded up communication and lent reports immediacy and freshness. It increased the popularity of the war correspondent as hero. But it also fuelled the growth of the popular press and yellow journalism, encouraging a style of journalism that favoured the drama and sensation of war over truth and accuracy. The new technology improved the means of reporting war but not the quality and reliability of the journalism.

PHOTOGRAPHY

The invention of photography and its development into a commercially viable technology of representation brought with it the possibility of bringing to the sensational and invented reporting of the yellow press a 'realistic' or even 'objective' image of war to the public. Without entering into a detailed history here, there are two aspects worth considering: photographic representation of war and the potential for manipulation and propaganda; and the impact of war photography on public opinion.

As William Howard Russell is recognised as the first war correspondent, Roger Fenton is widely regarded as the first photographer of war, if not a war photo-journalist. His photographs from the Crimean War show that 'while the camera does not lie directly, it can lie brilliantly by omission' (Knightley, 1982, p.15). They show a war in which everything is in good order, in which the troops are well fed, and in which officers and infantry mix freely in harmony. They also show the aftermath of battle minus the dead and wounded. After the Charge of the Light Brigade, Fenton wrote how he surveyed the carnage on the battleground and decided not to take any photos. He packed up and returned home, satisfied he had done his job (ibid). However, it must also be noted that Fenton was limited by the technology; photographic hardware in 1854 was still bulky and unwieldy, and limited exposure times made it impossible to capture movement and action within a single frame. Fenton's shots of the 'Valley of Death' in the aftermath of the Charge of the Light Brigade showed a largely empty terrain, clusters of spent cannon-balls the only visual evidence of what had passed.

Images of the casualties of war have always presented a problem for the military censors. Vietnam is often called the first living-room war for the terrible images of death and bloodshed that television brought right into people's homes. But Vicki Goldberg argues that the 'first living-room war' was not Vietnam but the American Civil War because it was brought home to a mass public through the pho-tographic image (Neuman, 1995, p.78). This, as Neuman argues, overstates the case. Photography was not a mass medium at the onset of the Civil War and even when it developed into the twentieth century, it never really achieved the same audience reach or impact as television did in the 1960s. Nonetheless, it added a dimension to the depiction of war that Fenton could not or did not explore. The Battle of Antietam, in the American Civil War, saw 20,000 dead and wounded in one day. The carnage was pho-tographed in explicit detail, showing, as Johanna Neuman puts it, 'bloated, gouged, twisted, grotesque figures in painful demise' (1995, p.78). There was nothing in these images to suggest the glory and heroism of war conveyed in the semi-fictional accounts of so many reporters. Yet these photos of Antietam, and of the war in general, did not turn public opinion against the war. There were no public protests, no political backlash. Neuman guesses that perhaps too few people had seen the photos, as they appeared in the newspapers or in a public exhibition in New York in 1862, for them to have had any real impact. She suggests the possibility that 'photography had to instruct before it could shock [and that] perhaps the emotional content of pictures was a learned response'(ibid, p.79). Such photos did not lead public opinion but followed it; they were viewed in a political context – the public will or lack of it to fight a war. Fur-thermore, memory and experience frame the photograph as much as the photographer. As Neuman puts it, sometime between Antietam and the Second World War 'the public had learned decipher horror, had been trained to focus on grief' (ibid, p.82).

In the two world wars, the military censored war photographers more severely than their reporter colleagues, and the penalties for breach of restrictions were much more severe. The fear was that pho-tographs packed an emotional punch that would weaken public support for the war effort. For example, in the First World War printed publication of material deemed by the military as helpful to the enemy incurred a 20-year prison term. For taking photos at the front, in the initial stages of the conflict at least, the penalty was death (ibid, p.81).

Photography has always been seen as a medium especially prone to cheating and manipulation. One of the most famous but now controversial war photographs is 'Death of a Republican Soldier' in the Spanish Civil War, 1936–39. It was taken by Robert Capa, one of the founders of the Magnum Photographic Agency, and apparently shows a Republican militia man falling to the ground at the instant of being shot. It made Capa famous as a war photographer and has since become an icon of the Spanish Civil War, reprinted countless times in historical accounts of that conflict. In 1974, Philip Knightley challenged its authenticity. What is significant about this photo for him, as it appeared first in *Life* magazine, was its dependency on the caption. On its own, the photo is ambiguous. It could easily be a photo of a soldier who had just tripped and fallen in training. It is blurred and unclear so we are unable to see if he really has been wounded. Only the caption fixes its memory: 'Robert Capa's camera catches a Spanish soldier the instant he is dropped by a bullet through the head in front of Cordoba.' Knightley set out to investigate the exact circumstances in which the photo was taken and discovered conflicting versions. One was that that Capa took the photo by sheer luck during a Republican assault on a Nationalist machine gun position. Sheltering behind a parapet, he lifted the camera up at full stretch and snapped blindly in the hope of capturing some of the action. This would hardly be extraordinary or controversial since much of the great action photography is taken by photographers who are good enough to make their own luck. Other versions of what happened are much more controversial. One has suggested that the photo was not Capa's at all but that of another photographer on the scene, while the *Daily Express* reporter in Spain with Capa at the time, O.D. Gallagher, claimed that it was a posed photo, set up for the photographers when they complained to Republican officers about the lack of good photo opportunities. Capa apparently bragged to Gallagher that the photo was even out of focus, making it look all the more genuine. However, highly respected journalists, such as the late Martha Gellhorn, who also reported the Civil War in Spain, and who knew Capa well, insisted to Knightley that the photo was genuine, that it was indeed a photo taken at 'the moment of death' of a republican soldier (Knightley, 1982, pp.193ff; Brothers, 1997, pp.178ff).

War photography can be used to good effect to represent war in all its horror but it can also be used to select certain truths and omit others, to 're-present' reality in a way likely to change or manipulate our responses to what is being done in our name, to perhaps even influence our opinion. Caroline Brothers looks at the photography of the Vietnam War, the Falklands War and the Persian Gulf War and makes key distinctions between each. The photography of the Vietnam War was, for her, characterised by its 'surfeit of realism', the notion that its stark representation of war helped, like TV images, turn public opinion against the war. In fact, many of the most celebrated photos from the war were not originally taken as anti-war statements. The photo by Eddie Adams of a South Vietnamese army colonel executing a Vietcong suspect (1968) appeared in newspapers around the world, 'firmly embedded in the rhetoric of American res-oluteness' and support for its South Vietnamese client against a ruthless enemy. As the dominant consensus about the war collapsed, the photograph was appropriated by anti-war protesters as evidence of the horror of war (Brothers, 1997, p.204).

Compared with Vietnam, the Falklands War of 1982 was charac-terised by the relative absence of photographic record. The British fleet set sail for the South Atlantic in April that year to retake the Falkland Islands from Argentina which had occupied them and claimed them as its own territory. It took with it a small, exclusively British media pool that included only two photographers. The navy and the military were determined not to make the same mistakes as the Americans in Vietnam and sought to impose strict controls on media reporting. They made the job of taking, developing and trans-mitting photographs especially difficult. For a good part of the Falklands War, remarked Robert Harris, 'the camera might as well have not been invented' (ibid, p.206). Only 202 photographs were transmitted, most of these contrived by the military for propaganda use. One of the most famous and deliberate propaganda photographs from the Falklands appeared in the *Sunday Mirror* as British forces retook the islands. Captioned, 'Cuppa for a Brave Para', it showed the residents of San Carlos welcoming British troops onto the island and appeared to symbolise everything that was British about these distant islands. A soldier stands by a very English-looking white picket fence drinking a very English 'cuppa tea'; an image that provides an instant connection between the Falklands and home, communicating even to the doubters what the war was about (ibid, 208). Most images of battle action came courtesy of war artists but, like the war artistry of the American Civil War, this was very much comic book depiction. It promoted the heroism of British forces and their liberation of British territory from enemy occupation; and it did this by recalling all the old myths of the Second World War – of the Blitz and the Battle of Britain – that were sure to bolster domestic public opinion in support of the war (ibid, p.207).

The Persian Gulf War in 1991 is now thought of as the perfect 'television war' and a case study in what Jean Baudrillard calls the 'hyperreal'. It was a war defined by the manufacture of suitable images, not of what actually happened but what the allies wanted us to believe happened. For that reason, Baudrillard and others have argued that the Gulf War did not take place. What we witnessed was a virtual war, a Hollywood spectacle. We were not allowed to see or know about the death of up to 200,000 people or the untold economic and environmental devastation wrought on Iraq and Kuwait. Throughout the war, technology that made possible almost instantaneous transmission of photographic images was of little use when the US military ground rules for the media explicitly banned 'Information, photography or imagery that would reveal the specific location of military forces or show the level of security at military bases or encampments' (see Appendix 5). Photographers were reduced to taking photographs from approved television footage at the media centre in Riyadh. Only occasionally did we get a glimpse of the reality. In the closing stages of what was euphemistically called the 'land war', a large column of Iraqi soldiers in military and civilian vehicles, most of them conscripts, fled in panic from Kuwait City and up the road home to Basra. It was cut off by the Americans at a place near the border called Mutlah Ridge and wiped out by Apache helicopter gunships in what they called 'the turkey shoot'. There is little photographic evidence of the carnage that ensued except for a gruesome photograph of the charred skeleton of an Iraqi soldier at the wheel of a burned-out army truck. It was published by the *Observer* newspaper in Britain but only after it was clear the objectives of the war had been met. The photograph, therefore, was effectively neutralised by the circumstances of its publication and simply served to illustrate, as picture editor Kenny McGrath put it, that 'war is a terrible thing'.[1] There was, however, military video footage of the slaughter and it was broadcast on television after the war, not on the news but on a programme in the Channel Four science and technology series *Equinox* (May 1991). The footage was taken from the cockpits of Apache helicopters in action at Mutlah

Ridge and its pictures of helpless soldiers being destroyed by missiles makes for chilling viewing. Relating back to the point Brothers makes about the photographs of the Vietnam War, one cannot help wondering if the release of such pictures during the war would have made much difference given the level of public support that had already been achieved by that stage by anti-Iraqi propaganda. Indeed, the demonisation of Saddam Hussein and his army was so effective that it persists in western public consciousness even today to such an extent that the country and its people are reduced to the grotesque caricature of the leader. It is in that context that the US and Britain are able to sustain and legitimise a sanctions regime that has sent the infant mortality rate in Iraq soaring to obscene levels.

Of course we cannot talk about photography here without reference to film and its role and impact in representing the realities of war.

NEWSREEL FILM

The Boer War is said by many to have been the 'first media war', certainly the first major conflict covered by what we now call the mass media: press, photography, and a new medium – film. William Dixon of the Biograph and Mutoscope Company arrived in South Africa to capture the action in motion pictures (Foden, 1999a). These prototype movie cameras were large, cumbersome and static in operation. In *Ladysmith*, Giles Foden's semi-fictional novel about 'The First Media War', Dixon is depicted as a character called 'The Biographer', a man who thinks himself defined by the uniqueness of this wonderful new medium; as if the specialist skills required to handle it set him apart from journalists such as Winston Churchill (*Morning Post*) and John Black Atkins (*Manchester Guardian*), men he spent time with socially as well as professionally:

> The Biographer wished he was elsewhere. These people, these colonels and aides-de-camp,...these civil servants and silver-tongued correspondents...they were like another breed. Even the way they held their bodies was different. Look at Churchill now, for instance, listening as another one of them blathered on. Even when he wasn't centre of attention, he had a patronizing air, a way of holding his head that said, 'I'm cock of the walk'. The Biographer never felt like that. He wished he had his big camera with him; with its armour in front of him – its huge elm-wood box, glass plate and hood – he felt protected, in control, unassail-able. (Foden, 1999b, p.34)

There was no doubt that, in the Boer War, film's time had come as a medium of news and information. But Neuman questions film's 'intersection with diplomacy and war, whether film mirrors truth or illusion, whether filmed propaganda should be sugar-coated or force-fed, whether leadership in an age of film can compete with its power to cast spells' (1995, p.121). In the Boer War, its illusory qualities were more apparent than its potential for authenticity. For the British, one of the problems of fighting the Boers was their invisibility – it was a bush war fought not in the open battlefield but by guerrilla methods of ambush and hit and run. The film cameramen who wanted to shoot pictures of soldiers shooting each other faced the same problem – the lack of battle action to film – so they made it up for themselves. For the still unsophisticated audiences at home, any film footage of the war was viewed as real just because it was film and it made an enormous impact (BBC2, *Timewatch*: 'The First Media War', 1995). For the first time, people were gathering as a public audience to 'watch the news' about a distant war rather than find out about it as individual newspaper readers. It was a new, immediate and collective experience that signalled the advent of the mass media age.

On the whole journalists were divided about film's potential as a tool of news; some saw it as no more than a tool of illusion. In the US, the newsreels brought home to people images of two world wars and are credited with helping to bring about American intervention in each case but they were confections – part news, part entertainment (or 'infotainment' as it is called today). Most newsreel battles were reconstructions, sometimes pure inventions, and they were cut with footage of natural disasters and human interest stories. American humourist Oscar Levant called the newsreel 'a series of catastrophes followed by a fashion show' (Neuman, 1995, p.123). Photography and film supplemented war reporting with images that lent some authenticity and realism, some emotional impact, to the printed word. But military leaders have realised their potential for propaganda and persuasion because of the ease with which the photographic image, still or moving, can be manipulated.

RADIO

Radio was just becoming established as a mass medium when the Second World War broke out in 1939 but throughout the 1930s the BBC had been developing methods of outside broadcasting that involved heavy, cumbersome equipment such as the Blattnerphone in 1931 which recorded sound magnetically onto a large reel of steel tape at 3 ft per second. In 1935, the Corporation experimented with gramophone-like machines that cut grooves on magnetic aluminium discs, instantly ready for playback. This was unreliable technology but it relieved radio broadcasting of the pressure to present every programme live (Hickman, 1995). With further streamlining, they would come into their own during the war when reporters had to relay their reports from remote frontlines like the deserts of Northern Africa. Just months before the outbreak of war, saloon cars were converted into mobile recording studios, featuring a single turntable called the mighty midget, capable of four minutes' recording time. The equipment did not require very much power and the recordings could be played back over telephone lines or even the less reliable shortwave radio transmitter. These studios were in effect the first ever BBC radio cars and they were used to report major events like the Battle of Britain from Dover on the south coast of England. For a major reporting operation like coverage of the 8th Army's North African campaign, the BBC fitted out a large van, nicknamed Belinda, which enabled multiple recordings to be made, transmitted, and broadcast within days. Developments like these helped reporters bring the realities of battle right into the living room with an immediacy and apparent authenticity which the printed word or photograph could never hope to match. Of course, for all its immediacy, for all its apparent authenticity, radio was still open to manipulation and censorship. But from the point of view of the war correspondent it offered a new style in reporting. Just like the telegraph, reporters had to match their style of address to the technology they were using. The telegraph forced the reporter to describe the various battles, and the conditions of war, in a sharper, more economical style. Radio forced the reporter to describe what was going on in a way that supplied the listeners with both words and images with a new intimacy, to communicate with the mass audience and the audience of one at the same time. The CBS journalist Ed Murrow understood this; so did Richard Dimbleby of the BBC. Murrow reported from Britain on the Second World War and was acutely aware that he was being used in a campaign to bring the US into the conflict. He took advantage of the relative leniency shown to American journalists by the censor to consistently remind listeners of the fact and to complain about the quality of available information about controversial or difficult events such as the Battle of the Atlantic or the allied retreat from Dunkirk (Knightley, 1982, p. 224). The BBC's War Reporting Unit made the Corporation's reputation as a serious news provider. Its regular *War Report* programme became essential listening for people with access to a radio and among its most famous correspondents were Frank Gillard and Richard Dimbleby. Dimbleby was present to witness the liberation of Belsen, one of the Nazi death camps, 'the most horrible day' of his life, and his first dispatch from there was deemed so shocking that his bosses back home at the BBC refused to believe it was true at first (Hickman, 1995, pp.189ff). Former BBC radio journalist Robert Fox has argued that the medium never lost that quality and that even by the late 1980s it was still 'the cleanest and quickest medium of serious journalism', a point vindicated by radio coverage of the Falklands War but lost on the politicians and broadcast executives (1988, p.15).

The broadcast potential of radio that made Murrow and Dimbleby famous also made it an ideal, seemingly instant and direct instrument of propaganda. 'Germany calling! Germany calling!' was the call signal of William Joyce, 'Lord Haw Haw', who broadcast crude German propaganda to whoever would listen in Britain. It had limited impact because it was broadcasting to a largely hostile and resistant audience. Fifty years later, in Rwanda, radio propaganda of a more sinister nature played a significant part in genocide. The privately owned *Radio-Television Libre des Milles Collines* (RTLM) was controlled by the Hutu extremists who carried out the slaughter of between 500,000 and 1 million people in a matter of a few weeks in April 1994. Its basic message was that 'Tutsis need to be killed' but it targeted anyone deemed a threat to 'Hutu power', including many Hutu people (Keane, 1995, p.10). Another of its murderous slogans, 'One Belgian Each', went out just days before the torture and murder of six Belgian civilians and ten Belgian paratroopers by the Rwandan Presidential Guard. It also issued detailed instructions on handling weapons and a methods class in effective killing (Misser and Jaumain, 1994, p.74). RTLM was dubbed 'Radio Television La Mort' as its true role became clear although an *Article 19* report has suggested that it did not so much incite genocide as actively organise it; the killing would have gone ahead with or without the help of RTLM (McNulty, 1999, pp.274ff). This is a short-sighted distinction to say the least. Yes, the killing would have gone ahead regardless but it would not have extended across such a wide geographical area and reached such genocidal proportions without the organisational power of RTLM. Organisation and incitement in this case are inextricably bound together; and, in some ways, organised killing on a mass scale is much more the significant crime than incitement. In his powerful account of the genocide in Rwanda, Philip Gourevitch writes that the station's propaganda may have been crude and inflammatory but it acted as an accurate weather forecaster of political developments in the country. It predicted the fate of President Juvenal Habyarimana days before he was killed on 6 April in a mysterious plane crash and hinted that 'there will be a little something here in Kigali and also on April 7 and 8 you will hear the sound of bullets or grenades exploding' (1998, p.110). So when Thomas Kamilindi, a reporter for Radio Rwanda, wanted to know what was going to happen in the wake of the assassination, he tuned his radio to RTLM and kept it tuned:

> The radio normally went off the air at 10pm, but that night it stayed on. When the bulletins ceased, music began to play, and to Thomas the music, which continued through his sleepless night, confirmed that the worst had been let loose in Rwanda. Early the next morning RTLM began blaming [the] assassination on the Rwandan Patriotic Front and members of UNAMIR (United Nations Aid Mission In Rwanda). But if Thomas believed that, he would have been at the microphone, not the receiver. (ibid, p.111)

TELEVISION

It has long been assumed in official quarters that pictures of dead or wounded American troops going out on television screens night after night took their toll on public opinion and turned it against the Vietnam War. As one critic put it, 'for the first time in modern history, the outcome of a war was determined not on the battlefield, but...on the television screen', while the US commander in Vietnam, General William Westmoreland, complained that 'television's unique requirements contributed to a distorted view of the war...The news had to be compressed and visually dramatic.' As a result, 'the war Americans saw was almost exclusively violent, miserable, or controversial' (MacArthur, 1992, p.132).

Those who pushed this view at the time pointed to the anti-war protests on the streets of American cities, even though those protests accounted for a tiny proportion of the population. Lawrence Lichty showed that although 'half of all TV reports filed from Vietnam were about military operations, most showed very little action'. He calculated that in a five-year period, from August 1975 to August 1970, about 3 per cent of all evening news reports from the war showed what he calls 'heavy battle' or footage of heavy incoming fire with images of US casualties: a total of 76 combat stories out of 2300 reports on the war (ibid, p.133). Hallin uses a much broader definition of combat footage than Lichty but reaches similar conclusions. In the period 1965–68, 22 per cent of all film reports from South East Asia included combat footage, and even then it was often shots of troops under fire from a sniper or a mortar position. Hallin also showed that 24 per cent of reports showed images of casualties; in the period 1965–68, 16 out of 167 stories showed a picture of a dead or wounded soldier (ibid).

The sort of coverage the American news viewer became used to is summed up well by Michael Arlen when he describes it as a 'nightly stylised, generally distanced overview of a disjointed conflict' that featured little or no serious combat footage (ibid, p.134). One reason for this was technological: instant satellite links were theoretically possible but far too expensive for even the big American news networks to afford. Journalists in Vietnam had to make do with canning their film reports and flying them back to their newsroom – a procedure that took two or three days. By that time, they were only good for background pieces or as TV wallpaper; and if the viewer ever did see scenes of battle or of war casualties, it was out of context, bearing little or no relation to current events. Richard Nixon remarked that TV coverage of the war resulted in 'a serious demoralisation of the home front, raising the question whether America would ever again be able to fight an enemy abroad with unity and strength of purpose at home' (Cumings, 1992, p.84). However, as the evidence suggests, critical television coverage was minimal and the majority of the population disagreed with the administration's war policy, not the morality of fighting the war in the first place. Public opinion turned against the war in Vietnam because the pro-war consensus among the political elites in Washington broke down. If there was any media effect, it was not the sight of dead and wounded night after night but of politicians appearing on the news debating the war. According to Lichty's analysis, in the period immediately following the Tet Offensive, three TV networks featured a rough balance of pro- and anti-war guests and by 1970 the number of critics exceeded the number of supporters. He concludes that, 'This opinion trend paralleled the trend in the publicly expressed opinions of many senators and congressmen, perhaps because senators and congressmen were so often those interviewed' (MacArthur, 1992, p.136). Hallin found that editorial commentaries on TV shifted after Tet from 4:1 for the war to 2:1 against. These shifts in media orientation away from a pro-war perspective are encapsulated in this recollection from Max Frenkel, executive director of the *New York Times*: 'As protest moved from the left groups, the antiwar groups, into the pulpit, into the Senate...as it became majority opinion, it naturally picked up coverage' (ibid).

Satellite, Cable and the Digital Information Age

The advances in satellite and cable television technology in the 1990s have changed the nature of live news. From being a novelty or special feature for the big set-piece event, the live broadcast from 'our own correspondent' on the spot became an essential guarantor of the news organisation's credibility and status in a hi-tech, competitive media market. The reputation of CNN was made in the late 1980s on its apparent knack of being in the right place at the right time with live, uninterrupted coverage of the most important world events of the period. The quality of its coverage at the time was derided by the major American network news programmes but these criticisms belied a certain nervousness, an attempt to distract from a crucial fact: CNN was there and they were not. The organisation was quick to shed its image as 'Chicken Noodle News' and build on the plaudits it received for its wallpaper coverage of the Gulf War. It continued to beat its rivals to the big stories of the 1990s. Contrast that with the British news channel, Independent Television News (ITN), which suffered in the late 1980s when it missed some big international stories, including the August coup in Moscow in 1991 and the assassination of India's president Indira Ghandi (McNair, 1994, p.93). Taking feeds from television news agencies was not good enough.

For some, the quality of broadcast journalism has suffered as a result of this competition for instant-fix news. In the early days of television coverage in Vietnam, there was the news crew of journalist, cameraman and sound-recordist, all tied to each other with electric cables. In the present satellite and digital age, there is just the journalist and the satellite uplink – no cables – yet the journalist is still tied to the demands of the technology. Brent MacGregor calls this 'palm tree journalism' in which all that is needed is a stand-up journalist and a suitable backdrop or prop to authenticate location and convey immediacy (1997, p. 184). Maggie

O'Kane of the *Guardian* tells the story of staying in an hotel in Srebrenica, Bosnia, during the Serb siege of the city. An American reporter in the room next to her spent his entire working day standing on the balcony doing live, stand-up reports, telling the same story, giving the same information over and over again. But while he was doing all that, where was he getting the time to be a real journalist, to go out into the city and see for himself what was happening?[2] Alex Thomson of *Channel Four News* says that routine television news tends to select a leading story and structure everything around that. Foreign news is no different. 'It's the headline story everyday', he says, and sometimes that is led by technology. He presents the following scenario to illustrate the reporter's predicament:

> You're in Pristina and something's going on and you've got...maybe a hour, hour and a half, to do a bit of filming; smash and grab something, put it together, come back because they want you live at the [satellite] dish for the lunchtime news. Smash and grab, edit, smell of burning rubber, get it over the bird [satellite link], fine! Up to the stand upper (to camera piece); is the hair straight?; tie straight? Great! Mic working? Fine! Fire away! Out again in the afternoon. Maybe you've got an hour, two hours if you're really lucky. Same thing. Smash, grab, live spot...for the 5.40...And then in the evening, fine, there may be nothing going on, or there might be, so you can to some extent recut more leisurely, and they want another live [spot]. How do you do it?[3]

Lindsey Hilsum thinks that ultimately this can only impair the ability of reporters to make proper judgements in complex crises:

> Obviously...if you are under constant time pressure...there is a danger of forming the wrong conclusion and there is a danger of making judgements too quickly because you have to get the story on the air.... So you have two dangers. One is making a wrong call, making a wrong judgement, misinterpreting because you haven't enough time to do enough research. And the second one is lowest common denominator journalism: 'On the one hand this, on the other hand that, I can't quite conclude because I haven't had time to find out. Lindsey Hilsum, *Channel Four News* in the middle of nowhere.' So you have to be very careful about that.[4]

Other journalists are more optimistic about the impact of technological change in the last decade. Nik Gowing is an enthusiastic advocate of the liberating potential of the new media technologies to compress still further the time and space it takes the correspondent to report fast-moving events across the world and to do that on a self-sufficient basis:

> To me it's actually the fascination with the dynamic of how information flows...The technology has arrived. It's cheaper – we can get satellite feeds for £3 per minute now whereas before it was £600 per ten minutes or something...So you've got the compression of the time line between gathering and transmitting the news and you've got the removal of filtering processes...No longer do you go through a cutting room as much, no longer do you go through editorial process, no longer do you go through the shipping of the film or the tape. It's got to be *now* because the technology lets you do that. You can sit in a hotel room in Dreadfulstan or somewhere or in a tent with a little generator and a tiny edit pack and a satellite uplink called *Livewire* or one of the new systems which means you can put that stuff out from the middle of nowhere, not necessarily in real time but close to real time. You don't have to rush back for four hours to a feedpoint or a hotel. You do it *now*...So you've got this compression there but at the same time you've got the broadening. No longer have you just got ITN, BBC, Sky...You've now got a fantastic broadening right across there and this enormous tree includes email, the internet, websites.[5]

Gowing recognises the danger of fetishising technology as an end in itself, of blinding oneself to its potential for manipulation. He is interested in the inherent contradictions of the information age between 'low-cost, high-penetration, highly mobile hardware and the quality of what we put out'. Does the technology help improve the quality of the end product, the actual reporting? There is in his business 'the temptation and the pressure...to get it out now and to get it out right but [these are] not necessarily the same thing'. He worries that 'a lot of people in this [news] environment haven't yet worked out the dynamic and the pitfalls...of this wonderful new technology...You may have someone on a satellite dish in the middle of a jungle but does that mean they're telling you good things which are accurate, enlightening you even more?'[6] David Halberstam writes that 'immediacy doesn't necessarily mean better, more thoughtful

reporting' and wonders whether 'the lack of satellites and comparative slowness of the transmission process in the old days permitted
the news desks...to act less as prisoners of technology than they do
today'. He argues that improvements in the technology of news have
seen an inverse decline of 'the editing function, the cumulative sense
of judgement – the capacity...to blend the visual and non-visual'
(1991, pp. 385–6). Philip Knightley thinks print journalism still has
an edge in the television age: 'A good picture to illustrate a
thoughtful report is still a bonus in quality print journalism, not an
imperative.' And, paradoxically, the costs of television news pictures
are so high that pictures of various conflicts around the world
invariably come courtesy of western news organisations. As a result,
'you can see how easy it is for the viewer of today's television news
to receive something of a one-dimensional view of the world' (1988,
p.13). Bob Woofinden believes that these fears are not well founded.
The major television news organisations put their editorial priorities
and resourcing issues first and that, in this respect, 'the technology
can only be a huge advantage' (1988, p.15).

There is also the political angle. The instantaneousness of news
that these technologies make possible can be used *against* journalism
as much as *by* journalism, what Gowing calls 'the information
boomerang'. He draws examples from his own research on the media
and the Great Lakes crises in Africa:

[You are] sitting in the desert or the jungle broadcasting the
horrors up on your [satellite uplink] and it's broadcast on BBC
World and the people who are committing this are sitting in their
villas nearby and thinking, 'Those people, they're spies!', whereas
in fact all they are doing is good journalism...That's a part of the
downside of technology. So you've got the accuracy and credibility problem and the other one is the...impact which can actually
be more profound that many people feel comfortable with.[7]

The BBC's John Simpson appreciates 'the standing danger that
because you can report 24 hours a day from anywhere in the world
that people will try to get you to do that and that... leaves less time
for finding out what's really happening...but I think everybody now
understands that so fully that that's been pretty much counter-
acted'.[8] During the NATO bombing of Yugoslavia from March to
June 1999, Simpson made hundreds of hours of broadcasts from
Belgrade without feeling confined to the spot for the next satellite

link. If he needed to go out he would simply put it off until he was ready. He dismisses the idea that reporters are burdened by the tyranny of technology: 'We're able to do what we pretty much need to do. Otherwise, the advances in technology are purely advantageous...We're in charge rather than the machine I think.'[9]

CONCLUDING REMARKS

The degree to which reporters are in charge of the machine is a moot point but it is clear that most if not all journalists are aware of the impact of new technologies and the opportunities and dangers that they present. Perhaps the most fatalistic view comes from Pete Williams, NBC correspondent and ex-Pentagon spokesman (during the Gulf War): 'I suppose there are purists who argue that sending back a live picture isn't journalism...It may not be journalism, but it is television, and that is a fact of life' (Dunsmore, 1996, p.4). Neuman argues that what is new today is not technological change so much as the sheer speed of that change, with some startling advances in brief periods of time (1995, p.7). But it is not just about speed. It is also about control. Technology is only as powerful and free as human agency allows. We need to examine quality as well as quantity, content as well as form. We need to get past the fetish of technology, of liveness, of instant news, and look at the nature and accuracy of the information being fed to us via the satellite link or the email news server or the website. We have to get past the postmodern hyperbole of technology as a liberating force and recognise its uses and abuses by powerful interests including, in this context, the governments and the military of all countries, whatever the political or economic system.

Part II

The War Correspondent in the War Zone

4   Journalists in the War Zone: From Crimea to Korea

> We did not know much about war but we were determined to get acquainted with it as quickly as possible.
>
> Arno Dosch-Fleurot, watching the German invasion
> of Belgium, 1914, in *Through War to Revolution*, 1931

The main concern in this chapter is to put contemporary war reporting into historical perspective. In the broadest sense of the term, there have always been 'war correspondents' on hand to chronicle the major wars and battles of ancient and modern history. John Carey (1987) gathers together some fascinating examples of these first-hand accounts in his *Book of Reportage*: The Burning of Rome in AD 64 (Tacitus), a Dinner with Attila the Hun, c. AD 450 (Pricus), or the Sack of Antwerp by a Spanish Army in 1576 (Gasgoigne). The historian Joesphus claimed to be witness to the Siege of Jerusalem in AD 70 when 'no respect was paid even to the dying...in case they were concealing food somewhere in their clothes, or just pretending to be near to death'. He mentions a woman with a child so ravaged by hunger that 'she killed her son, roasted the body, swallowed half of it, and stored the rest in a safe place' (ibid, p.16). There is an especially graphic account by Bartolome de Las Casas of atrocities in the West Indies carried out by Spanish Conquistadores, c.1513–20. It was not an isolated incident but consistent with their brutal methods of conquest and repression of the region's indigenous populations. De Las Casas had even taken part in it himself until he became a Dominican missionary and spoke out against such brutal repression:

> The Spaniards with their Horses, their Speares and Lances, began to commit murders, and strange cruelties: they entered into Townes and...Villages, sparing neither children or old men, neither women with child...but that they ripped their bellies, and cut them in peeces, as if they had beene opening of Lambes shut up in their fold...They tooke the little soules by the heeles...and

crushed their heads against the clifts...They put others, together with their mothers, and all that they met, to the edge of the sword...I have seene all the aforesaid things and others infinite.... And forasmuch as sometimes, although seldome, when the Indians put to death some Spaniards upon good right and Law of due Justice: [the Spaniards] made a Lawe betweene them, that for one Spaniard they had to slay an hundred Indians. (ibid, pp.82ff)

Compare De Las Casas' account of the Spanish Atrocities with this report of another atrocity, this time in the Middle East over 400 years later. It is by Robert Fisk, then of *The Times*, reporting the massacre by Christian militias of Palestinians in the refugee camps of Chabra and Chatila, in Beruit, Lebanon, September 1982:

They were everywhere, in the road, in laneways, in backyards and broken rooms, beneath crumpled masonry and across the top of garbage tips. The murderers – the Christian militiamen whom Israel had let into the camp to 'flush out terrorists' fourteen hours before – had only just left. In some cases the blood was still wet on the ground.When we had seen a hundred bodies, we stopped counting...Down every alleyway there were corpses – women, young men, babies and grandparents – lying together in lazy and terrible profusion where they had been knifed or machine-gunned to death...Another child lay on the roadway like a discarded flower, her white dress stained with mud and dust...The back of her head had been blown off by a bullet fired into her brain. (ibid, pp.679ff)

Common to these very different accounts is the immediate, powerful impact of word and image. But Josephus and De Las Casas and other such writers and historians were partial eyewitnesses and only a few of them worked under the institutional constraints of today's news media: the requirement to be objective, the pressure of the deadline, the editorial process, the mass readership. Whereas De Las Casas is writing to a limited, educated elite in the small and limited world of mediaeval times, Fisk reported the massacre at Chatila in the mass media age. So when we talk of war correspondents and war reporting it is essential to narrow our field of inquiry, to root the progress of the 'luckless tribe' in the nineteenth century and the development of truly 'mass media'; to trace the development of a professional identity – the journalist as 'war correspondent' – and identify the various commercial, political and technological dynamics that shaped and directed that development.

THE CRIMEAN WAR, 1854–56

The Times sent William Howard Russell to report on the Crimean War in 1854. Some call him the greatest war correspondent there ever was and although this is debatable he provided much better reportage than readers of *The Times* had been accustomed to up until then. He was an establishment figure, never too critical of the officer corps, not critical enough of the conditions of the rank and file; but he was still influential in changing military and political policy in respect to the Crimean war and other conflicts which he reported for his paper. Russell was interested in the detail of battle, the technicalities of tactics and strategy, the graphic accounts of death and injury on the battlefield. In his report on the Battle of Alma, for instance, he describes the first advances with a sense of admiration and awe:

> The troops presented a splendid appearance.The effect of these grand masses of soldiery descending the ridges of the hills rank after rank, with the sun playing over forests of glittering steel, can never be forgotten by those who witnessed it. Onward the torrent of war swept; wave after wave, huge stately billows of armed men, while the rumble of the artillery and tramp of cavalry accompanies their progress. (Lambert and Badsey, 1994, p.56)

Yet he draws this scene of the great battle on a more intimate human scale, reminding the reader of what war really involves and marking his ability to convey the multidimensionality of war:

> At last, the smoke of burning villages and farm houses announced that the enemy in front were aware of our march. It was a sad sight to see the white walls of the houses blackened with smoke – the flames ascending through roofs of peaceful homesteads – and the ruined outlines of deserted hamlets. Many sick men fell out, and were carried to the rear. It was a painful sight – a sad contrast to the magnificent appearance of the army in front, to behold litter after litter borne past to the carts, with the poor sufferers who had dropped from illness and fatigue. (ibid)

Although he dubbed himself the 'miserable parent of a luckless tribe', Russell was not the only journalist to report on the Crimean War (Knightley, 1982, p.4). He was soon joined on the front by Edwin Lawrence Godkin of the *London Daily News*. Russell was interested in the strategy and tactics of war and battle, while Godkin focused more on the human angle, on the psychological effects of battle on the individual. But both journalists were appalled by the inadequacies in British military leadership, and the terrible conditions suffered by the troops (ibid, p.10). Russell wrote to his editor that a once proud army had been reduced to a sorry collection of 'miserable, washed-out, worn-out spiritless wretches'. And while he agonised over his criticisms of the military leadership, his editor John Delane encouraged him to, 'Continue as you have done, to tell the truth and as much of it as you can, and leave such comment as may be dangerous to us who are out of danger' (ibid, pp.10ff).

Russell's criticisms of the military in the Crimea may seem measured by today's media standards but they attracted vehement protest among the officers at the front and back home in England. The military were particularly outraged by reports revealing troop and artillery deployments, arguing that once these found their way into the pages of *The Times* they would be picked up in Moscow and lend the Russian army much valuable intelligence. Delane agreed and ordered Russell to confine his reporting to past events even though the Russians learned about British military tactics and movements on the battlefield, or through its spy network, not from the pages of *The Times* (Knightley, 1982; p.13; Hankinson, 1982, p.58). The French army imposed strict censorship on the French press, and tried to make a case with Britain for excluding journalists altogether once their armies went into action (Hankinson, 1982, p.57). Hankinson, however, argues that the British Army could not have excluded journalists from the Crimean front even if it wanted to. Public opinion at home had expanded due to the increases in the electoral franchise and the growth of literacy and, since newspapers were powerful organs for amplifying such opinion, there would have been uproar had there been any attempt to exclude the correspondents. The alternative, censorship, would have been problematic, too, for the same reasons, but it could have been achieved through a workable system agreeable to military and journalists alike. In the end, the Commander of British forces, Lord Raglan, froze journalists out, offering them no information or assistance. As Hankinson remarks, 'It was the policy of the ostrich and it was to cost [Raglan] dearly' (ibid, p.55). The military's experience of this new breed of journalist influenced the introduction of formal military censorship commonplace in most wars since. Sir William Codrington, the new Commander-in-Chief at the Crimean front, issued a general order in February 1856 prohibiting correspondents from reporting military details of value to the enemy on pain of removal from the front. Although the war ended before the order came into effect, it was to make its impact on how subsequent wars were reported (Knightley 1982, pp.15–16).

THE AMERICAN CIVIL WAR, 1861–65

When Russell went to report the American Civil War in 1861, he soon lost heart in it and some professional and personal problems damaged his reputation. His Northern sympathies rested uneasily with *The Times'* pro-Southern editorial line and he eventually returned to Britain. The only journalist in England who was worthy to take his place was Edwin Godkin but he was ill at home for most of the war and came to it too late to make a real impact. The other journalists from England were of a lesser quality and so openly hostile to the North that even their editors urged them to say a good word about the North. With both sides vying for the high moral ground, it was vital that British public opinion should be well informed by the press but, according to Knightley, the coverage by *The Times* in particular was far from glorious and caused serious diplomatic distrust between Britain and the North that lasted long after the war. Part of the problem was that the proprietor, editor, and foreign manager were ignorant about the US and ill-equipped to report the war as an important historical development. This combination of partisan and ignorant editorial policy with inadequate journalism at the front damaged *The Times'* reputation as a paper of record. When the war ended with victory to the Union, the editorial staff became embroiled in bitter recriminations about how they could have got it so wrong (Knightley, 1982, pp.34ff).

It was not just *The Times* whose reputation suffered in the Civil War. In spite of the opportunities it offered journalists to shine, the conflict marked, for many, a low-point in the history of war reporting. Knightley writes that most were 'ignorant, dishonest, and unethical' and filed some of the most 'inaccurate,...partisan and inflammatory' copy of the war (ibid, p. 21). Objectivity had yet to develop as a guiding ethic in the practice of journalism. Reporters were young and inexperienced for the job of war correspondent and intense competition between newspapers nurtured a culture of sensationalism and jingoism in their coverage. Journalists saw no problem in reporting defeat as victory if that would help maintain public morale and sell newspapers. They would go to any lengths, it seemed, to scoop their rivals with a breaking story. Battles were reported that had not taken place, towns were invaded by armies that had not reached them, journalists were praised for reports they had simply invented, and war artists indulged in a high degree of artistic licence to sketch non-existent battle action. One journalist tried to interview a mortally wounded soldier, begging him not to die until the interview was finished and promising him that his last dying words would be published in 'the widely-circulated and highly influential journal I represent' (ibid, p.26). The story was hardly any different among Southern correspondents. In general, journalists refrained from reporting negative news about the war such as dissension in the ranks, the punishment of deserters, racism in the army, rivalries between eastern and western regiments in the northern armies, inadequate medical facilities at the front, and civil resistance to conscription. Knightley mentions the honourable exceptions – Ned Spencer of the *Cincinnati Times* or Samuel Wilkinson of the *New York Times*, for example – reporters who may not have made a name for themselves but who nonetheless covered the war with integrity and sensitivity to the horror and brutality of the conflict (ibid, pp.31ff).

A contributory factor in the poor coverage might have been the antagonistic relationship between reporter and soldier. General Sherman hated the press and saw their presence at the front and on the move with the army as a burden and an unwarranted interference in the conduct of the war (ibid, p.27). A correspondent for the *New York Tribune* wrote in April 1865 that 'a cat in hell without claws is nothing [compared] to a reporter in General Sherman's army' (Hammond, 1991, p.5). The General saw journalists among other things as 'dirty newspaper scribblers who have the impudence of Satan', as 'spies and defamers' and 'infamous lying dogs'. The day would come, he was sure, 'when the press might surrender some portion of its freedom to save the rest or else it too will perish in the general wreck' (Ewing, 1991, p.19). Just before Christmas of 1862, he issued an order, directed mainly at war correspondents, that 'Any person whatever, whether in the service of the United States or transports, found making reports for publications which might reach the enemy giving them information and comfort, will be arrested and treated as spies' (Lande, 1996, p.110). His colleagues were none too sharp on press relations either. General George Meade, for example, had reporter Edward Crapsey put backwards on a horse with a sign round his neck, 'Libeler of the Press', and chased out of camp to the tune of 'The Rogue's March'. However, on that occasion, reporter solidarity was such that Meade's name was left out of future dispatches, a factor said to have done some damage to his career ambitions (Knightley, 1982, p.27). Another officer commanding, General Burnside, would have had William Swinton of the *New York Times* shot for espionage had it not been for the intervention of General Grant (Roth, 1997, p.6).

Some of this flak was aimed at newspapers as well as individual reporters. The Union government prosecuted those that publicised information likely to aid and abet the enemy or compromise military security; and closed down those that printed material harmful to the Union war effort. The *Chicago Times* was closed down temporarily for criticising President Lincoln (ibid, p.6). By 1864, the Union Secretary of War, Edward Stanton, was so concerned about the state of public morale that he took on the role of propagandist, 'dispatching' his own reports 'from the front' complete with favourable embellishments, strategic omissions, and downsized casualty figures (ibid). Southern papers were allowed a greater degree of freedom of reporting and of opinion. The Confederate President, Jefferson Davis, promised freedom of the press in his inaugural address and, unlike President Lincoln in the North, he never closed down a newspaper during the war. This, in the early stages of the war, was perhaps more by default than enlightened military policy; the authorities simply did not have the resources to police and censor journalists. By 1862, the Confederate Army at the Potomac tightened existing reporting restrictions. All reports had to dispatched through the military censors and correspondents were banned from the front; the breach of these restrictions would be treated and dealt with as a criminal act (ibid).

Looking back at his many angry, bitter clashes with the journalists, General Sherman came to recognise the need to find some compromise between the military and the press. 'So greedy are the people at large for war news that it is doubtful' he conceded, 'whether any army commander can exclude all reporters without bringing down on himself a clamour that may imperil his own safety. Time and moderation must bring a just solution to this modern difficulty' (Ewing, 1991, p.29). Ironically, some forty years later, war correspondent Henry Villard found himself in sympathy with Sherman's original hard line; the presence of the press on the front line, he thought, 'must lead any unprejudiced mind to the conclusion that the harm certain to be done by war correspondents far outweighs any good they can possibly do. If I were a commanding general I would not tolerate any of the tribe within my army lines' (ibid). These conflicting requirements for secrecy and publicity continued to influence the relationship between military and journalists in subsequent conflicts during the final decades of the nineteenth century, a period known, ironically enough, as 'the Golden Age' of the war correspondent.

FROM THE 'GOLDEN AGE' TO WORLD WAR, 1865–1914

The disillusionment and cynicism that infected journalism during the American Civil War were not symptoms of some new malaise. They were endemic to the evolution of a commercial and fiercely competitive press in the nineteenth century. The decades that followed the American Civil War, up until the First World War, are commonly regarded as the 'golden age' of the war correspondent but reporting in this period had more impact on the circulation figures of major newspapers, and in feeding into the popular myths of war as glamorous adventure, than it had in influencing people's opinion against war (Knightley, 1982, pp.42ff). In America, for example, the Battle of Wounded Knee in 1890 was a last stand for the Sioux and for native American resistance to white expansionism but most of the reporters who arrived to cover the story saw it as an opportunity to make a name for themselves and to this end they were given to considerable creative license. An op-ed article in the *Omaha Bee* complained that reporters overplayed every minor event as hugely significant, to see 'an outbreak in every breeze, a bloody encounter in every rustling bough' (Kolbenschlag, 1990, p.1). According to native American writer Bright Eyes (Suzzette la Flesche) and her husband T.H. Tibbles, the young city reporters were highly skilled in cutting 'new inflammatory stories...out of the whole cloth' (ibid, p.16). There were exceptions such as Charles Cressey of the *Omaha Bee* and Gilbert Bailey of the *Chicago Inter-Ocean*. The *Philadelphia Public Ledger* (5 January 1891) declared Cressey to be quite unlike his more famous colleagues in that he 'relates facts as he sees or hears them and leaves criticism to others. He deserves honourable mention for keeping a cool head and sticking to the facts instead of glorifying himself after the usual fashion of war correspondents' (ibid, p.17). Gilbert Bailey wrote original feature stories and background to the uprising that favoured putting down the uprising but none the less saw the need for a change of attitude towards the Sioux, to see them as people who deserved just treatment. His views represented quite an advance on the generally negative press treatment of the Sioux case. Generally, though, reporters and their newspapers attacked each other for poor, inaccurate reporting , each one of them at the same time occupying a morally superior position (ibid, p.27).

Some contemporary observers, such as Richard Harding Davis, saw 1914 and the beginning of world war as marking the end of the Golden Age of war correspondents. However, the real blueprint for modern military censorship was the Japanese model during the Russo-Japanese War of 1904–05. The American journalist and novelist, Jack London, went to report the war with 'gorgeous conceptions' of the war correspondent, based on the romantic accounts of journalists who reported General Gordon's fall at Khartoum in the Sudanese uprising in 1885. London became a war correspondent to 'get thrills' but instead he and the small contingent of journalists who made the journey to Tokyo found themselves up against nothing but 'delays and vexations'; a vast military bureaucracy that could not see that journalists could help promote the cause. There were a total of 14 articles reporting regulations (Sweeney, 1998, pp.549ff). These effectively kept western journalists well away from the front and under strict censorship. As Knightley puts it, 'What it came down to in the end was that, in the eyes of GHQ, the ideal war correspondent would be one who wrote what he had been told was true, or even what he thought was true, but never what he knew to be true. Given these restrictions, the war correspondents might just as well have stayed in London' (1982, p.79). Most of them eventually gave up and returned home but one or two stayed and made an impact, especially the Italian reporter, Luigi Barzini, of *Corrierra della Sera,* whose knowledge of military tactics won him considerable kudos with the Japanese military. He wrote extensively on the decisive Battle of Mukden (1905) and with such clarity of detail and grasp of strategy that the Japanese used his reports as part of the war studies curriculum in their military academy. More to the point, Barzini was the only reporter to fully appreciate the wider geopolitical implications of the Japanese victory, the rise of a new regional power and the first military victory of an Asian power over a European power (Roth, 1997, p.23). But Michael Sweeney makes a crucial point about the way in which Japan dealt with foreign war correspondents: that it was not uniquely eastern but learned from historical precedent, from the way in which other militaries had dealt with journalists; not so much their restriction of movement as the denial of factual information, censorship by omission (1998, p.555).

Thus, from the onset of the First World War in 1914, Britain and France similarly learned from the past. The British officer corps made no secret of their hostility to journalists at the front, branding them outlaws and spies, and their concerns were fed by decades of experience going back to the Boer War in 1899 and the Sudan expeditions of 1898, even as far back as the Anglo-Zulu War of 1879. These conflicts saw the rise in the popularity of war as a story in commercial popular journalism. Its emphasis on the human angle of war rather than on the technical and strategic aspects, and the speed at which news could be dispatched from the front, helped to raise the status of war correspondents and make their presence at the front an uncomfortable fact of life for the military officer class which viewed them as a burden and a threat to operational security. The commander of British forces in the Anglo-Zulu War, Lieutenant-General Lord Chelmsford, complained in a bitter letter to the Secretary of War that it was 'more probable with such a large number of newspaper correspondents in camp, that many false impressions may be circulated and sent home regarding our present operations either intentionally or ignorantly'. He resented the journalists whom he felt were 'always ready without insufficient data for their guidance to express opinions on every conceivable military subject *ex cathedra*' (Laband and Knight, 1996, p.v). One of Chelmsford's officers, Sir Garnet Wolsely, saw the correspondents as a 'race of drones [and a] newly-invented curse to armies' (Hankinson, 1982, p.243). Nonetheless, the correspondents themselves, people such as F.R. MacKenzie of the *London Standard*, and Francis Francis of *The Times*, identified closely with the might and right of the imperial cause and if they were ever critical it was of issues of leadership and strategy. They saw the officer class as primary sources and saw little benefit in alienating them with undue criticism. Conversely, the officers appreciated the benefits of a 'good press' for their reputations and careers so they tended for the most part to cultivate good relationships with the correspondents. The only significant exception to this cosy relationship was the antipathy felt by Chelmsford towards Archibald Forbes whose persistent criticisms of his leadership damaged his standing in military and political circles back home in Britain (Laband and

Knight, 1996, p.viii). British commander Lord Kitchener was especially hostile to war correspondents and tried to impede their movements and obstruct their work in every possible way (Knightley, 1982, p.54). 'Out of my way, you drunken swabs!', was his dismissal of correspondents in Sudan, setting the tone for his approach to press relations in the First World War. Still, his antipathy to journalists did not blind him to their uses and he was never beneath the occasional subversive letter to the press to advance his career ambitions (Royle, 1989, p.46).

It was no surprise to the press in the First World War that Kitchener should adopt a policy of the strictest censorship and control. Correspondents were refused official accreditation in the first year of the war and they had no choice but to submit to an official drip of information from the newly formed Press Bureau which censored British Army information before passing it on to the press and around the world. The Bureau's communiques were usually old news that the newspapers already knew about because it was published elsewhere (Farrar, 1998, p.5). The aim essentially was to do or say anything but not mention the war, an objective clearly on the mind of Winston Churchill, himself a former war correspondent, when he talked about the 'fog of war'. In the first few months of war Britain and France treated all journalists the same, wherever they came from: they were free to report anything they wanted except what the war was really like. Lloyd George told C.P. Scott, editor of the *Manchester Guardian*, that if people really knew what was going on in the war, it would be stopped immediately: 'But of course', he said, 'they don't know and can't know' (Knightley, 1982, p.93). The British discouraged neutral correspondents from moving between fronts with the threat that if they were caught, they would be shot as German spies. The Germans subsequently introduced this ruling, too, so that most neutral journalists decided to stick with one side or the other for the duration and became fully immersed in the propaganda war (ibid, p.99). It was a situation that provoked Philip Gibbs of the *Daily Telegraph* to conclude that 'By one swift stroke of military censorship, journalism was throttled' (Farrar, 1998, p.9). The picture was hardly any better with the Russian army on the Eastern Front; indeed, it was probably worse. The few western reporters to make it there were very much on their own; they enjoyed little or no privileges, access or facilities, and were rarely allowed to visit the front line (Washburn, 1982).

There were early instances of voluntary censorship in which the press chose not to report significant events such as the mobilisation of the BEF (British Expeditionary Force) to France. How such mass movement of troops could be kept secret was not considered but there was a vain hope that the War Office would reward the press for playing a responsible and patriotic role. The official argument was that censorship had to be imposed blanket fashion since it was impossible to predict or anticipate what information would or would not be useful to the enemy (Farrar, 1998, p.11). The attitude to journalists who tried to operate outside of these restrictions was unforgiving. Any reporter found in the field of combat would be arrested, stripped of his passport and deported back to England. They were 'outlaws', *persona non grata*. Journalists in this period were not used to the official daily briefings and press releases so common in war reportage today so they depended on a high degree of mobility and flexibility to gather information and build credible reports and stories (ibid, p.12). But how could they do this if they were treated as potential spies or had their reports so severely delayed or heavily censored as to render them useless as news? As Farrar shows, the ultimate effect of the War Office policy on the press in this early phase of the war was to create an information gap that bred uncertainty at home and lent tawdry respect to rumour. Philip Gibbs wrote how the press became so desperate for information that they would report 'any scrap of description, any glimmer of truth, any wild statement, rumour, fairy tale, or deliberate lie' if it would fill the vacuum (ibid, p.14).

However, there were also at this time *un*accredited correspondents in France and when the fighting began they sent back dispatches that undermined official censorship. Arthur Moore of *The Times* and Philip Gibbs of the *Daily Chronicle* moved around France, relying on fortitude and luck to avoid arrest and get real information on events at the front, especially strategically important battles such as that of the Marne and the first battle of Ypres. Their accounts often presented a very different picture of the situation from that provided by the military, particularly the change of strategy from fighting along mobile fronts to the static trench warfare for which the First World War became notorious (ibid, pp.25ff). The War Office publicly denied their very existence but was careful at the same time to place restrictions on their dispatches: 'No correspondents are at the front', it said in a press release, 'and their information, however honestly sent, is therefore derived at second or third hand from persons who are in no position to tell coherent stories and who are certain to be without the perspective which is necessary to construct or understand the general situation' (ibid, p.22). The government eventually made some concession to the rising public clamour for news from France but it was, to use Farrar's term, 'renovation' rather than complete overhaul. An official army correspondent, Colonel Ernest Swinton, was assigned to GHQ in France in September 1914 and charged with the job of writing articles on military operations (also subject to censorship) with the byline 'Eyewitness' (ibid, p.23). Swinton however was not a journalist and his 'dispatches' were written in turgid military-speak unfit for public consumption. Crucially, though, it was never intended as an alternative source of public knowledge about the war; it was simply a cover for continuing the policy of non-information, of censorship and propaganda (ibid, p.24).

The real breakthrough in this situation came in March 1915 amid continued public debate about the role of correspondents at the front. Four journalists were invited to visit British GHQ (General Headquarters) during the battle of Neuve Chapelle; others joined the Admiralty Fleet on its way to the Dardanelles where plans were afoot to open up another front and put pressure on German forces. As a result, news from Neuve Chapelle reached the front pages back home within days rather than weeks (ibid, pp.47ff). Furthermore, in May 1915, the military finally granted permanent, pooled accreditation to five war correspondents under strict censorship and control: Philip Gibbs (*Daily Telegraph, Daily Chronicle*), Herbert Russell (Reuters), William Beach Thomas (*Daily Mail, Daily Mirror)*, Perry Robinson (*Daily News, The Times)* and Percival Philips (*Daily Express, Morning Post*). Their reporting from and movement in the war zone were governed by the War Office's 'Regulations for Press Correspondents Accompanying a Force in the Field'. There was also an official register of accredited reporters who could be trusted to comply with regulations and not betray military information to the enemy by accident or design (ibid, p.4). Correspondents were to be accompanied at all times by military minders, invariably officers who despised journalists and made it their business to obstruct them as much as possible. They had the power to read and censor not only journalists' dispatches but also their private mail. Once reporters typed up their dispatch, it was given to their minder who vetted it before sending it onwards to GHQ where it was telephoned to the War Office and from there by hand to the newspapers. Neither the

War Office nor the newspapers could edit or alter a dispatch once it was passed by GHQ, France. There was little or no resistance to any of this from the five pooled correspondents or their newspapers (Knightley, 1982, p.80). Farrar passes a severe verdict on their performance. 'The introduction of journalists to the Western Front could have helped the Home Front in their search for the truth', he says. 'What was created, however, was a group of correspondents who conformed to the great conspiracy, the deliberate lies and the suppression of truth.' These correspondents, with their honorary officer ranking and uniforms became part of the establishment and their primary job, to report news of the war as truthfully and accurately as possible, became an inconvenience (1998, p.73).

As the First World War went on, public opinion in Britain became more apathetic. The government tried desperate measures to renew its propaganda campaign against the Germans, including the revival of false atrocity stories like that of the factory that boiled the corpses of German soldiers to produce glycerine for munitions. Many British soldiers at the front read or heard of the stories and were able to write back and say they were false. One knock-on effect of wide public scepticism was a reluctance to believe true stories such as Turkish atrocities against Armenians (Knightley, 1982, p.88). If the journalists in the First World War had not become propaganda tools and if censorship had not been so rigid, what stories should or could they have filed? The real stories, the stories not fit for public consumption, included the stalemate at the front that turned the war into one of attrition with millions of dead and injured, the shortage of arms and ammunition at the front, the use of black soldiers from the colonies to save the lives of white soldiers, the bitterness and hostility between officers and troops (ibid, pp.92ff). There is the possible exception of Charles a Court Repington, a military correspondent who rarely visited the front line. He specialised in strategy and tactics and he enjoyed privileged access to the highest ranks of the military and diplomatic corps. His articles were crafted from on- and off-the-record information, comment and analysis, and on reports by other journalists from the front (Royle, 1989, p.112). He is best known for breaking the story of the 'Shells Crisis' in which the BEF suffered a severe shortage of artillery munitions. The story was originally sourced to Field Marshal Sir John French whose relationship with Kitchener was strained and difficult. French blamed the retreat at Mons on strategic failure on Kitchener's part but moreover on the shortage of shells and machine guns at the front.

Repington reported these allegations in *The Times*, provoking a furious political row at home. When the BEF suffered further setbacks and heavy losses at Auber's Ridge, Neuve Chapelle and Festubert, it fuelled a crisis of government in which Asquith was forced to ask for the resignation of his cabinet and pave the way for the formation of a coalition government. (There were of course other factors influencing the crisis such as the U-boat campaign which culminated with the sinking of the ocean liner, the Lusitania, the Zeppelin raids on London, the Gallipoli disaster, and the high casualty rate in France.) However, calls in *The Times* for Kitchener's resignation provoked a public clamour of support for the commander who kept his place in the new cabinet but lost control over munitions to Lloyd George who formed a new Ministry of Munitions (ibid, pp.124ff). Royle gives Repington considerable credit for his role in changing policy on munitions but argues that he had to get his story by deceit and subterfuge, even if in some ways that was forced on the journalist by the tight censorship policy that prevailed at the time (ibid, p.133).

A look at the work of journalists from neutral countries in the early stages of the First World War provides some useful comparisons with those from the combatant countries. All parties to the conflict had an interest in good public relations when it came to handling such journalists, especially Americans. Britain and France wanted the US to enter the war, Germany wanted them to stay neutral. This meant that in the early stages of the war, American correspondents were able to report stories that were officially censored or embargoed, like the German army's first use of gas at the front which Britain wanted to keep secret in case it should spook public opinion. America remained neutral up until 1917 and its newspapers were so starved of information that they would send over amateur correspondents in the vain hope they might get accredited; over 20 had made the journey to neutral Austria by mid-October 1914. They were to say the least naive adventurers and the type of correspondent lampooned in the Evelyn Waugh novel, *Scoop*. One identified himself as a 'special correspondent' of the Transcript Press, a Boston publisher. He had bet his friend a box of cigars that he would make it to the front and return home for Christmas: 'Hence my determination to smell the smoke of battle in order to puff the cheroot of peace' (Crozier, 1959, p.39).

Accredited journalists were none too keen on these new arrivals and accused them of being too ready to believe everything they were told about German atrocity stories, without interference from the censor. The reality was rather different. Knightley argues that American correspondents were less gullible when it came to atrocity stories and some of them expressed concern about the nature and reach of official censorship. Westbrook Pegler of the United Press news agency was censored when he reported on the high incidence of fatal pneumonia among American troops at the front and that this was being covered up by the authorities. He was soon recalled when the army persuaded United Press that he was too young and inexperienced for war reporting. He wrote that 'Censorship is developing more in the news interests of the military than in that of the American reader' (Knightley, 1982, p.114). A leading American journalist in London wrote that: 'The news hungry public was often misled in that period...News, lies, local color, human interest, fakes: all went down the public gullet in gargantuan gulps' (Crozier, 1959, p.41). The American correspondents fought hardest against censorship and intimidation and some of the best even went home rather than compromise their professional integrity, a principled stand that was very rare then and almost unheard of nowadays (Knightley, 1982, p.103). For the initial period of the First World War, while America remained neutral, American press coverage was better, more comprehensive, and certainly more impartial than anything available in the pages of the British, French or German newspapers. A poll asked 367 proprietors which side had their sympathy – two-thirds expressed no particular preference. Editors, too, were careful to preserve neutrality in their selection of war news (ibid). However, once the US entered the war in 1917, the situation for American correspondents predictably changed. US Army Censorship was managed by a committee of ex-journalists and ex-army officers and, in its short life, its job was bolstered by the Espionage Act of 1917 and the Sedition Act of 1918, which respectively legislated against aiding and abetting the enemy and criticising the conduct of government or military (Kirtley, 1992, p.475). In effect, these Acts were catch-all legislation used to control the press with impunity.

The key characteristics of most reportage from the front in this period were the exaggeration of military success, underestimation of casualties, and little or no sense of the true reality of trench warfare. When the hard questions were asked on the Home Front, the truth of what was happening came as a shock to all. Farrar takes issue with Knightley about the degree to which journalists became propaganda mouthpieces but it is difficult to escape the conclusion that both authors agree on the basic outcome: subservience among reporters to the military and, as a result, public ignorance at the home front. They and many other writers agree that the 'Golden Age' of the war correspondent came to a close during the First World War; reporters were no longer the free-booting adventurers of the Spanish–American War or the Boer War. Not everyone thought such an age ever existed. An article in the *Daily Mail* defended the First World War correspondents against critics who hearkened back to reporters like Archibald Forbes whom, it was thought, would have done a much better job. 'There is a great deal of nonsense spoken about the old school of war correspondents', said the writer. 'The truth is they were not supermen at all' (Farrar, 1998, p.206). In the latter stages of the First World War, argues Farrar, they 'yielded to military pressure and became a propaganda tool. They betrayed the trust of their readership' (ibid, p.226). Reporters came to accept the idea of systemised restrictions on both their reporting and their movement; it seemed to them that being near the front, bivouacked in some chateau under strict military supervision, was better than sitting at home relying on second-hand news. It was to prove a costly compromise. Henry Nevinson described how correspondents 'lived chirping together like little birds in a nest', wholly dependent on the military to feed them news (ibid, p.227).

THE SECOND WORLD WAR, 1939–45

War correspondents during the Second World War were known in the armed services as 'warcos'. By 1944, as the allies pushed the Germans out of France and Belgium, there were 150 warcos from Britain and the US all filing stories to 278 million readers worldwide 'like the scriptwriters of a long running soap opera' (Collier, 1989, p.178). They were fitted out in officers' uniforms, including caps, Sam Browne belts and arm badge with the gold letter 'C' for correspondent. They were forbidden to carry arms, although if captured and held as POWs (prisoners of war) they could assume the status of captain. However, an American press officer remarked that when at large the warcos 'assumed the rank of field marshal...and recognised no conventions' (ibid). The warcos had come to expect good treatment from the military without considering the cost in terms of professional integrity and independence. Alan Moorehead of the *Daily Express* admitted that 'Like the children of very wealthy parents it seemed quite natural to us that we should occupy the best houses and hotels, that we should have at our command cars, motor launches, servants and the best food' (ibid). The big question mark, of course, hung over the parents. What would their attitude be to their spoilt and unruly children? One of indulgence or discipline? It is instructive to compare the British approach to control of the media with that of Germany in the early stages of the Second World War and then to compare both of these with the new, public relations approach taken by the US army when it eventually entered the war in 1941.

In Germany, all agencies of communication were brought under the direct control of the state so that journalists were conscripted along with film and radio producers, printers, artists, writers and photographers, into the ranks of the Propaganda Division of the Army. They were given basic military training and were sent to the front to fight when necessary. But their principal role was as propaganda shock troops: they were to help to keep up morale on all fronts, and to damage enemy morale (Knightley, 1982, p.204). The German approach to neutral correspondents, especially Americans before the US entered the war, was rather more seductive. Its Ministry of Propaganda under Goebbels facilitated neutral corres-pondents through its Foreign Press Department. They were given a range of perks and privileges (extra rations, petrol expenses, special exchange rates among others) and a free hand to report what they wanted. However, in practice, all communications out of the German theatre of operations were carefully monitored and jour-nalists who filed negative copy were intimidated or even arrested for spying. As Knightley suggests,this was an easy charge to make in wartime where the line between journalism and espionage is a rather fine one; its effect was to encourage self-censorship. Still, the conditions experienced by foreign correspondents in Berlin in the early stages of the war were much more favourable than those prevailing behind allied lines and it was little wonder that over 100 journalists based themselves there (ibid).

The British way was just as effective but far from seductive or subtle (ibid, p.202; pp.205ff). The government used the Emergency Powers Act to censor all public and private communication out of the country that was thought to be of use to the enemy. The media – which now included radio as well as the press – were subjected to the same reporting restrictions as in the First World War. A limited number of correspondents were allowed to the front under the watchful eye of a senior Ministry of Information minder, called

'Eyewitness' as in the First World War. They were subjected to strict procedures of accreditation and essentially became part of the BEF. Furthermore, their dispatches from the front were censored so they would not undermine morale at home. Four British correspondents accompanied the BEF to the Maginot Line in France where they worked in a pool system. The system of media control in France was so stringent that by the time a correspondent's dispatch reached the newspaper it was barely news any more. Such was the dearth of hard news and skilful media management from the Ministry of Information, *The Daily Express* complained that Britain would need to launch a leaflet drop on itself to inform its citizens about the course of the war so far (ibid, p.205). Its correspondent O.D. Gallagher suggested that British Army public relations was so ineffective that it would be better to adopt the German system instead. After pressure from the military, Gallagher was recalled from the front and sent around Britain to report on civil defence arrangements (ibid, p.207). His crime had been to think the unthinkable.

The approach of American reporters to British censorship was to fight it. Ben Robertson was reporting a dog fight between German and British planes mid-Channel and reported the loss of three Spitfires to seven Messerschmitts. But one of the censors on duty in the Ministry of Information struck out the references to British losses. Robertson took exception and appealed upwards, eventually to the Minister himself, Alfred Duff Cooper, who agreed to let it through. For Robertson, the main obstacle was not so much the system in place as the individual censor, often lowly ranked and poorly paid, and quite unwilling to stray from the rules (Collier, 1989, pp.49ff).

Robertson and his compatriot colleagues were used to a different culture of information and expected openness and public relations skills from their military. The US Army saw public relations and news management as a vital part of overall strategy; as General Dwight D. Eisenhower put it to a meeting of American newspaper editors, 'Public opinion wins war' (Knightley, 1982, p.299). Considerable resources were afforded to the job of accommodating and controlling the burgeoning demands the media were making for information about the latest developments in the war. Military officers became adept at handling journalists and catering to their professional requirements. The concern among the military was to strike a working balance between necessary censorship and good public relations, a desire to bring reporters on side, accommodate them as much as possible, give them stories and pictures, and be mindful of the impressions the military journalists would bring back home after the war (Braestrup, 1985, p.30). Eisenhower told reporters that it was 'a matter of policy [that] accredited war correspondents should be accorded the greatest possible latitude in the gathering of legitimate news' and that 'Public Relations Officers and Conducting Officers give...war correspondents all reasonable assistance' (ibid, p.31). Of course the the power to define 'legitimate news' rested with the military. American reporters were subjected to censorship but they were allowed easy access to the front, accompanied always by a public affairs officer. The facilities offered to the American press corps by the US Army were looked at with envy by reporters from other countries including Britain. American field commanders were more open with reporters; British commanders were more suspicious. American reporters; were treated as active officers and given room and equipment to do their job, including the services of a press officer; while British reporters were watched closely at all times by a duty escorting officer and were subject to a whole raft of reporting restrictions and censorship procedures (ibid, p.41).

Braestrup notes that the US Army allowed journalists in on the planning of major operations such as the D-Day landings and both parties got to know each other quite well. 'The journalist had time to understand the problem and the plan – and hence gain some basis for later assessments of what actually took place' (ibid, p.28). Amphibious landings by the US Army in Europe and the Pacific were 'set-piece affairs' well planned in advance, including accommodation of a select number of journalists. Just before the Normandy landings, reporters based at army headquarters were assured that they would be well looked after by the Public Relations division which would offer them 'the very best in information and communication'. They were assured they had 'true friends' among the Public Relations Officers, some of whom were reporters themselves and who knew a good news angle (ibid, p.36). The public relations strategy did not quite work in practice when the invasion finally went ahead. The contingent of reporters with US forces was small and severely stretched. Reporters found themselves isolated and unable to access communications facilities. John McVane of NBC remarked on 'All the vast public relations preparations and only a lieutenant there to help us' when he tried to report on the Omaha beach landing (ibid, p.40).

The treatment of journalists at the Normandy landings was not flawless but it was a great improvement on earlier operations such as the disastrous raid on Dieppe when reporters were largely kept in the dark, given little or no information and subjected to unreasonable censorship (ibid, p.41). It was also true that improved military public relations did translate into better or more extensive coverage of the war by the American news media. The Asian and Pacific theatres were not well covered at all simply because there were not enough reporters to cover every battle. Important battles such as the famous Battle of the Bulge at Bastogne in December 1944 went unwitnessed by American reporters (ibid, p.27).

This was not to say that all sections of the British armed services were lacking in public relations skills. The British Army in the North African theatre was taking a very different, more media friendly approach (Knightley, 1982, pp.290ff; Hickman, 1995, pp.155ff). For the British Army, the North African campaign was a chance to shine against the enemy in apparently wide open and empty spaces without having to worry too much about civilian casualties. Furthermore, it distracted from their own deficiencies in the European theatre of war where it was becoming apparent that defeat could only be averted by American intervention – both financial and military. The war in the desert also appealed to the warcos. When the offensive began, in December 1940, six reporters accompanied the British armoured brigades. Within a year and a half, there were 92 of them, and more arriving by the day (Knightley, 1982, p.289). General Montgomery was charismatic and dynamic and he appreciated the value of a friendly and amenable press corps for self-promotion and propaganda in his personal duel with the German Field Marshal Rommel. He went so far as to regard journalists as elements of his staff (ibid).[1] BBC correspondent Frank Gillard talks about 'the kind of relationship which could develop in this war between a war correspondent and the commander-in-chief' and says that it was 'crucially important to a correspondent that he should be recognized and trusted as a member of the Army family, even though he could never allow the army to use or manipulate him. This delicate relationship was greatly strengthened if it was seen that the correspondent was approved of in the top ranks of command' (Hawkins, 1985, p.12). Duly approved of, and some with egos greatly inflated, the warcos saw little problem with this and some even considered giving up the job to enlist. They reported the desert campaign as a romantic adventure in which the British triumphed and where even the enemy displayed chivalry and military greatness.

Yet for all the public relations, few journalists ever got close enough to the front lines to witness a single tank battle. Alan Moorehead of the *Daily Express* recalls that they 'were simply conscious of a great deal of dust, noise and confusion' (Knightley, 1982, p.292). And the PR approach did not extend to the few women correspondents accredited in the Second World War and who turned up to report the action in Northern Africa. Army Command barred women reporters from working in active combat zones and were especially irked whenever they caused a fuss and made difficult demands for equality with their male colleagues. The head of the British Army's Press Division, Lieutenant Philip Astley, wondered why women reporters could not just be content with special 'visitor status' and facilities (Sebba, 1994, p.153).

Phillip Knightley distinguishes between the ostensible aims and the real aims of the censorship regime in the Second World War. Ostensibly, it was to keep the public informed about their army at the front, while at the same time making sure nothing got published that might aid and abet the enemy. But the real purpose was to manage the public mood in support of the war effort and encourage recruitment, to cover up military mistakes at the front and quash criticism of the conduct of the war. It was a systematic mobilisation of propaganda and manipulation of public opinion. Although journalists soon realised this, few if any confronted the system. They went along with it because they either thought the situation would change for the better or that the war would soon be over. The criticisms and reservations were saved for their postwar memoirs when it was too late to have any real effect. A Reuters correspondent admitted that journalists were simply propagandists for their governments, mere cheerleaders: 'It wasn't good journalism', he said. 'It wasn't journalism at all' (Knightley, 1995, p.45).

THE KOREAN WAR 1950–53

Some veteran American correspondents of the Second World War compared their coverage of the war with the media's experiences in Korea and Vietnam. In the Korean War, General MacArthur repeatedly refused to provide a formal system of censorship and regular briefings which, he thought, was impossible. Subtly, he shifted the burden of censorship onto reporters themselves, trusting on their good sense not to compromise military security or undermine the authority of a field officer with 'unwarranted criticisms' or personal attacks (Braestrup, 1985, p.50). Reporters felt a deep sense of unease about this and actually demanded from MacArthur direct censorship and 'uniform guidance' with reporting (ibid, p.50; see also Adams, 1986, pp.27ff). According to Braestrup, journalists feared that MacArthur's permissive policy would put increasing pressure on them to disclose more information than their rivals. They also thought the lines of transgression too vague. How was a reporter to judge what might compromise security or endanger lives? And when did a reporter cross the line to make 'unwarranted criticism' of army operations or damage the prestige and pride of American forces? Where were the definitions and ground rules? For all their fears and anxieties, the voluntary code remained in place until the end of 1950 during which time, said the US 8th Army censor, 'the disclosure of security information by correspondents was virtually a daily occurrence' (Braestrup, 1985, p.52).

However, the situation changed radically when the Chinese army turned the tide of the war against UN forces from mid-September 1950. Suddenly, the need for tighter security and secrecy of information became more pressing but it was not until 20 December that the Far Eastern Command (FEC) imposed a system of censorship in which all media material relating to the war would be submitted first for clearance. A Press Advisory Division was set up and based at the FEC public information office in Tokyo for the purpose of censorship. Field censorship in Korea was handled by a Press Security Division attached to the US 8th Army (ibid, p.53). It was estimated that 90 per cent or more of reporters favoured this formal system of censorship because it lifted the burden of self-censorship and eased competition with rivals. Some however tried to get round the new restrictions through loopholes and subterfuge and, as a result, invited further tightening of restrictions. But Braestrup argues that despite the imposition of formal ground rules in December 1950, the FEC attitude was still relatively lax throughout the war compared with other conflicts, before or after Korea, and the army rarely took drastic action against errant reporters. Journalists were allowed considerable latitude to criticise and analyse military operations, and to portray the war in its full horror. During the peace talks, they spoke out against misleading or inadequate UN briefings. Notably, says Braestrup, the military did not blame 'the security lapses, mood swings, exaggerations, or forebodings' of journalists for the growing dissatisfaction at home with the war (ibid, p.54).

Australian correspondent Wilfred Burchett reported the Korean War from a radical perspective and he always thought that the real 'press war' in Korea was between journalists and their American press officers (1980, p.174). The most interesting phase of the war, as far as the role of journalists is concerned, came as it drew to a close with the ceasefire talks in Kaesong. The UN was deeply divided over bringing the war to a close and Burchett, along with Chinese journalist Chu Chi-p'ing and Alan Winnington of the British *Daily Worker*, found themselves in the position of unofficial briefers for journalists attached to the UN command. This happened, said Burchett, because of the 'suppression, distortion, and untruthful accounts of conference proceedings given by the official UN spokesmen'. Other international media outlets covering the talks increasingly took to lifting the accounts of these journalists and publishing them alongside reports of news agencies because their reports were generally found to be more accurate than those using the UN as a chief source (ibid, p.165).

A significant example of how this worked concerned a crucial battle of words over the final line of demarcation that would define the ceasefire settlement: the 38th parallel. Using the UN as diplomatic cover, the Americans tried to get the line pushed back 35 miles from the existing Chinese-Korean front. The Chinese and Koreans argued that the existing positions on either side of the 38th parallel more or less reflected the original balance of forces and seemed a fair enough compromise for a settlement. The UN command produced a map to support its identification of the line but western journalists found themselves cross-referencing the three reporters over the precise demarcation line in question because there was 'an obvious discrepancy between what they were *told* and what we *knew*' (ibid, p.166; emphasis in the original). The UN map released to the western press was a fake, something the UN press officer, Brigadier-General William P. Nuckols eventually admitted. In response, the UN launched a propaganda counter-offensive in which it contrived a breakdown of negotiations, one provoked by the Chinese-Koreans and resulting in their banning of western journalists from Kaesong. Before Burchett and his two colleagues had a chance to offset the crisis and point out that only one day's talks had been cancelled it was too late. Contact between the press and both sides had broken down, with UN chief liaison officer Colonel

Andrew J. Kinney (USAF) claiming it was all down to communist obstruction, and that the communists were the ones who banned the press (ibid, p.166). This pattern of disinformation of the press by UN press officers, and the habit of accredited journalists of cross-checking with Burchett and his other two colleagues, continued throughout the ceasefire talks and their frequent crises and breakdowns. It presaged a new phase of military–media relations that would define and be defined by future international wars and the invasions and interventions so beloved of the US and its allies throughout the Cold War.

CONCLUDING REMARKS

In a period of a hundred years from the Crimean War to the Korean War, reporters and the military have fought on contradictory principles: the military's need for secrecy and the journalist's need not just for facts and information but also news. Yet all the evidence points to a rapprochement in this period, with the military moving away from the chauvinistic assumption that the journalist has no business in the war zone. Some American and British military leaders in the Second World War recognised the benefits and advantages of a favourable domestic press in wartime in terms of propaganda, morale on the Home Front and even their own self-promotion. Eisenhower knew it and Montgomery certainly knew it.

For their part, reporters learned that it was pointless adopting a purist, principled position of independence. As in all major wars since Crimea, many war correspondents learned to strike a deal with the military that would guarantee all-important access to 'authoritative' information. As Wilfred Burchett realised in Korea, the question of whether 'authoritative' information was accurate was another matter entirely.

Korea was the war in which journalists expressed uneasiness with the trust General MacArthur was prepared to invest in them to report 'responsibly', and to censor and regulate themselves: suddenly, direct censorship seemed much less onerous. But if there was one war that seemed to herald a break from the fatally compromised relationship between the military and the media, it was Vietnam. Journalists were apparently free to roam the war zone unhampered by military restrictions, to criticise and challenge and question, and to fatally undermine military morale and the American will to win. All of these were myths, of course, but after the way they were used to justify a backlash against the media in which the military asked the vital question whether they could any longer countenance the presence of the journalist on the front line. The first real test of this question was not an American war but a very British war over the tiny Falkland Islands in the South Atlantic and the answer was very nearly 'No, there is no room at all for the media in the war zone.'

5 Journalists and the Military since Vietnam

One of the most enduring myths in the recent history of war reporting is the 'Vietnam Syndrome', the widespread belief that the mainstream American media were opposed to the Vietnam War and openly hostile to the US military and its South Vietnamese clients; and that as a result of their critical coverage they lost the war for the US. This of course bears little or no relation to the media's actual coverage of the war, yet it has shaped and influenced political and military control of the media in subsequent conflicts from the Falklands War to the American invasions of Grenada and Panama and in the Gulf War in 1991 (Hallin, 1986; MacArthur, 1992; Williams, 1993).

THE VIETNAM WAR, 1965–75

The following discussion of the American media's relations with the US military in the Vietnam War relates to the period between 1965–75 during which military involvement was at its most direct; so-called US military advisers were in place long before this, helping the South Vietnamese regime put down the nationalist and communist insurgents, collectively labelled the Vietcong. The turning point during this period came in 1968 when the North Vietnamese army launched a surprise offensive against the South Vietnamese regime on the traditional Tet holiday. From then on, the consensus among Washington elites about the conduct of the war began to leak. Popular support also waned, apparently because of hostile media coverage and the nightly images of dead and injured American soldiers. By 1975, American resolve had finally collapsed; total withdrawal swiftly followed.

Both the Kennedy and Johnson administrations were extremely sensitive to 'negative' news from Vietnam and, by extension, negative domestic comment and analysis in the elite press. Negative news was essentially any news that contradicted the official line that the military was making progress in winning the war (Braestrup, 1985, p.62). The White House and the Pentagon consistently tried to counter every piece of 'negative' news with optmistic assessments and projections and Johnson even went so far as to second military commanders in Vietnam, including General Westmoreland, to help sell the war at home which Braestrup describes as 'an unprecedented use of the military to achieve domestic political objectives' (ibid, p.63).

The history books offer numerous examples of the freewheeling journalist in Vietnam, undermining military security and public morale with daily reports of tactical blunders, strategic incompetence and the terrible rate of attrition suffered by American troops for vainglorious ends. The reality was quite different. Reporters like David Halberstam and Neil Sheehan cultivated good relationships with their military sources, most notably Lieutenant-Colonel John Paul Vann. They also got on well with the rank and file and delighted in hitching rides on the combat helicopters, describing their experiences in the first person plural. With few exceptions, the American press corps in Saigon were ordinary hacks who knew where their sympathies lay (MacArthur, 1992, p.118).

Halberstam, who reported for the *New York Times*, is still thought of by liberals in the West as an exemplary war reporter: bold and courageous in the pursuit of truth in spite of the criticisms ranged against him at home for his reporting of the Vietnam War. In late 1963, the CIA produced an analysis of Halberstam's 'lugubrious and pessimistic' reporting which, although accurate with the facts, drew conclusions from those facts that seriously impugned his objectivity (ibid, p.116). Some of the most conservative sections of the American media also took exception to Halberstam's subversive journalism. Halberstam himself recalled how the *New York Journal – American* accused him of being 'soft on Communism', and 'paving the way for a bearded Vietnamese Fidel Castro' (ibid, p. 119). President Kennedy wondered aloud to *New York Times*' publisher Arthur O. Sulzberger if he was planning to move Halberstam somewhere else (ibid, p.120). In fact, like almost all of his colleagues in the Saigon press corps, he was a patriotic journalist who questioned certain operational and strategic decision-making that undermined the war effort against the Vietnamese communist and nationalist insurgents. As Neil Sheehan wrote of him, Halberstam was an example of 'the genius of the Anglo-Saxon society of the Northeast for co-opting the talents and loyalty of outsiders with its social democracy. A society that would give...the grandson of immigrant jewish peddlers a Harvard education and a job at the *New York Times* was innately good, incapable of perpetrating evil in other lands.' Halberstam was 'full of gratitude to that society and wanted to spread its good' (Sheehan, 1989, p.321) and rarely questioned the morality of US involvement in Vietnam or indeed anywhere around the world. In his book, *The Making of a Quagmire*, he wrote of his belief that 'Vietnam is a legitimate part of [America's] global commitment... perhaps one of only five or six nations in the world that is truly vital to US interests. If it is this important it may be worth a larger commitment on our part but if so we should be told the truth, not spoon-fed cliches as in the past' (Braestrup, 1983, p.4).

Halberstam, Sheehan and others were pressured not so much for what they believed or wrote but because of the ideological battles raging on the home front over what was happening on the ground in Vietnam. Anyone who questioned any aspect of official policy was at best 'a liberal', at worst a 'communist'. It all depended on the nature of the critique and the context of its presentation. The more vital the policy to the economic and political interests of the state, the further left the critiques were regarded. Mildly critical journalists became unpatriotic subversives who, as the famous war correspondent turned establishment columnist Marguerite Higgins complained, would love their country to lose the war so they could be proved right (MacArthur, 1992, p.120). Peter Arnett writes that 'Caught between the truth of what we saw and the nation's sense of patriotism, the Vietnam reporters became something like outcasts, destined to defend their professionalism for the rest of their lives' (1996).

This sets in brief context the daily American military briefings in Saigon, and explains why they quickly became known as 'The Five O'Clock Follies'. These were simply designed to feed the news media with a daily 'hard news' story but were not taken seriously by most journalists because they were based on 'hasty, fragmentary, inevitably inaccurate field reports' of action in a theatre of war where there was no actual front line, moving or stationary (Braestrup, 1985, p.63; 1983, pp.17ff). Only the American aerial bombardment passed as 'hard news' despite the fact that it was entirely detailed in army press releases; journalists were not allowed to accompany the aircrews on bombing sorties. The myth of heated clashes between spokesmen and journalists was, Braestrup suspects, more about journalists giving vent to frustrations about the lack of real news than sharp, perceptive reporters holding out tenaciously for the 'truth'. Any such journalists knew the truth was not to be had in the briefings. And as Braestrup points out, official optimism had become such a devalued currency over the first few years of war that journalists in Saigon 'were inclined to discount all optimistic assessments by official spokesmen, even as they dutifully reported them' (ibid, p.64). John Pilger recalls from his own experience that reporters like himself regarded the Follies as 'a bit of theatre' in which some journalists amused themselves by tormenting the briefer:

> In fact I went down there and filmed the briefer...and asked him ABC questions like, How many men were serving in Vietnam?, How many people were killed by friendly fire?, How many men were killed by accidents?, How many helicopters fell out of the sky because they were badly serviced? They threw him into a panic. He couldn't even tell me how many men were in the country. So from my point of view they were useless.[1]

Jacques Leslie reported the war for the *LA Times* from 1972 until July 1973 when he was expelled from the country for his habit of reporting inconvenient exclusives: the torture of women prisoners, corruption and ceasefire violations, and even a conspiracy by South Vietnamese army generals to smuggle valuable used artillery shell cannisters out of the country for a very profitable return. These stories were possible because Leslie cultivated good official *and* unofficial sources. 'The result, of course, was that I was finally kicked out of the country in July, 1973, an act the US Embassy heartily endorsed.'[2]

Drew Middleton of Associated Press reflects that in Vietnam, as in Korea, no one was quite sure what the ground rules were so the military were much more wary of talking openly and freely with journalists (Knightley, 1982, p.299). There were about 40 American and foreign journalists in Saigon in 1964, increasing to more than 400 by summer 1965 when daily briefings were provided for 130 correspondents. By 1966, there were 419 journalists from 22 countries, 179 of which were American (Braestrup, 1985, p.64). The most troubling aspect was that, with few exceptions, the Follies became for the vast majority of reporters the principal source of information about the war. Pilger reveals that out of 649 journalists accredited to the Saigon press corps from 1968, only about eight made regular forays into the field (2001, p.263). Jacques Leslie remembers it differently. He says that 'most journalists, unless they were too frightened or concerned for their safety, got out of Saigon – the good stories weren't in Saigon'. He accepts credit for being the first

American correspondent to foray into Vietcong territory 'only because of the arrival of the ceasefire in late January, 1973. Before that, it was impossible – anyone trying before that was likely to enjoy the fate of my friend Alex Shimkin, a *Newsweek* stringer, who blundered into Vietcong territory in 1972 and was immediately killed.' Leslie does not see his actions as particularly daring or heroic. It was about being sensible and about being a good journalist. He had simply nurtured good contacts and sources, in this case Vietcong, who assured him that with the ceasefire in place he would be safe and that he would be treated well. As he points out, 'it wasn't laziness on the part of other journalists that kept them out – rather, it was a quite reasonable fear of being killed, and the dearth of sources like mine'. Once he set the example and showed it could be done, others followed in his footsteps, some of them quite literally 'to the very village I'd visited, until the village chief told them they were taking up too much of his time, and to pass the word to stop going there'. The majority of journalists never considered meeting the Vietcong because they had nothing to learn. The VC were the enemy, they were evil; end of story. Leslie's bureau chief, George McArthur, was a Vietnam 'hawk' 'who rarely left Saigon for any reason, relied on his CIA sources for many if not most of his stories, and probably figured anyone who pulled off the feat would be treated to nothing more than a Potemkin Village-like performance for his efforts'.[3]

Pilger, Braestrup and many other critics discount the myth that the media lost the Vietnam War and firmly point to political divisions at home, and poor news management at the White House, as part of the problem (see Hallin, 1986; MacArthur, 1992; Pilger, 2001; Williams, 1993). Braestrup himself reported the war and, like so many of his American colleagues in the press corps, supported its fundamental justification. Thus, he argues, the real folly was Kennedy's and Johnson's habit of accentuating the positive while doing little or nothing to progress the war on the ground, of which the briefings in Saigon were merely an extension. Nixon took firm and positive action on the ground first and then sold it to the media but there was still a significant credibility gap there that could not be closed. Braestrup argues that any administration sending troops to war must prepare a clear media strategy and 'a sturdy resolve...not to gloss over difficulties' (Braestrup, 1985, p.75).

The prevailing myth of a hostile media quickly took root in military thinking and fed into the perception that as a result of their opposition the media lost the Vietnam War for the US. The US Army was convinced for the wrong reason they made a mistake with their open media policy in Vietnam. However, it was a convenient delusion because the record suggests a good working military–media relationship in Vietnam. The system of censorship that existed was indeed relatively open and relaxed but as Jane Kirtley shows, the press corps in Saigon was a well-behaved lot 'for out of approximately 2000 correspondents, only six were cited for violations severe enough to warrant revocation of their credentials' (1992, p.476). But the US Army made up its mind that in future its attitude to media reporting would be different, certainly more restrictive, and was to learn much from the successes and failures of British military and political information policy during the Falklands War in 1982. The American military was impressed with British information control but not with their Public Relations and media management.

THE FALKLANDS WAR, 1982

When the Falklands crisis moved onto a war footing in 1982, the British armed forces struggled to formulate an information policy and media strategy. They too fell victim to 'Vietnam Syndrome'. As far back as 1970, Air Vice-Marshall Stewart Menaul had bemoaned coverage of Vietnam, concluding that 'television had a lot to answer for in the collapse of American morale'. At the same time, an MoD Director of Defence Operations advised colleagues to ask themselves: 'Are we going to let television cameras loose on the battlefield?' (Glasgow University Media Group [GUMG], 1985, p.8). With thinking like this it was little wonder that their approach to media management in the Falklands was so problematic. A limited number of British journalists were allowed to accompany the fleet to the South Atlantic: only 29 correspondents and photographers – all of them British – were assigned to various pools on board the Royal Navy ships and the amount of help and assistance given to them was minimal. The government and military line was that reporting restrictions were necessary and vital to safeguard operational security and the lives of the troops. However, critics argued that it extended far beyond such terms of reference and was designed to ensure coverage that would convey a favourable impression of the war at home (GUMG, 1985; Harris, 1983; Morrison and Tumber, 1988; Mercer et al, 1987). Journalists such as Brian Hanrahan (BBC) and Michael Nicholson (ITN) complained bitterly of heavy-handed censorship; they eventually took to prefixing their reports as having being censored but this word itself was censored (GUMG, 1985, p.9). In a report for the Home Office, Valerie Adams argues that many of the problems experienced between the military and media were down to oversight or to specific failures of planning by the Ministry of Defence (MoD) which failed to think in advance about how the media should be handled. For their part, journalists failed to understand some very practical, operational limits prevailing aboard ship (1986, p.4). None of this however should detract from the reality of direct and deliberate censorship of the media during the Falklands War. It operated on three levels:

- direct censorship and control by the MoD in the South Atlantic
- restraints imposed by the lobby briefing system
- self-censorship by journalists in the name of military security or in respect to public opinion.

Direct Censorship and Control of the News Media by the MoD in the South Atlantic

Unlike the army, with its media experience in Northern Ireland, the navy was not accustomed to having journalists aboard their ships and had the government not intervened there would have been no media presence in the Falklands at all. Once on board and at sea, the media pools were at the mercy of their military minders. They had no facilities for sending reports via satellite and were forced to rely on ship communications to get their copy home. In many cases this was made extremely difficult; phones were mysteriously busy when a journalist wanted to send a report on a dramatic development, especially when things were going badly. From a naval point of view, journalists expected to dispatch copy via ships communications when it suited them but it soon got to the point where almost 30 per cent of traffic was press copy, not a situation the Navy could easily tolerate for obvious operational reasons (Adams, 1986, p.14). The effect of all this on the quantity and quality of coverage was serious. In some instances, unfavourable reports or pictures took days to find their way to the newsroom, by which time they were stale and useless as news.

Restraints Imposed by the Lobby Briefing System

Things were no better for journalists reporting from the home front. The Ministry of Defence's public relations department was headed by a civil servant, Ian McDonald, whose attitude to media management was so negative that he was quickly dubbed the 'Minister for No Information'. He would appear before the assembled media and read out brief, perfunctory statements; questions from reporters or off-record briefings were not allowed. The MoD's public relations officers (PROs) were even less helpful. They were 'relatively junior people, lacking the authority, the experience, or perhaps the ability to negotiate successfully' (Adams, 1986, p.14). Walter Rogers reported the briefings for ABC and thought that the British journalists were too passive. If they had stood up for themselves and demanded better treatment, the MoD would have given in sooner (Philo and McLaughlin, 1995, p.155). The Canadian CBS correspondent, Morley Safer, thought that the major difference between the MoD briefings and the Five O'Clock Follies was that in the MoD briefings, the journalists knew less than Ian McDonald; in Vietnam, the journalists knew much more than the hapless briefer, 'at least those...who'd been out of Saigon at all' (Pilger, 2001, p.261). But McDonald's approach was soon challenged from within the MoD itself, namely from PR professionals like Neville Taylor who believed that it could give the media what they wanted – news and pictures – but on its own terms. By the middle of May 1982, off-the-record briefings were restored.

Self-censorship by Journalists

In many ways, the MoD had no need to adopt such heavy-handed information management. It could rest assured that in a spirit of patriotism and a general atmosphere of fear most British journalists and their editors, on public service television as well as in the press, were easily persuaded to practice a large degree of self-censorship. The principal and ultimate tool at the MoD's disposal was the D-Notice which prevented publication of information thought by the authorities to compromise military security. But Morrison and Tumber have shown that apart from a set of standing orders issued three weeks before the Argentine invasion, no D-Notice was ever imposed during the conflict itself. Instead, the MoD favoured a more ad hoc arrangement in which journalists would seek informal guidance by telephone or meeting about whether to include certain information. In effect, journalists were cooperating with a system that put the onus of censorship not on the authorities but on themselves. Three criteria influenced the selection of combat footage for primetime television news: military security, standards of taste and decency with respect to pictures of dead and wounded, and intrusion of privacy with respect to interviews with families of troops killed in action (1988, pp.220ff).

Implications

A Commons Defence Committee inquiry into military–media relations during the Falklands War, led by Lord Beech, heard evidence from media and government and concluded, perhaps not surprisingly, that the basic goals of information policy had been successfully met, the war was won and no serious breaches of security had been committed by journalists. The Beech Report concluded that in wartime disputes will always arise about what constitutes 'operational security' but, crucially, 'where there are conflicting views...the military view must prevail'(Adams, 1986, p.161). The inquiry also looked at two other policy issues: the public's right to know and the government's duty to withhold information for security reasons. It recognised that censorship and propaganda had a place in concealing information from the enemy and also deceiving the enemy. 'Propaganda in itself is not objectionable', it reported, 'and it certainly need not involve lying and deception' (ibid, p.15).

Valerie Adams argues that journalists are not always in a position to judge and determine the boundaries of operational security and therefore they differ about what justifies censorship (ibid, pp.161ff). Max Hastings saw his reporting as much 'an extension of the war effort', giving help and succour to the troops when needed (ibid, p.47), while David Fairhall of the *Guardian* remarks that 'Much of what suspicious journalists regarded as news management could probably be explained as a mixture of ignorance, wishful thinking and a natural desire to put the best light on things when seen from a particular point of view' (ibid, p.53). Mike Nicholson accepts that 'sensible censorship' is inevitable and to be expected but he also talks about 'idiot censorship, total blanket censorship by men who are too cowardly or too arrogant to allow things to happen as they should'. He is also aware that there is disinformation, and that 'it's terribly, terribly hard to know when you're being lied to. It's not until afterwards that you realise you *have* been lied to...I mean we're always the puppets here and unless you say to them, "I'm not going to report anything you say because I think you're going to lie to me", what do you do? It's a Catch-22!'[4]

Mercer et al identify a crucial difference between the British and American information culture. The US Department of Defense (DoD) advocates public openness and accountability in accordance with the constitutional principles. 'Propaganda', it says, 'has no place in [DoD] public affairs programmes' (1987, p.4). The British MoD public relations staff seek to inform the public of its activities, also, but in wartime its primary function is of propaganda, in other words to 'create a favourable climate in support of these activities by the use of the news media, films, exhibitions and literature' (ibid, p.5). Journalists may see this as quite ironic given the MoD approach to briefings but the Ministry was nonetheless successful in 'creating a favourable climate' in support of the war against Argentina. Indeed, the British approach was watched carefully by military planners in the US. In a US Army journal, Commander Arthur Humphries drew a vital lesson from news management during the Falklands. Criticising British heavy handedness in their dealings with the news media, he advised that the military must give regular and friendly media briefings, and cultivate a relationship with the media based on mutual trust. This, he believed, would ensure 'the flow of correct information' and prevent 'faulty speculation'. He also accused the British of failing to 'appreciate that news management was more than just information security censorship. It also means providing pictures.' The crucial lesson, however, was control: 'Control access to the fighting, invoke censorship, and rally aid in the form of patriotism at home and in the battle zone.' Whatever about the rhetoric of free speech and democracy, 'the Falklands War shows us how to make certain that government policy is not undermined by the way a war is reported'. Humphries recommended that 'to effect or to help assure "favourable objectivity" you must be able to exclude certain correspondents from the battle zone'. In sum, then, Humphries advised that military planning 'should include criteria for incorporating the news media into the organisation for war' (MacArthur, 1992, pp.138–40).

Adams concludes that 'given the accessibility of many potential theatres of war and the immediacy of modern systems of communication, the problems raised by information-handling, and by the speculation and commentary surrounding operations in the South Atlantic in 1982, seem likely to pale into insignificance' in any future conflict (Adams, 1986, p.194). Only a year after Argentina invaded the Falklands, the US invaded the tiny Caribbean island of Grenada on 25 October 1983. Retired US Army General John E. Murray argued against media presence in the combat zone on the grounds that 'engaging the press while engaging the enemy is taking on one adversary too many'. It also appeared from opinion polls that media outrage notwithstanding, a majority of Americans supported the decision taken to exclude journalists from Grenada when it mattered (Braestrup, 1985, p.21). It seemed from the way their media strategy unfolded that the military were learning lessons about control first before thinking about public relations.

THE AMERICAN INVASION OF GRENADA, 1983

The aim of the invasion of Grenada, what the Americans called 'Operation Urgent Fury', was to overthrow the Grenadan government, itself imposed by military coup d'etat days earlier, on the grounds that it had allowed Soviet and Cuban forces to build up a military base there. The unease that the coup had caused among Grenada's neighbouring islands, and the apparent threat to resident American students on the island, was adequate pretext for the Reagan administration to order an invasion. It was left to the US Army and Navy to decide how to manage things. A feature of their approach was to keep the news media in the dark as much as possible (Braestrup, 1985, p.86). Secretary of Defense James Baker even excluded his spokesman, Larry Speakes, from National Security Council (NSC) planning; Speakes did not learn of the invasion until it had begun. The spokesmen at the Pentagon and at the State Department were told of the plans just before the invasion began but neither told Speakes. The reasons for excluding those who routinely dealt with press enquiries was the conviction among planners that spokesmen would be forced to lie to the press to keep the secret and therefore undermine their integrity as press officers (ibid, p.88). The military convinced the administration that the need for absolute secrecy in advance of the invasion was paramount for maximum surprise of attack and the ultimate success of the invasion. In his report on the invasion to the Joint Chiefs of Staff, in 1984, Admiral Wesley McDonald, insisted: 'The absolute need to maintain the greatest element of surprise in executing the mission to ensure minimum danger to US hostages...and to the servicemen involved in the initial assault dictated that the press be restricted until the initial objectives had been secured' (ibid, p.90).

Operation Urgent Fury was quite an improvised affair and pitted quite a small force against a rather noncommittal defence. The problem of how to deal with the media at large during the initial phases also seemed improvised. Again, the Pentagon left that to the commanders closest to operations, Admirals McDonald and Metcalf (ibid, p.92). Joseph Metcalf was the commander in the field and he devised a system of relaying information, most of it inaccurate and fragmentary, from the USS *Guam* to the Commander of the Atlantic Fleet (CINCLANT) in Norfolk, Virginia. Officials there used this information to form the basis of press releases. Looking back at his role in handling the media during the operation, Metcalf was unapologetic: 'I cannot duck the issue', he said, 'I had a great deal to do with keeping [the media] out. I think I did the right thing' (ibid, p.93). Moves to accommodate the media were made only after the operation was carried out and its objectives secured. A Joint Information Bureau (JIB) was quickly established at Grantley Adams Airport in Barbados. This had no direct link to Admiral Metcalf. To contact him, JIB officers had to do it through the American embassy, who rang CINCLANT in Virginia,who in turn contacted Metcalf and back again (ibid, p. 94). Metcalf finally gave permission for a small press pool to come onto the island from Barbados.

From the outset, the military excluded the news media from their immediate area of operations; up to 300 journalists were confined to a military base in Barbados. Even when the military finally agreed to allow a media presence on the island, on 27 October, they only allowed 15 reporters and photographers, 12 from the major American media and three from Caribbean media (ibid). ABC reporter Mark Scheerer recalled the mood of frustration among reporters in Barbados at being corralled away from the action and given inadequate facilities (four telephones between 300 reporters); and the heavy-handed, hostile approach of the USAF, whose officers routinely went 'bonkers' and confiscated film and audio tape. Press briefings were constantly cancelled and then never materialised and the pool list for Grenada kept changing (ibid, p.98). Thomas E. Ricks of the *Wall Street Journal* had a similar tale of woe: 'There are no press briefings, no press releases, no nothing. Some television cameramen have been sitting here in the airport for six days. They talk half-seriously of storming the barricades' (ibid, p.99). Once in Grenada their movements were restricted to guided tours of preselected locations, restrictions that were were not lifted until 30 October. There was only a trickle of information available during that period to Americans keen enough to look for it: ham radio broadcasts at first, threadbare press releases from the Pentagon, American students 'rescued' from the island, and reports from various Caribbean media (ibid, p.19). An ABC crew captured the first news pictures of US Marine activity at Grantley Adams airport but, to their dismay, their material was held back from broadcast when the station's Pentagon correspondent 'waved the story off' after a briefing from a 'trusted' DoD source (Hertsgaard, 1988, pp.206ff).

The news media were furious at their treatment but the only formal legal challenge against the media restrictions came from an unlikely source: the pornography publisher, Larry Flynt. He filed suit against the Department of Defense in the Washington Federal District Court and sought an order preventing further government restrictions on the media in Grenada on the grounds that it was unconstitutional. The court did not decide on the case until the following June, 1984, when it granted the government motion to dismiss the complaint as 'moot': in other words, as being a unique situation that was unlikely to recur. The court also ruled, crucially, that restrictions on reporters in the theatre of military operations was up to the military commander in the field (Kirtley, 1992, p.478). The indignant media were more successful with their call for a public inquiry into the affair. Led by veteran US Army Major-General Winant Sidle, it finally reported in August 1984 with a number of recommendations aimed at improving military–media relations in the event of future conflicts. The Sidle Commission advised that:

- the media should cooperate voluntarily with security guidelines
- the military should pay more attention to its relations with the media
- the military should help the media with logistics wherever or however possible in coverage of military operations
- any pooling system should as big as possible but kept in operation for the minimum time possible.

The military's response to Sidle was to create the official DoD media pool that became so familiar in the Persian Gulf War in 1991. According to the DoD, this would involve a select group of journalists ready at a moment's notice to go with the first wave in any military offensive. The pool was originally only created as a temporary, stop-gap measure that would satisfy both the media's need for information and the military's need for security at the critical moment of an operation. Eventually the rest of the media pack would join their advance colleagues when the situation would allow. The pool when it arrived on the island was given a restricted guided tour of what the guide called 'some of the most important aspects of the operation' (Braestrup, 1985, p.96).

Braestrup puts the Grenada coverage into some historical perspective when he compares it with the Normandy landings in the Second World War, the American intervention in the Dominican Republic in 1956 and several operations in Vietnam, when the US handled the media more or less well than might have been expected. Journalists were generally free to move round Vietnam but their reporting of several operations was restricted by news embargo, or they were banned from the battle zone altogether. The key and crucial difference in Grenada was, says Braestrup, 'both an attitude and a lack of planning by the Pentagon and the White House'. The lack of on-the-ground guidance, of well-informed and experienced press officers, or of proper press briefings and press releases in Barbados and in Grenada itself meant that reports that passed for news were based almost entirely on erroneous Pentagon briefings (ibid, p.104). However, Braestrup blames the media for lack of imagination and laziness, in that it was possible at the time to see from the contradictions between various official sources, between CINCLANT and the Pentagon and the White House, that there were inaccuracies and exaggerations and lies, and to ask some hard questions. 'Oddly enough', says Braestrup, 'the [media] seem to have devoted more of their energy to agonising over why they were excluded than on redeploying their man power and seeking to piece together the full story during the weeks that followed Urgent Fury' (ibid, p.109). Braestrup rather lets journalists off the hook here. Martin Hertsgaard points to a much more fundamental problem: the 'remarkable tendency' of the US media to accept government information as the 'basic truth' rather than think about its strategic value as propaganda, as was clearly the case with the Grenada invasion (1988, p.209). It was also evident that the restrictive media policy throughout the operation had been 'a major coup for the "bad cop" faction within the [Reagan] administration who favoured taking a hardline against the press' (ibid, p.236).

THE AMERICAN INVASION OF PANAMA, 1989

The test for the Sidle recommendations, and the DoD's new pooling system, came in December 1989 with 'Operation Just Cause', when American forces invaded Panama to overthrow President Manuel Noriega. Ostensibly, the operation was a 'drugs bust', only using about 24,000 US troops (Southern Command and 18th Airborne

Corps) instead of the customary drugs squad. Its real purpose was to secure American interests in the crucial Panama Canal Zone, with its bases, installations and commercial interests, before the Panama Canal Treaty returned the area back to Panama in 1999. Martha Gellhorn was in Panama City to report the operation and she saw it as a clear message to the developing countries of central and south America: with the Soviet Union in retreat, the US was the only superpower in town. She tells the story of how she tried to cash some travellers's cheques in Panama City only to find most banks closed because of the upheaval wrought by the invasion. She eventually found the Swiss Bank open for business but it was an international bank dedicated to transferring large sums of American dollars around the world; it did not cash traveller's cheques. Gellhorn left the bank with the thought that '24,000 armed men, attack helicopters, tanks and riotous disorder...had not interfered for an hour with international banking' (Gellhorn, 1994, p.270). It did however interfere with media reporting. Sandra Dickson convincingly shows that coverage of the invasion by the American press was ideologically skewed towards a narrow, status quo explanation of why the invasion was launched and what it hoped to achieve. She points to the dependence of the news media on institutional sources such as the State Department and the Pentagon which, she correctly argues, is linked to professional and instutional routines. However, she barely mentions the means by which those sources forged that dependency and restricted public understanding of the invasion's geopolitical and strategic impulses: the media pooling system (1994, pp.809ff).

William Boot defines the DoD media pool as 'A select group of combat journalists that is never permitted to see combat. Sometimes referred to as "the public's eyes and ears"' (1990). (William Boot is the pen name of Christopher Hanson of the *Seattle Post–Intelligencer*.) Up until the latter half of the operation, journalists were corralled like cattle at isolated American bases, well away from the action. The US Army Southern Command only briefed journalists once during the four days of the pool's deployment, while its 'media centre' was beset with technical problems which caused serious delays for the transmission of copy and photographs (Hoffman, 1991, p.92).

The International Centre on Censorship pointed out that during the invasion, the pool was 'activated' too late to be of any help to journalists (Philo and McLaughlin, 1995, n.8). However, this was exactly what the US Secretary of Defense, Dick Cheney, had intended. He made no apologies for it but mollified media hubris by commissioning an enquiry into what happened, led by Fred S. Hoffman. The resulting Hoffman Report (1990) criticised the Department for excessive secrecy and noted that the reports sent back from Panama by the news pool were of 'secondary value' (Hoffman, 1991, p.93). It made 17 recommendations for improving the situation in future operations, among which were that in advance of future operations, the Secretary of Defense should state his or her official sponsorship of the media pool, and that the DoD should monitor the development of a public affairs strategy that includes proper accommodation of the media. The pool should be briefed regularly by senior officers and coordinated by public affairs officers and escorts from the section of the armed services involved in the operation. For their part, the pool participants should share all 'pool products' – news pictures and copy – with the other participants. The report also recommended that proper channels of communication and accountability be kept open throughout all stages of an operation so that problems and difficulties be rectified on the spot or as soon as possible thereafter. As an adjunct to this, there should be regular liaison between media and military to discuss any problems and clarify rules and responsibilities in the event of future operations; the armed services might also consider incorporating the media pools into military exercises (ibid, pp.105ff). In response, Dick Cheney welcomed the report but said he '[did not] agree with all the facets of it in terms of recommendations'. He accepted responsibility for his policy of secrecy and explained that he was 'very concerned about the possibility of premature disclosure of the operation [which would have] created enormous problems for us, obviously, and put at risk the lives of the men conducting the operation' (ibid, p.108). Effectively, it was 'thanks but no thanks' to Hoffman.

THE PERSIAN GULF WAR, 1991

In both Grenada and Panama, the military control of the media was highly successful and effective but it was arguably let down by poor public relations. They kept the media in one place away from the battle zone but not on side and 'on message'. In the Gulf War, they exercised some public relations with the help and cooperation of a good number of journalists present. The Pentagon was ecstatic with the result, what assistant Secretary of Defense Pete Williams celebrated as 'the best war coverage we've ever had' (Boot, 1991, p.24). The media reaction, after the war was over, was somewhat less ecstatic. Two aspects of the military's handling of the media in the Gulf stimulated considerable debate: the news pools and the daily media briefings and conferences. In each case, the acquiescent posture of the assembled journalists contrasted with the sceptical, critical response of their colleagues in Baghdad to Iraqi efforts at public relations.

The News Pools

Six army Public Affairs officers were appointed to manage the media in the Gulf. Alex Thomson (1992) provides a colourful picture of these officers. Their coordinator was Michael Sherman who usually directed the Navy's PR office in Los Angeles and who was nicknamed 'Hollywood Mike' for his consultancy work on movies like *Top Gun*, the *Hunt for Red October* and *Flight of the Intruder*. As early as 13 August 1990, just nine days after Iraq's invasion of Kuwait, Sherman and his team were responsible for setting up the main military briefing room and TV studio in the International Hotel in Dhahran and of course the now familiar news pools or 'Media Response Teams' that would be allowed to accompany troops on certain operations. John Fialka (1992) argues that when the news media came to the Gulf, they expected a long Vietnam-style war of attrition in which they could move around on different fronts. Instead, what they got was a short and remote aerial bombing campaign followed by a brief 'land war' that evidently could not accommodate large numbers of journalists. Media pressure for increased accreditation on the news pools overloaded and finally collapsed the system. It led to bitter competition between informal media cartels among the news pools and to pedantic squabbling among journalists over definitions, rules and privileges (ibid, p.8). Some journalists came prepared for a particular type of war, often with surreal results. Robert Fisk of the *Independent* remembers them well:

One guy turned up from a small town [American] newspaper...wearing camouflage costume and he had boots with leaves painted on – Saudi Arabia of course has no trees as you're aware. And some of them came along in desert camouflage would you believe, from the Gulf, and turned up in Kosovo where there are leaves and trees and grass. These guys! Who are these people?

What possesses them to behave like this? It's definitely not journalism, not the kind I'm involved in anyway.[5]

As the Gulf War entered its final stages, Pete Williams told the US Senate Committee on Governmental Affairs that the pool system was a compromise and designed for three reasons: 'It gets reporters out to see the action, it guarantees that Americans at home get reports from the scene of the action, and it allows the military to accommodate a reasonable number of journalists without overwhelming the units that are fighting the enemy' (1995, p.334). This was a very positive spin on the pooling system that gave no clue to its function as an instrument of control. The control was inbuilt and depended on one crucial dynamic: the degree to which the media would play along with it and effectively police themselves. The system bred an overweening competitiveness among them and some went so far as to inform on other journalists such as Robert Fisk, who tried to operate outside the system. As Fisk argues, the last thing a journalist needs in the difficult environment of a war zone is for his or her colleagues to report them to the authorities.[6] John Fialka remembers that in-fighting among the American news pools was ceaseless and they were organised and controlled from within according to different priorities. There were arguments over what exactly was being pooled: the information or the correspondents? The 'big three' American networks – NBC, ABC and CBS – objected to their correspondents having to do stand-ups on CNN. The photography pool was 'a plutocracy' run by the elite of three news magazines, *Time*, *Newsweek* and *US News and World Report*, and two press agencies, AP and Reuters (1992, p.37). This cosy arrangement was blown apart just as the war started when the newspaper photographers appeared in force and demanded fairer play from the 'Big Five' in terms of shared use of materials and shared responsibility for running the pool. The stakes were high. John MacArthur mentions the freewheeling French photojournalists who dubbed themselves the 'Fuck the Pool pool' that, by operating outside the system, captured some of the best images of the war (1992, p.155).

The pool also nurtured a culture of grievance and encouraged poaching and plagiarism of pooled dispatches; there were even paranoid suspicions that 'foreign reporters' were looking for material from the American news pool attached to US military units (Fialka, 1992, pp.32ff). Fialka and the other journalists in his pool 'discovered that the military had also found ways to make working conditions there more difficult. We encountered multiple layers of control, at least one of which always seemed to be there. Barriers seemed to raise automatically to blur the reality; buffers were always at the ready to blunt the sharp edges of truth' (ibid, p.55). Maggie O'Kane remembers how this reached its nadir during the American invasion of Haiti in 1994 when journalists, crazed by the competition the pooling system engendered, embarked on something of a witch hunt for reporters who made it to the island unaccredited and by unorthodox means.[7]

Margaret Blanchard sees the Gulf War as the 'first time in American history (that) reporters were essentially barred from accompanying the nation's troops into combat' (1992, p.6). The news pools offered journalists very little in the way of first-hand action with the possible exception of the Iraqi incursion into the Saudi border town of Khafji, or the final skirmishes in Kuwait City as the Iraqis withdrew in some disarray. They saw little or nothing of the brief and much vaunted 'land war'. Instead they found themselves watching planes taking off from air bases and returning or cruise missiles launched from ships in the Persian Gulf; or even worse still, watching CNN and NBC in their hotel rooms for the real action in Baghdad. Thus, Pete Williams' argument, that the media pools would allow journalists to see the action, was quite disingenuous in one way, but weirdly accurate in another.

Some journalists questioned the pooling arrangement while others – such as Robert Fisk of the London *Independent* and Chris Hedges of the *New York Times* – refused to work in it altogether and were dubbed 'unilaterals' or 'freelancers' by the military. Fisk points out that such labels were totally pejorative; he was a full-time staff journalist with a British newspaper, not a freelancer. The term 'unilateral', on the other hand, appeared to be purely a military moniker too readily accepted by journalists themselves.[8] Hedges writes of his experiences with other unilaterals and how troops in the US and Egyptian army units subverted the rules to allow them unofficial passage in their successful bid to reach Kuwait City before its liberation. Their success was 'due in part to an understanding by many soldiers and officers of what the role of a press is in a democracy. These men and women violated orders to allow us to do our job' (1991, p.27).

In spite of the obvious vagaries of the media pools, most journalists cooperated with the system in something of a Faustian bargain. Kate Adie says the media and the military must 'do a deal and they must do it publicly – that is the pool';[9] while Martin Bell talks about the need for trust between journalists and their military minders:

> It's essentially part of being a journalist, understanding people and seeing soldiers as human beings and not as numbers in an order of battle. It does help, if you're reporting on soldiers, to have been a soldier. They get alienated by daft questions from reporters who don't know the difference between a brigade and a battalion. And they'll simply tell you more if they trust you more. I never saw that as a hindrance to good journalism; it was a help to it.[10]

Indeed, British journalist, Mark Urban, suggests there is a key difference between the American approach and the British approach:

> The Americans will try to short-circuit the gap between reality and publishable reality by telling lies sometimes and it's very rare that you catch the Brits doing that. I mean when they said in the Gulf War that they were not targeting Saddam it was plainly rubbish...We know absolutely it was their intention to try and kill him if an opportunity presented itself...it was a patent lie. You get other occasions when they're flustered, like when the Iraqis went into Khafji, where they're not exactly lying but they're on the hind foot and they're talking rubbish. The Brits are more trustworthy in that respect.[11]

That judgement may come as a surprise to journalists who have tried to report, independently, other more contentious conflicts in which the British have been directly involved such as Malaysia and Northern Ireland where disinformation and psychological operations have been used to create a 'favourable climate' for effective propaganda (see Carruthers, 1995; GUMG, 1985, Miller, 1994). Michael Nicholson learned a bitter lesson in media–military trust from his reporting of the Falklands War:

> [My] first instinct was to believe what the military were telling me. But of course it transpired that they were telling lies. People you trusted or thought you trusted were lying to you for their own military purposes and sometimes for their own reputations...[When] you go to war with Brits, with your own people, there is this naive assumption you're on the same side and you all want that side to win and therefore they can be trusted.

But they don't trust you. That's the whole point of the aggravation that happened out there and in the Gulf. The military do not trust the journalists which I think was unfair...It was constant hostility.[12]

And so what if the Americans do lie? In the US, journalists are citizens, not subjects, and like all American citizens they enjoy the right to access public information, a principle not lost on General Grant in the American Civil War in his efforts to develop a practical censorship policy. So although, as Blanchard argues, there is a long history in America of military and political manipulation of the media in wartime (1992, p.16), the citizen journalist has at least some constitutional avenues for countering the pernicious effects of the control culture. In Britain, few such avenues exist. There is a vague notion in British culture of 'the people' but they are 'loyal subjects' of Her Majesty rather than 'citizens' of a republic; no constitutional conception of the citizen or citizen's rights yet exists, although there is now recourse to human rights law in the European Union. As the party of government, Labour pays lip service to the concept of freedom of information yet bolsters the culture of denial and secrecy in government departments and the intelligence services. At the time of writing, plans are being made to further bolster these measures after the terrorist attacks on New York and on the Pentagon on 11 September 2001, all the more worrying when public acquiescence is obtained amid widespread revulsion, fear and anxiety.

The Briefings and News Conferences

If the pooling system brought out the worst in journalists, the picture was hardly any better when they assembled in the briefing rooms in Dhahran or Riyadh. While the pooling system kept journalists well away from the real action, the briefings kept real information away from journalists. But they did nothing to escape the accusation that they let the military get away with it. They did not ask hard questions of the briefers who, wrote Henry Allen of the *Washington Post*, made them look like 'fools, nitpickers, and egomaniacs...dinner party commandos, slouching inquisitors, [and] collegiate spit ball artists'. All in all, they constituted 'a whining, self-righteous, upper middle class mob' (Fialka, 1992, p.62). John MacArthur's criticisms are milder but no less damning. Journalists were made to look 'so bumbling and informationless...contrasted as they were with the purposeful and self-assured military briefers'

(1992, p.151). Added to this are the charges that they failed to challenge the slick Pentagon videos of 'smart bombs' hitting their targets with questions about their real accuracy and the actual ratio of 'smart bombs' to conventional, 'dumb' munitions used. Had these questions been asked, had journalists investigated further, with some research, they may have been able to ascertain that only 7 per cent of all munitions used were smart weapons. Instead, the briefings were like video war games that played to the whoops, cheers and laughter of the assembled journalists, most if not all seemingly forgetful of the reality that human beings were dying in their tens of thousands under some of the most lethal firepower ever deployed – 'smart' or 'dumb'. Their amnesia was probably induced by a directive from General Schwarzkopf that the briefings were not going to turn into the 'Five O'Clock Follies' of the Vietnam War when briefers offered daily body counts. There was to be no body count, only weekly bomb damage assessments. Journalists were given details of how many tanks or artillery pieces had been knocked out but nothing about estimated casualties amongst the soldiers who presumably manned them (Thomson, 1992, pp.97–8). This was restricted information according to the extensive media ground rules at the military's disposal (see Appendices 3 and 4) but, as Massing argues, an experienced and resourceful journalist could easily extrapolate from the welter of statistics the military *did* release on a daily basis (1991, p.24).

The most damning indictment of these journalists must surely be that they did not ask the right questions at the right time and recognise that the briefers were military officers with a war to sell, not messengers from heaven speaking the gospel truth. As in all wars, there were honourable exceptions but not enough to make a real difference. The impact of these briefings and the easily processed images they provided made for 'good television' and certainly filled many slack hours of saturation coverage during the first week of the war. In London, two senior BBC journalists, anchor David Dimbleby and defence correspondent David Shukman, played and replayed the first video images from the briefing rooms as if they were analysing a soccer match, using laser light pens to circle targets and bring home to the viewer that this was indeed a hi-tech, low casualty war where bombs and missiles were so smart 'they are able to destroy [a military target], no doubt kill all the occupants of it, but without causing casualties amongst the civilian population around' (18 January 1991). Smart bombs indeed. Journalists might wonder in response what useful information could be obtained from briefers who responded to questions in terms such as 'We just don't discuss that...I can't tell you why we won't discuss it because then I'd be discussing it' (Thomson, 1992, p.83). But blaming the military for the briefings is rather futile; the briefings and the information policy that supported them fitted into a highly successful and effective military public relations campaign from the very outset of the Gulf crisis in August 1990 when Iraq invaded Kuwait. Like entertaining a party of children, the briefers kept the journalists occupied and out of harm's way. The children for their part got their ringside seat at the circus and wanted to keep it.

Media Responses to Iraqi Propaganda in the Persian Gulf War

British and American media coverage of the war was not confined to the home studios or the briefing rooms in Saudi Arabia. Some journalists based themselves in Baghdad and the test would be how they responded to Iraqi news management tactics. In the first few days, journalists such as Brent Sadler (ITN) and Peter Arnett (CNN) came under some political flak in Britain and the US where critics thought their presence in Iraq was being used by Saddam Hussein for his own propaganda purposes. As Walter Goodman put it, 'Much of the abuse was strictly political. The Scuds came mainly from the right' , from critics who worried about images of civilian casualties being beamed around the world (1991, p.29). Typical of the type of material the critics had in mind was an ITN film from Baghdad that showed cruise missiles whizzing overhead on their way, it was assumed, to preprogrammed targets, probably the first footage of these missiles being fired in anger. The reporter was led by an Iraqi minder to the aftermath of the attack where he reported that 'simple gunfire' brought down at least one of the much vaunted hi-tech missiles. He also went to a hospital filled with casualties from the attack and interviewed a doctor and civilian eyewitnesses. The report ended with a woman in a UN track suit shouting to camera, 'This is not a game! These are human lives!' (1 February 1991). Mark Urban thinks such reports expose the myth that the media helped to sanitise the war and explain why they attracted such opprobrium from conservative media critics:

> The reason I believe it's erroneous is because the images of the suffering...were under the control of Saddam Hussein who was so stupid that he kicked out all but three of the [western] journalists

when the war began. If Saddam Hussein had allowed access, and allowed people to drive all over the country, then I think the effects would have been very different. We saw that there was a wobble in public opinion after the Amiriyah shelter bombing and we can only speculate, for example when a British Tornado dropped a laser-guided bomb on the market in Falujah and killed it is believed 160 civilians, what would have been the effect in the UK if Jeremy Bowen or John Simpson had been allowed to go there and say, 'We did this. The Brits did this', with all the sort of gore and suffering and screaming which comes about when something like that happens.[13]

However, the record shows this to be an over-optimistic assessment. The western news media did report some examples of Iraqi 'gore and suffering' but generally dismissed it as propaganda. For example, Urban's reference to the Al-amiriyah bomb shelter is an interesting case. A bomb shelter in the Baghdad suburb of Al-amiriyah, packed with civilians during a bombing raid, was hit by a missile, killing all or most of the unfortunate occupants. As Urban would expect, many good western journalists filed harrowing dispatches but the problem was what happened to them when they reached the newsroom for broadcast. Independent Television News (ITN) cut the most difficult footage on the grounds that it was 'too distressing', an extension one could say of their policy during the Falklands War. However, the BBC's treatment of a report from Jeremy Bowen stands out for the way in which it was so effectively interrogated and emasculated by the news anchor. In a recorded two-way with Bowen in Baghdad, Peter Sissons questioned him within the strictures of the Pentagon claim that the bomb shelter was a military command and control bunker. He left no doubt whose account he believed:

> *Sissons*: A few moments ago I spoke with Jeremy Bowen in Baghdad and asked him whether he could be *absolutely sure* there was no military communications equipment in the shelter which the allies believe was there?
> *Bowen*: Well, Peter, we looked very hard for it. I'm pretty confident, as confident as I can be, that I've seen all the main rooms.
> *Sissons*: Is it *conceivable* it could have been in military use and was converted recently to civilian use?
> *Bowen*: Well, it would be a strange thing to do...

Sissons: Let me put it another way, Jeremy, is it possible to say *with certainty* that it was never a military facility? [emphasis in the original]

At that point, Sissons closed the interview with the caveat that Bowen was 'subject *of course* to Iraq's reporting restrictions' (BBC, 18.00, 14 February 1991; emphasis added). Another ITN report from Iraq surveyed what the allies called 'collateral damage', damage to civilian populations. It showed footage of children in hospitals, and images of bombed out houses and churches; but right from the introduction, the news anchor raised the suspicions of the viewer in less than subtle terms. The footage, we were told, was taken by an ITN camera but 'operated by a *Jordanian* cameraman', the implication being that we could trust the camera but not the operator because of his Arab origins. The film report runs with pictures alternatively labelled as being from 'ITN', 'Iraqi TV' and the 'Iraqi Ministry of Information' while the journalist underscores his voice-over report with the heaviest qualifications. The pictures 'show extensive damage caused, *the Iraqis say*, by allied bombers...an image of life in Iraq that Saddam Hussein is anxious for the world to see and believe'. This is followed by a sequence of images 'supplied by the Ministry of Information [which] as propaganda graphically illustrates the suffering [and is] being used as a weapon...as a means to influence world opinion'. The problem, the reporter says, is that 'Iraqi-supplied material draws natural suspicions about its authenticity'. For example, over images of civilian casualties, he comments that they are 'claimed by Iraq to be recent victims of the bombing but they have not been independently verified as such' (21.45, 26 February 1991). Goodman gives an example of similar attempts by American reporters in Iraq to signal images of civilian casualties as Iraqi propaganda (1991, p.30). Contrary to Mark Urban's hunch, then, the Gulf War was a sanitised war partly because the western news media played a key role in constructing it as such. Under fire from politicians at home, reporters were sensitive in the extreme to charges of being propaganda dupes. Western-supplied material did not raise 'natural suspicions about its authenticity'; presumably any such suspicions that existed would have been classed 'unnatural'.

BOSNIA AND THE 'EMBEDDED MEDIA'

Relations between the media and UNPROFOR Bosnia were generally good and never reached the depths of antagonism plumbed during the Gulf War. The media were much freer to move about at their own personal risk – explaining perhaps why so many were killed and injured. But Bosnia did not mark an end to the evolutionary process evident ever since Vietnam. The US military had clear ideas both of their objectives in Bosnia and of how the American media might help them meet those objectives. The general commanding the American sector in Bosnia was William L. Nash. His three goals in respect to dealing with the media were to: gain support of the American public for the conduct of the operation, maintain the morale of American troops, and use the world's media influence to promote compliance with the Dayton Accords among the former warring factions (1998, pp.132–3). To these ends the planners came up with the concept of 'embedded media', which was really a less restrictive version of the pooling system. Reporters (about forty of them) would accompany troops on the ground for two weeks and get 'a more nuanced picture of our activities by allowing them virtually free access to the soldiers and commanders'. This of course required a revamp of the Joint Information Bureau system to ensure tighter coordination between levels of command and avoid embarrassing and unnecessary conflicts (ibid, p.132). A significant component of the Nash approach and which was not seen in the Gulf War was his idea of allowing journalists to be present at points of conflict as a means of demonstrating the 'transparency of our operations and the firmness of our purpose'. Nash gives the example of Linda Patillo of ABC News who witnessed one such confrontation between a US Army Colonel and a Bosnian Serb Commander in spring, 1996. Nash was delighted with the public relations derived from the story Patillo sent back. It 'portrayed a "real life situation" in which armed conflict could have broken out at any minute. [It] showed the preparedness of [our] forces, their resolve to do their duty, and the colonel's...professionalism and calm nature in the execution of his duty. What a great story to show the American people!' (ibid, p.133). Nash concludes that 'it is essential that the military and the media engage *before* they need to do so' and that requires a break from traditional thinking and a recognition that 'good policy and good execution usually result in good stories...Don't sweat the spin. Work the issues wisely' (ibid, p.135). It is worth noting here the emphasis on getting out 'a great story'; at no stage in his article does Nash mention 'censorship' or 'propaganda'.

British soldiers serving with UNPROFOR were given clear guidelines for handling unsolicited media enquiries in Bosnia and these also indicated the shift from direct censorship to spin. An *aide mémoire* instructed them on the following easy-to-remember principles of handling the media:

- the media are not hostile
- handled well they will promote the unit's image
- poorly treated the opposite applies
- they will report on us as they see us
- things unsaid are rarely regretted.

If in any doubt, the anxious soldier should utter one of two statements:

1. 'We are here to help UN relief supplies get through to those in need.'
2. 'We do not support any side. That's not our job. We are just here to help the needy.'

CONCLUDING REMARKS

Back on the Home Front and behind the scenes, there have been some attempts since the Gulf War to create some meeting place between journalists, military and academics to discuss issues of media censorship and the freedom of information. Mike Nicholson argues that when it comes to the media, the military seems to focus too much on learning how the news media work and tells a story of a social encounter with the British military that neatly sums up the problem with so much emphasis on training the new officer classes in modern methods of handling the media:

> I was once asked at some dinner by some admiral, if this was a wonderful thing to do, wouldn't this make things easier in the future? And I said no, of course it won't make things easier in the future. Nothing will ever change. All you're doing is learning our tricks, that's what it's all about. You're spending money employing us to come and talk to you because you want to know how we work. But you'll never let us know how you work. And he shut up after that.[14]

An American collection of essays edited by Lloyd J. Matthews, entitled *Newsmen and National Defense: Is Conflict Inevitable?* (1991), highlights a gulf of misunderstanding between the military officer class and commercial mainstream news media. For example, journalist Richard Halloran surveyed a sample of US Army officers to discover their principal perceptions of the media. Chief among these were: that the media were an all-powerful entity (with the 'newspaper man' and the 'press' being the sole representatives of the 'media') with a liberal agenda that was instinctively anti-military; also that journalists were just in it for the money or to 'sell newspapers', that journalists were not really professionals, that unlike the military they reported they were not accountable to the public, that they were usually inaccurate with the facts, that they only 'printed' bad news, that they relied on unnamed and unattributable sources, that they often published classified material and used unauthorised information without thought about the consequences, that war and defence correspondents often lacked military knowledge or experience, that they took up precious military time and resources, and, worst of all perhaps in the eyes of the US military, they just lacked patriotism (1991, pp.39ff). Other individual contributions to the volume, such as Sarkesian (1991, pp.61ff), crystallise the inherently contradictory assumption that the media are staffed by liberal elites from top to bottom and are run by all-powerful corporations, in some cases corporations such as General Electric and Westinghouse which are instinctively anti-liberal in their business practices and that arm the US military with missile and radar systems. Yet as William Hammond argues in the same volume, the US military has developed an acute sense of public relations as a cure for all these ills in the military–media relationship. However, he warns that after the sales pitch and the ad campaign, 'sales still depend on whether the product itself fulfills...expectations' and on the fact that 'the truth has greater ultimate power than the most pleasing of bromides' (1991, p.15).

Military public relations over this period, then, has become more effective than direct censorship of the type familiar in both world wars. One could say that by the end of the 1990s it had become the new censorship. Serious examination of the most critical phases of the Falklands War, the invasions of Grenada and Panama, and the Gulf War, shows that these operations were carried out with most journalists under the thumb and the public in the dark. In this regard, the pooling system was successfully 'activated' in every instance while journalists, on the other hand, were effectively *deac*tivated. As Martha Gellhorn wrote after the Gulf War:

In the Falklands, Grenada, Panama and the Gulf War, our governments have shown a fine skill in controlling and manipulating the press. The press is shown what the government thinks fit when the government ordains. The press is treated to military briefings instead of finding out for itself. An accompanying officer or minder is always at hand. The result of this press management...is that we have had no real press coverage. In the interests of 'national security' or any phrase they wish to use, our governments have decided to neuter the press in war time. (1993, p.340)

The Gulf War marked this new approach to military PR and showed that the problem is not so much the extent and nature of reporting restrictions; the focus on these alone lets journalists off the hook and deflects the blame onto their military minders. The problem is how journalists respond to propaganda from what they might see as their 'own side': their unwillingness to challenge reporting restrictions, their enjoyment of the razzmatazz of the briefings and their susceptibility to disinformation and dissemblage, and their failure to corroborate source information against alternative material. But there are lessons from 'abroad', from journalists in parts of the world not known for their celebration of the freedom of the press such as Russia. In the first Chechnyan War, from 1994 to 1996, the Russian Army was ruthless in its attempts to intimidate the Russian and international media away from the story of its brutal war with Chechnyan rebels. Public opinion in Russia suggested that the army had considerable popular support to do what it deemed necessary to win. A favourite tactic was to suspend accreditation procedures at critical moments in the conflict and to tell journalists that their safety could not be gauranteed. Yet Russian journalists simply sought out alternative sources in the age-old tradition of good reporting (Peters Talbott, 1996, p.48). As a result, they were able to resist the twin pressures of government censorship and economic constraint to 'break Soviet traditions of passive reporting and provide Russian readers with a broad array of views' on the Chechnyan conflict (ibid, p.51). They were praised for 'the frankness of their coverage' and their criticisms of the government's conduct of the war, 'the first time in Russia's five year democratic experiment that [they] have played such a role' (Rutland, 1996). Things have changed since then, of course; Russia has been fighting a second, still more brutal campaign in Chechnya while the unstable political and economic climate at home has taken its toll on the concepts of freedom of speech and media pluralism. Yet the Russian media's experiment with independence has shown their western counterparts that there is always a space in which journalists can ask hard questions of their military and political leaders in a war situation; and a space in which they can be resourceful enough to access alternative sources of information.

6 Lessons Learned? The Media, the Military and the Kosovo Crisis

> If you don't trust the military, and they're the ones dropping the bombs, who are you going to trust?
>
> Mark Laity, BBC's Defence Correspondent at the NATO media briefings during the bombing of Serbia in 1999[1]

> In a democracy, a journalist's job is to challenge authority – it's even more important for him to do it when a democracy is at war – but if he doesn't do it [then] put on a uniform and join the Territorial Army and go and fight. Otherwise you're not a journalist.
>
> Robert Fisk, of the London *Independent*, on asking hard questions at the NATO briefings[2]

After every major war since the Crimea, journalists have spent considerable column inches and air time agonising over the way in which they were cowed and controlled by the military and the dreadful implications this all had for freedom of the press and democracy: too late then of course to put things right and take a stand. The Gulf War of 1991 in particular was a high point for the military and a low point among many for the war correspondent. However, news coverage of the American bombing of Iraq just before Ramadan in 1998, and NATO's bombing of Serbia in 1999, provided two further opportunities to see if the media had learned any lessons at all from the Gulf War in dealing with organised attempts to influence and control their reporting.

BOMBING IRAQ, 1998[3]

The Gulf War officially ended in April 1991 but since then American forces have maintained a 'low level' but sustained bombing campaign against targets in Iraq. In practice, 'low level' usually means concealed from public knowledge but no less lethal in execution or effect. However, there have been moments during this period when bombing raids have been ratcheted up and brought to us live on television amid intensive propaganda; moments such as 16 December 1998 when the attention of the American people was distracted away from impending impeachment proceedings against President Clinton over the Monica Lewinsky affair. What was called 'Operation Desert Fox' in the West, the Iraqi media called 'Operation Monica'. *Channel Four News* opened with an ironic intercutting of images of war over Baghdad and war in the US Congress. Their Washington correspondent sent this dispatch from Capitol Hill:

[Two] political parties literally digging trenches for themselves and now slogging it out one by one, hour after hour. The hatred is almost visceral, the fury quite latent...The President is urging unity at a moment of conflict with Iraq but here on the battlefield of Congress there is only the dialogue of the deaf...Republican after Republican literally throwing the book [US Constitution] at the President; Democrat after Democrat lining up to defend the President, painting *Apocalypse Now*, and here in Washington, not in Baghdad. (19.00, 18 December 1998)

Once again, a powerful military operation was sold to us as a necessary blow to Saddam Hussein's reputed biological and chemical weapons capability which, we were continually told, appeared to expand all the time in the 1990s in spite of a comprehensive programme of disarmament by the United Nations weapons inspectorate (UNSCOM), and successive American bombing missions. Thus, an avowed aim of Operation Desert Fox was to 'degrade and diminish' still further Saddam's mythical military capability, especially his 'weapons of mass destruction'. Most American and British TV news reporters were oblivious to this contradiction and internalised the military line instead. The truth – as even US Secretary of Defense William Cohen was eventually forced to admit – was that there was no guarantee that any of the 'command and control' targets contained such weapons. As former UN arms inspector Scott Ritter put it, 'We're hitting empty buildings and we're killing innocent civilians' (BBC1, 18.00, 17 December 1998). Yet, newscasters and reporters lapsed into unreflective 'wow journalism' and continued to treat the bombing raids as militarily justifiable. They fed contentedly on the usual statistics about numbers of bombing missions and their success rates, or the types of planes and weapons used; all presented to them in military briefings by the British Ministry of Defence or at the Pentagon with the help of missile videos and before-and-after displays of satellite reconnaissance photography. Even experienced journalists such as BBC World Affairs Editor John Simpson seemed happy to endorse the 'weapons of mass destruction' line. There was 'no alternative' to the bombings, he said, 'because Saddam Hussein has all these absolutely obscene weapons which he's shown his willingness to use in the past' (BBC1, 21.00, 18 December 1998). Simpson was perhaps referring to the gassing of an entire Iraqi village in the Iran–Iraq war of the 1980s. The attack was barely noticed or reported in the West and there were no bombing missions proposed to 'degrade and diminish' Iraq's military capability. Iraq was still at that time a friend of the West in the wider battle against the common enemy, Iran and its revolutionary Islam.

It was clear that the bombing raids on military and political targets, and on Saddam Hussein's many palaces around the country, were aimed purely at intimidating and containing him or, in the propaganda phrase that belied the true aim of the bombing campaign, 'putting him back in his cage'. News reports suggested that Saddam Hussein's many palaces and Ba'ath Party buildings around the country housed deep underground bunkers that supposedly contained stocks of chemical and biological weapons which the Iraqis had apparently managed to hide from UNSCOM. Propaganda such as this had the beauty of not only justifying the bombings per se but also explaining away awkward questions about their ultimate lack of success. Mark Urban reported the doubts of a weapons expert that 'the strikes will have done much more than batter some bad taste architecture'. Group Captain Duncan Lennox, editor of *Jane's Air Launch Weapons*, pointed out that the 'allies' had not yet developed the weapons to pierce these deep bunkers and destroy their deadly contents. However, Urban suggested that 'one reason Saddam's weapons programmes are such difficult targets is that there's so little of them left. UNSCOM has destroyed everything it knows about...Intelligence analysts are divided as to whether Iraq actually possesses any chemical or biological weapons at all.' He cited a Pentagon analysis that accounted for all but two of the 819 SCUD missiles Iraq imported from the Soviet Union in the 1980s, and referred to a Whitehall intelligence estimate that the country had just a handful of its biological and chemical weapons left. 'It's for this reason', Urban concluded, 'that American officials are careful never to say that Iraq actually possesses weapons of mass destruction and missiles' (BBC2 *Newsnight*, 17 December 1998). Indeed not;

they only had to suggest the possibility and the pliant media would do the rest. This is the joy of the background briefing.

As for the 'weapons of mass destruction' the allies were using to such devastating effect on Baghdad, they were celebrated by reporters and news anchors for their accuracy and apparent ability to distinguish between military targets and civilians. On 17 December, the first full day of bombing, NBC coverage featured a report on the type of weaponry available to the 'allies'. In its tone and hyperbole, it resembled a promotional video for one of the big American weapons manufacturers. Opening with archive footage of an atomic test, the reporter intoned, 'Firepower: it no longer means a mushroom cloud.' He continued over pictures of weapons tests, sounding like Q, James Bond's quartermaster:

> Today, smaller and smarter counts. The goal? Hit targets without killing innocent civilians around them, fire from high up and miles away to keep pilots out of range of anti-aircraft guns and missiles, convert good old fashioned dumb bombs to smart ones, [to camera] and shoot missiles that can home in on targets no bigger than this [arms outstretched].

The reporter turns to the development of weapons that can be guided by satellite (rather than 'good old-fashioned' laser beam?) for even greater accuracy; such technology would have the capacity for not last-minute but 'last-second adjustments'. Over more test video footage of missiles hitting military bunkers, complete with helpful arrows, he exclaims excitedly that 'Targeters, bragging they no longer aim for something as small as a door, claim they can aim for a door *knob* and hit it!' With no hint of irony, the reporter asks: 'But are these claims sometimes over-stated?' Apparently not, a military consultant tells him: the accuracy of 'smart bombs' today has improved by up to 15 per cent on the Gulf War of 1991. The reporter raves on about 'improved bunker busters' that 'penetrate deeply' through two or three levels to the assigned target, cluster bombs that can disable an entire airfield, and other 'robot-like weapons'. The military consultant concludes that 'Science fiction is here! In the next ten years it's going to be all we're using!' It is ironic that among the key targets of American bombing were Iraqi aircraft hangars that 'possibly' contained pilotless, robot planes, or what the MoD in Britain called 'drones of death', that 'might' be used to carry 'possible' weapons of mass destruction. Science fiction indeed.

All this was a rehearsal of the old Gulf War formula: smart, hi-tech bombs mean low civilian casualties. Two British TV journalists discussed with amazement how Iraqi civilians were still going about their normal business even during the air raids. 'I suppose', said one, 'it's implicitly a compliment to those special weapons the Americans are using...It does appear that these smart weapons, as the Pentagon calls them, are proving pretty effective. It does appear they're taking out fairly systematically those chosen targets' (ITN, late night coverage, 17–18 December 1998). The BBC's correspondent in Baghdad spoke of the 'degree of trust that these so-called smart bombs are hitting very specific targets and I doubt that anybody in Iraq, at least not the population at large, think that they are the actual targets of these bombardments' (BBC1, 18.00, 18 December 1998).

Whenever it was impossible to ignore the inconvenient matter of casualties, reporters were careful to exercise a degree of scepticism totally lacking in their parroting of allied propaganda. Report after news report from Baghdad cautioned that the Iraqis were 'anxious' to make capital out of civilian casualties and that, even though their estimates were quite conservative, in the tens rather than the hundreds, they were 'impossible to verify'. Television pictures from hospitals or the site of destruction by allied bombs only 'seemed' to show casualties and were to be treated with caution because as John Simpson put it, 'civilian casualties make the best propaganda' (BBC1, 21.00, 17 December 1998). Houses or factories were only ever 'apparently hit'. An ITN reporter visited the ruins of a house 'after apparently being hit in last night's bombardment'. Even though the reporter could see for himself that it was actually hit by an American missile, and even though it was recorded and self-evident, he warned that it could not be verified. So while ground-level pictures of the aftermath of bombing in Baghdad are 'apparent' and 'impossible to verify', grainy cockpit video of missiles hitting their targets can be taken at face value: 'Well', said an ITN anchor after an MoD briefing, 'obviously successful strategic bombing' (17.30, 18 December 1998). The effect of these caveats and qualifications is to numb the public consciousness to the reality of a civilian populace under fire: the daily risk of death and destruction. It took NBC anchor Tom Brokaw to enter a note of unqualified compassion into such euphoric coverage. He cautioned his viewers that 'However you feel about Saddam Hussein, you must also remember that there are innocent people who are in harm's way on the ground tonight in Baghdad as well' (17.00, 17 December 1998). There were also a few examples on

British television news of thinking journalists who learned the lessons of the Gulf War and asked some real questions. They understood that Pentagon and MoD briefings played the same role as Iraqi briefings: selecting only the most convenient facts and material to get a particular version of events across to the media. After one such MoD briefing, BBC reporter Ben Brown noted that:

> At briefings like this, the press is only shown what the military select and this is part of a propaganda war, aimed at countering Iraqi claims that allied air strikes have caused civilian casualties. Today's video display...is reminiscent of the Gulf war over seven years ago; now as then it is a somewhat sanitised view of an armed bombardment in which no one is seen to die. (BBC1, 21.00, 18 December 1998)

Julian Rushe remarked on *Channel Four News* how 'carefully selected images of clinical warfare are seductive' but should not distract us from 'what we are not being shown or told':

> We weren't told this morning if any...planes were inside the hangar when it was hit. We weren't told how many bombs missed their targets but we know they sometimes do. We weren't told what the long-term strategy actually is and we still haven't been told the definition of the jargon of this war. 'Degrade and diminish' means what exactly? (19.00, 18 December 1998)

Such exceptional moments apart, the reporting of the bombing of Iraq in December 1998 did not depart too far from the abysmal record we saw in the Gulf War in 1991. News anchors and reporters were still susceptible to briefing materials and their automatic reflex response to military public relations was to couch facts and material in safe, harmless language and present them as part of a consumable package for primetime news. On the other hand, NATO's bombing of Serbia, just months later in 1999, provides us with a contrasting case study of a failure of military public relations and its consequences for how the media respond to military briefings in comparable conflicts of the future.

BOMBING SERBIA, 1999[4]

Jake Lynch reported from the NATO briefings in Brussels for *Sky News* and argues that in the main, 'journalists were prepared to accept the fundamental framing of the conflict which NATO was conveying, namely that this was all the fault of Slobodan Milosevic for being unreasonable/evil as the case may be and that therefore the only way of resolving it was to coerce the Serbs into backing down. That fundamental proposition about the conflict was internalised, unexamined, by journalists despite the unease and criticism and anger on the part of many of them at the texture of the NATO contact with us shall we say.'[5] This is a crucial point but it would be wrong on that basis alone to simply dismiss as irrelevant the resistance of some journalists to NATO spin control. It would be wrong also to see the NATO media pool as entirely determinant of a story's presentation on the news.The evidence from news bulletins is revealing.

NATO planes committed up to thirteen 'blunders' in the course of the bombing campaign on Serbia and Kosovo: these were 'accidental' bombing of civilians, including a Serbian train on 12 April and a convoy of Albanian refugees heading out of Kosovo to Albania two days later on 14 April. NATO's unconvincing presentation of most of these blunders, particularly the refugee convoy incident, opened up an information vacuum and offered spaces in primetime television news where, away from the infectious atmosphere of the briefing rooms, journalists could ask awkward questions about what they were being told.

On 12 April 1999, NATO bombers hit a civilian train as it crossed a bridge, killing nine passengers. Just two days later, on 14 April, NATO planes hit two Albanian refugee convoys in two locations near the Kosovar town of Djackovice as they headed south-east to the Albanian border. Up to seventy refugees were reported dead in the aftermath of what were horrific attacks. Their lethality – the sophistication and relative accuracy of the weapons used – pointed to NATO but the organisation in Brussels denied involvement right up until the last moment when the evidence could no longer be denied. Indeed, in both tragedies there was an acute awareness among many journalists of the high propaganda stakes involved. NATO's attempt to explain the attack on the civilian train was seen as a defeat in the propaganda battle. An ITN correspondent remarked that 'There is no doubt that this attack has handed the Serbs a propaganda weapon' (ITN, 23.00, 12 April 1999). And in a dispatch from Belgrade that drew flak direct from Downing Street, BBC World Affairs Editor John Simpson pointed out that 'This isn't just a military conflict; it's a propaganda one as well and in Yugoslavia, NATO isn't winning the propaganda war' (BBC1, 21.00, 12 April 1999). For all that, however, the media response was relatively muted; TV news headlines that evening generally reproduced NATO's bullish 'faith in bombing':

> NATO reaffirms its faith in bombing and admits bombers may have struck a passenger train, killing nine. (*Channel Four News*, 19.00)

> NATO's put its faith in a bigger and longer bombing campaign against the Serbs but it's admitted hitting a train by mistake reportedly killing at least seven passengers. (BBC1, 21.00)

One reason for the low-key response may have been that the train and its passengers were Serb and that this was not going to make an impact on western public opinion. In a discussion of the incident on Newsnight, Mark Urban noted that 'it's also being realised by NATO commanders that civilian casualties on the Serb side, which at first they were very afraid of, are not a factor to be worried about...there hasn't been public uproar in NATO countries and I think to some extent that will embolden them to hit more targets like those bridges' (BBC2, 12 April 1999; emphasis added). In January 2000, NATO admitted that the cockpit video of the train crossing the bridge at the moment of impact had been speeded up on replay at the original NATO briefing. This seemed significant because NATO's defence at the time was that the pilot had no time to abort the attack when he saw the train approach the bridge. Had the video been manipulated in service of this defence? Jamie Shea says it was 'a cock-up' rather than conspiracy: 'There was no manipulation there.' The video had been speeded up to facilitate immediate bomb damage assessment and this was not picked up when it was subsequently made available for the media briefing. Shea investigated the matter when it came to light and had it checked out to see if at normal speed the tape undermined NATO's defence. 'In fact it doesn't change it – the slowed down video does not show the train appear upon the bridge before the pilot released his munitions...it was not a case of a deliberate attack on that particular train on the bridge.'[6]

NATO was able to neutralise negative coverage of the train incident because it presented a plausible explanation which journalists were happy to accept without further question. But the bombing of the two Albanian refugee convoys was a different story. Conservative estimates put the death toll at 70 people but nothing could detract from the horror of the attack and the images coming back to western publics via the news media. NATO took nearly a week to provide a detailed, plausible account of what happened and in that time struggled to put its version across in a clear and credible manner. Even Alistair Campbell admitted as much himself in a speech to the Royal United Services Institute in London (7 July 1999). 'The real problem', he said, '[was] that different things were said in different parts of the operation as we speculated and thought aloud before the facts were known. The resulting confusion was damaging' (Campbell, 1999, p. 33). There were too many different sources offering differing versions of the incident at different times. NATO in Brussels was contradicted by the Pentagon in the US which was in turn contradicted by the British Foreign Office or MoD. This created an information vacuum, a space in which journalists began to ask critical questions of the official version.

Contrary to my original expectations, overall news presentation of the incident was sceptical and at times even critical, much more so than it had been with respect to the train incident. Breaking news headlines were open-minded as to what exactly happened and who was really responsible: in other words they did not automatically accept NATO claims or denials at face value. The BBC led with: 'Serbs blame NATO. NATO says the planes attacked a military target.' The news anchor introduced the lead item on the story in the same open-minded vein but described the incident in the strongest terms: 'A column of refugees has been massacred in Kosovo...Nick Witchel on the massacre and *who may be to blame*' (21.00; emphasis added). ITN reported the competing claims from NATO and the Serbs and asked 'Who do we believe?' (22.00, 14 April 1999), while *Channel Four News* asked: 'Have NATO bombs killed Kosovar refugees by mistake? Serbia and some refugees say they have' (19.00). The American media also kept an open mind. CNN led with 'A scene of death and devastation in Yugoslavia. Was it the work of NATO or the Serbs?' (17.00), while NBC stated: 'The terrible price of war: did NATO make another tragic mistake?' (17.30).

The British and American news media were well aware of the terrible irony of 'deaths from among the very population the war was designed to save' (*Channel Four News*, 14 April 1999). For *Newsnight*, the stark fact remained that 'NATO pilots dropped bombs: dozens of refugees they were supposed to be protecting were killed' (14 April 1999). An ITN correspondent reported 'the one inescapable fact...that these people have been subjected to an attack as foul as anything experienced by the Kosovar people in this conflict' (18.30, 15 April 1999).

Awareness of the propaganda war was more acute than it was in response to the bombing of the train:

> Claim and counterclaim as dozens of refugees die in attack. (ITN, 22.00, 14 April 1999)
> NATO and the Serbs blame each other for civilian deaths in Kosovo. (CNN, 17.00, 14 April 1999)
> we are in the maelstrom of a propaganda war...(*Channel Four News*, 19.00, 14 April 1999)
> a battle partly for public opinion...(BBC1, 18.00, 15 April 1999)
> a war of claims and counter claims. (ITN, 13.00, 15 April 1999)

There were also some extended references to the propaganda war. *Newsnight* led with the proposition that 'This is either one of the most cruelly effective pieces of war propaganda in recent years [on the part of the Serbs] or NATO has made a terrible mistake.' The news presenter remarked that 'If NATO's political leaders thought they could fight a war without any casualties they were brutally disabused today', and asked Defence Secretary George Robinson 'whether the whole campaign isn't now more concerned with saving NATO's face than anything else?' This followed a feature item on a 'propaganda war' in which 'our leaders...bombard us daily with words, demonising Milosevic like hellfire preachers' (BBC2, 14 April 1999). The BBC's lunchtime bulletin the next day featured an extended discussion on the issue in which the news anchor put it to his guests that 'Propaganda is not a word we like but you could argue that actually that's what public affairs officers for NATO should be engaged in, it's a weapon of war'(13.00, 15 April 1999; emphasis added). *Channel Four News* asked, 'Is Milosevic winning the propaganda war?', and opened a detailed news item with the remark that 'both the Alliance and Yugoslavia's treatment of the news of the tragedy has emphasised just how important propaganda is in war'(15 April 1999).

Claim and Counterclaim: TV News Assesses the Evidence

The initial, official reaction to the incident from NATO in Brussels and from the Pentagon was that the Serbs did it. How would journalists react to that? Would they accept the official line at face value until proven otherwise? Or would they handle it with as much caution as Serb claims? The BBC's Defence Correspondent in Brussels, Mark Laity, came under fire from critics for his passive response to NATO claims. In one of his first assessments of the convoy tragedy (21.00, 14 April 1999) he simply reported the NATO line without apparent awareness of its inherent leakiness. While the news presenter was 'not entirely clear what NATO is saying', Laity showed no such doubts:

> *Laity*: Well what they are saying is that they are *very confident* that they attacked a military convoy...and that the pilots came back saying they are confident they hit military targets. Now *that would preclude the idea of them hitting tractors* or something of that kind because clearly they're easily identifiable as non-military, because that's what they're saying: *absolute confidence* that they hit a military convoy. (emphasis added)

Yet Laity belies a complete collapse in this 'absolute confidence' when he closes thus: 'By implication they're saying they did not hit those civilians but *they're not absolutely certain*. They're still investigating reports. *Privately there's a lot of suspicion* about what is going on there' (emphasis added).

Much of the uncertainty in the immediate wake of the bombing lay in the fact that NATO in Brussels was taking its cue from the Pentagon in Washington, where NATO Commander Wesley Clarke briefed aggressively against the Serbs only to retract when some facts began to emerge. Little of this got through to British TV news. Jim Miklaszewski, NBC's Pentagon correspondent, reported at first that 'NATO and the Pentagon claim allied warplanes bombed only military vehicles, not civilian, and that the refugees were part of the convoy, with military tanks and trucks at either end...Wesley Clarke first told *Bloomberg News* it was Serb troops themselves who killed the refugees in retaliation...But tonight the Pentagon says the initial reports of Serb retaliation appear to be wrong' (17.30). The NBC correspondent did not comment on it but this did not constitute a Pentagon admission that it was NATO, not the Serbs. The Pentagon just had a different version. CNN reported that 'the Pentagon says it's getting reports, still unconfirmed, that Serb helicopters and aircraft are attacking clusters of displaced Albanians inside Kosovo' and carried a statement from spokesman, Ken Bacon, that 'We're hearing from refugees coming into Albania that there have been attacks against refugee convoys by Yugoslav aircraft' (17.00). Twenty-four hours later and it was more apparent than ever to Jim Miklaszewski that NATO and the Pentagon were not briefing as one: 'Tonight NATO claims it still can't say just what happened to all those civilians...One senior Pentagon official told NBC he's "mystified" by NATO's silence. And NATO tonight is denying nothing' (17.30, 15 April 1999). CNN was headlining on 'NATO's deadly mistake' and reporting that 'there are still more troubling questions tonight about the attacks on those convoys...and it could be even worse than first imagined'. News anchor Bernard Shaw remarked that 'There's been a lot of conflicting information coming from Belgrade, NATO and the Pentagon about the attacks.' The programme spoke to Paul Watson, the *Los Angeles Times* correspondent in Kosovo, who reported that the NATO bombing raids were forcing the pace in mass population shifts out of the province, and not just to Albania – convoys were heading north to Serbia (17.00).

NATO took another five days to finally present a definitive account of the circumstances surrounding the convoy attack and during that time, and quite independently of the NATO media pool, news presenters and correspondents assessed the contradictory evidence with the sort of scepticism and open-mindedness seriously lacking during the Gulf War in 1991 and the bombing of Iraq in 1998. 'The question remains', said the *Channel Four News* reporter, 'what were NATO planes doing in the area and why did they decide to attack these convoys which included tractors and cars?' (14 April 1999). Later that evening, *Newsnight's* probe opened with this cautionary gambit 'You won't find any starker examples of Dr Johnson's adage that *truth is the first casualty of war* than today's deaths in Kosovo.' Correspondent James Robbins considered NATO's case but cautioned that '*NATO has missed military targets and hit civilians before* and tonight in Brussels the Alliance spokesman, Jamie Shea, was *much more guarded in his response*' (emphasis added). The next day, 15 April, NATO admitted that in fact there had been two vehicle convoys hit in different locations in the Djackovice area and that one of those, a refugee convoy, may have been hit by NATO planes. The NATO line was that if this was the case it was regrettable but that the bomb was dropped 'in good faith'. The ironic *Guardian* headline the next morning quoted the military briefer: 'When the pilot attacked, they were military vehicles. If they turned out to be tractors, that is a different issue' (16 April 1999). However, the trickle of information and lack of hard evidence only served to sow more confusion among the news media about what exactly happened and

operation, in May, the Spanish newspaper *El Mundo* published what was purported to be an internal NATO report lamenting the poor state of NATO battle-readiness when it came to launching its media and public relations campaign (Goff, 2000, p.18). Shea says that the document was 'not without value' but nonetheless denies it was official or that its unauthorised release had anything to do with him or anyone in his office. He does however concede that there were problems. He explains, for example, that just as the operation got under way he had to send half his staff to Washington for NATO's 50th anniversary summit and so he was 'really flying by the seat of my pants for the first four or six weeks'. The lesson, he says, is 'that we have to have a big [media] organisation, even if we don't need it, from day one. It's better to have it and not need it than not have it and be found wanting.'[10]

In 1996, then US Secretary of Defense William Perry spoke in the abstract about the pressure for the instant response to media queries:

> The pressure...is to say something...If you simply say, 'I don't know what the facts are. We're going to have to take a couple of days to find out,' that's not very satisfying. Therefore the continual pressure is, 'Well, what do you think it is, what do you believe has happened? If that's happened what do you think you ought to do?' You can resist those but you resist them with great difficulty. (1996, p.125)

There is suspicion in some quarters that with the Kosovo crisis, NATO's press office laboured too much under the weight of media expectation in the 24-hour news cycle. Alex Thomson refers to 'a kind of culture of information intimidation' whereby NATO was 'caught up in this desperate need to furnish this media beast with information at top speed'. He suggests that 'They don't have to give daily briefings if they don't want to – give a weekly briefing! I mean they make the rules!'[11] Jake Lynch of *Sky News* was aware of 'a lot of acrimony behind the scenes [due to] the fact that Jamie Shea wasn't given the information' about the exact circumstances of the convoy bombing. Yet even at that, and this is from a purely NATO perspective, Shea 'inadvertently gave us more information than he should have done'.[12] Shea tells it differently. Far from being denied information by the Pentagon at such a crucial juncture, he was the one who held it up in the first instance because he thought it inadequate and in the long run detrimental to NATO credibility:

But I was partly responsible because when the military did come forward on Day Two with a so-called explanation, I canned it and sent them back to the drawing board which made me obviously not the most loved person at the time, not only with the military but of course with all the journalists who thought I was indulging in some kind of cover-up operation. But having listened to the military briefing after two days I decided that it simply didn't answer the questions and rather than giving an inadequate briefing that was only going to expose us to ridicule, I preferred to not have anything until we could present the whole story. It was either all or nothing. Either we put all the facts on the table and say everything we know and answer all the questions and tell the journalists that we have come clean or we don't say anything. But I didn't want this (situation) of giving one explanation on Day One and giving an alternative explanation on Day Two and looking silly. Partial explanations are often worse than nothing.[13]

Not only that, he says, but the Pentagon, in the shape of spokesman Ken Bacon stepped in behind him and added some punch to his position: 'I'm very grateful to Ken who said, "Look, we've made this commitment to journalists to own up even if it is going to be embarrassing to us and we can't renege on that." He used a phrase which I've used often myself: if we are not honest in admitting our failures, they won't believe us when we claim successes.' The military, he says, were concerned with getting on with the campaign, not expending time and resources on an investigation for the media. 'But eventually...I think we got the message through, that this was so important in terms of Nato's public image and credibility, it was as important explaining this as getting on with fighting the conflict itself. And towards the end that was understood. The trouble is that in any organisation you often need a failure to turn a situation around...And it woke people up to the reality of conflict...that this was a real conflict with real consequences and that therefore we had to adjust.'[14]

The adjustment came during the PR crisis over the refugee convoy bombing. Alastair Campbell, press secretary to Prime Minister Blair, stepped in to urge a revamp of NATO's PR operation, an intervention Shea thinks was decisive. 'There was a blockage there', he says, 'and sometimes in organisations you need people with clout to overcome those blockages. When prime ministers thump the tub they get things done much faster than when Jamie P. Shea, the NATO spokesman, thumps the tub.'[15] Any intervention by Campbell into controversial issues or events is bound to become a story in itself in the British media and Jake Lynch notes that Campbell's influence extended much further and deeper than simply supporting Shea's efforts with human and material resources. It shaped the whole presentation of information and material which was to 'sort of ration out small nuggets of information and wrap around that as much material as you can in order to project the kind of story you want to project'. In other words, 'It had been very effectively New Labourised in that they thought stories. They decided from day one to try and control the agenda and did a reasonable job of it.'[16]

It is true that a good majority of British and American journalists accepted the fundamental rationale for bombing Serbia and Kosovo; an observation that can be extended to many left-of-centre intellectuals and academics who waved the NATO flag for bombing on behalf of Kosovar Albanians in spite of the rather dubious legal grounds on which the bombing campaign was carried out. There was a liberal, humanitarian consensus abroad that squeezed out radical dissent more effectively than was the case during the Gulf War in 1991(Chandler, 2000; Chomsky, 1999). It is also the case that most journalists at the briefings were too willing to be fed information and digest it as transparent accounts of events on the ground rather than as selective and self-serving presentations of those events. Mark Laity, however, takes a clear and unapologetic attitude to military sources, the briefings and the information they release. 'If you don't trust the military', he says, 'and they're the ones dropping the bombs, who are you going to trust? Who are you going to talk to? What you want to do is you want to talk to the operators, the players, the doers, that's NATO. You don't go and speak to a bloody academic do you?' He rejects as unfair the criticisms of his performance during the briefings and on air and points out that he was one of the few journalists who badgered the briefers about the circumstances of the convoy incident – about whether there was not one but actually two separate attacks on two separate convoys. 'So in a sense it was me who tied them up into knots', he argues, 'not the hostile journalists who were committed. It was the uncommitted journalists who tied them up into knots by asking them knowledgeable questions and in fact it was the ones who actually knew what they were talking about that tied them up into knots, not the ones who were making tendentious political points.' He insists that:

The challenge for journalists is not to get all worked up because somebody has spun you; the challenge is to spot the spin and take it out. And given the choice between no information which is to a degree what we were getting earlier on and spun information, what we were getting later, give me spun information every time...I've got the facts and in there there's layers and layers of priorities and prejudices and I've got to take them apart and say that's the key fact. And if I don't spot it then more fool me and good luck to them. It's a game. So spun information: they spun a lot but to my way of thinking they did not lie in between. They got things wrong but they were not deliberately lying. Sure, individuals might have but corporately I do not believe NATO were.[17]

One of the 'committed' journalists Laity has in mind is Robert Fisk whose dismissal of Laity and most of his colleagues at the NATO briefings is withering: 'Most of the journalists at the NATO briefings were sheep. Baaaa Baaaaa! That's all it was.'[18] Jamie Shea is, perhaps not surprisingly, complimentary of the journalists in the NATO media pool whom he calls his 'customers' against critics such as Fisk who 'accuses the press at NATO of slavishly following the Shea line whereas in reverse the charge I would put to him is that in order to distance himself from that he's totally dismissive of everything we did. It's an opposite form of extremism. I've got more time for a lot of [journalists] who were basically in the middle, that listened to us but came to their own balanced, professional judgement on things. But Fisk seems to have an excess of moral perfectionism.'[19]

This is an extraordinary slight on a journalist of such experience and knowledge but typical of the attacks made against him when he showed up on one occasion at the briefings to ask questions about the real extent of 'ethnic cleansing' in Kosovo, more specifically the relationship between NATO bombing and the exodus of Kosovar-Albanians across the border into Albania. His attack on the majority of journalists present that day no doubt fed their resentment and ill-feeling but the crux for him is his integrity as a journalist and he would not see his reporting of Kosovo as 'extremist' or as 'moral perfectionism'. He suggests, instead, that insults and intimidation from 'the bad guys' is the price the good journalist has to pay for telling the truth:

[If] you cannot write with passion, if you cannot say, 'This was a civilian target, Nato said it was military, it is not, it is a hospital,

I've been there, I've seen it', etc. If you can't do that, you go home. There's no point in being there. And if the price of that is to be abused by Nato or whatever then that's the price you have to pay. Then...you have to take on the bad guys, I'm afraid, you have to do it. If these people are going to intimidate you into writing like Reuters, which is their intention, then you must leave your job, you're finished.[20]

And while 'uncommitted' and 'knowledgeable' journalists such as Mark Laity asked questions when NATO was on the back foot about the detail and circumstances of the refugee convoy incident, they were content to sit back and graze after the organisation got its act together and, as Jake Lynch puts it, got 'New Labourised'. Jamie Shea takes this as a compliment to the way in which NATO recovered the public relations initiative in its presentation of the the bombing of Serbia:

I'll never forget one of my final briefings...at the end of May when we had another one of these incidents, number 13, when Nato struck a block of flats in a little town on the Montenegran border...I didn't wait for journalists to ask me for the information, I came straight out with it because I had all the information without having to wait for five days and no journalists asked me a question, not one!, whereas a couple of months earlier Djakovice had become the single dominant issue. It was almost by that time treated as what the French call a *fait divert*, a passing little story of no great significance. We made more of it than the press did at the end. It was almost a reversal of roles.[21]

The majority of journalists present at the briefings will cringe to hear Shea say that and so they should; Shea very definitely got the measure of them. However, passivity in the NATO media pool should not imply universal obeisance. It would be academically spurious to present a critique of news coverage that did not at least give credit for more sceptical journalism when and where it was due. Richard Keeble (1999) and Philip Hammond (1999, 2000a), for example, are very critical of British media reporting of Nato's operation in Serbia and Kosovo but they present insufficient evidence to argue, as Hammond does, that the coverage was 'highly conformist' (Hammond, 1999, p.63), or to support the conclusion that 'one casualty of the Kosovo war was British journalism, although some sources maintain it was already long dead. In its place we have propaganda' (ibid, p.67). The evidence from this study of news coverage of the campaign suggests that in the case of the British news media, at any rate, there was real media counterweight to NATO spin, not among the media pool in Brussels, or among those journalists in Kosovo, but in the news rooms back in London and to a much lesser extent Washington, DC (see Herman and Petersen, 2000, on CNN's coverage of Kosovo). I think that is significant. Television journalism in Britain might be ailing but it is certainly not dead.

CONCLUDING REMARKS

Many journalists seem to forget that in wartime the military need them as much as they need the military and that the propaganda war is as much directed at domestic or friendly opinion as it is against 'the enemy'. The reporting of the bombing of Iraq fell into the same patterns as the Gulf War coverage: especially the readiness to take every piece of official information as factual and transparent without question or without alternative. Again if, in Kosovo, correspondents were even half as sceptical about NATO's propaganda as they were about Belgrade's, and they had every reason to be, then they would have done a decent job. They are journalists, after all, not Jamie Shea's 'customers'. However, the performance of some sections of the western media during the Kosovo crisis provides a saving grace. It was good to see a newscaster such as the BBC's Anna Ford doing the job her defence correspondent should have been doing and showing a healthy scepticism and disrespect for NATO blandishments. It was good to hear David Sells on *Newsnight* cast a cold eye on the crude propaganda spewing forth from senior Cabinet Ministers. And it was good too to see John Pilger, Robert Fisk and Paul Watson unsettle in their own different ways the humanitarian consensus for bombing Belgrade. There is much to admire in western journalism as there is much to criticise and it is important not to let one blind us to the other. In fact, any critique that does so is really just a polemic.

The conflicts and military operations mentioned in this section of the book represent fascinating case-studies in the development of modern military public relations in the twentieth century to a point in the Gulf War when these techniques appeared to replace the need for formal and direct censorship of the media. They were, for the most part, fought by national or supranational militaries along conventional military lines. In that sense, it has been convenient and useful to draw a line of historical development in these techniques and gain a long perspective on the way in which journalists have responded. Just as there is a tradition of the sort of fearless, independent reporting of Howard Russell, there is also a less valorous tradition of passive obeisance to military and political diktat. But there is a weakness with this approach that I want to correct in the next section of the book. That is that not all supranational wars are fought directly and conventionally as in the two world wars and that not all wars fought conventionally are supranational. One of the defining conflicts of the twentieth century was the Cold War, a conflict of ideas and systems as much as 'nations' and 'regions', a conflict of strategic influence and permanent propaganda on a bewildering number of simultaneous, shifting fronts. Perhaps it was the engagement of hearts and minds in this war that made journalism so central to its sustenance.

Part III

The War Correspondent in Crisis

7 Reporting the Cold War and the New World Order

1989: the year of revolution in Eastern Europe. At least that was the story television brought home to us every day. The emergence of a competitive democratic opposition was very newsworthy for countries so long governed by the one-party state. A month after the June elections in Poland, triumphant Solidarity deputies took their seats and, 'Suddenly there was an outburst of democracy!' (BBC1, 13.00, 13 November 1989). John Simpson reported from the Spartacus Cafe in Budapest, 'the information centre for the brand new opposition parties [where] "You can't afford to miss a single day's newspapers at the moment!", someone said, "It's like a new country everyday!"' (BBC1, 21.00, 10 July 1989). When the East German government promised 'free, universal, and multiparty' elections, the news focused on the newly legalised opposition group, *New Forum*. This 'cutting-edge of democracy' was not so much a political party as a pressure group of politically interested professionals (*Channel Four News*, 9 November 1989). Their chaotic, ad hoc news conferences provided a spectacle of western democracy, of 'normal politics' (BBC1, 21.00, 9 November 1989).

The principal theme of the East European revolutions was 'people power', which echoed the fall of the Marcos regime in the Philippines and implied that 'the people' could achieve anything if they took to the streets *en masse* and in peaceful protest. The opening of the Berlin Wall was reported as a government 'giving way to the parliament of the streets'. Even the security forces were 'forced to retreat in the face of people power'(BBC1, 21.00, 10 November 1989). On BBC's *Newsnight* programme, live from Berlin, newscaster Peter Snow welcomed his reporter 'who's walking into the studio with a large brick in her hand'. It was a piece of the Berlin Wall. After years of western neurosis about what it represented, Snow laid hands, priest-like, on it and exclaimed to his gathered studio guests, 'I don't think this Wall's going to last as long as Hadrian's Wall. It looks pretty flimsy, doesn't it?' (10 November 1989).

The first few scenes in the Romanian revolution seemed to fit the 'people power' theme with ease: the Romanian people toppling Nicolai Ceaucescu, invading his palace and throwing its contents onto the streets. When they took over state television and formed a new government live on air, the images recalled the days of New Forum in East Berlin, or Civic Forum in Prague. Of all the scenes from the East European revolutions, this seemed the closest to anarchy, to real 'people power' as opposed to the media confection. But when that power was extended to the summary trial and execution of the Ceausescus, the shaky black and white video images of their bodies suggested something much more sinister and calculated. Looking back on the 'revolutions' and the whole sweep of events in Eastern Europe throughout the 1990s, Alex Thomson accepts that themes of 'people power' and 'freedom and democracy' were less than adequate for explaining these fast-moving events:

I mean, Romania was the great lie there. What happened in Romania? Was it the fall of Ceaucescu? Was it the collapse of communism? Well of course it was all of those things but in fact...what we're actually seeing wasn't a revolution, it wasn't an upsurge of the people like the Velvet Revolution in Czechoslovakia a few weeks before. It was actually more like an in-house coup. So the Romanian example is quite a good one to bring in, in the sense that the overall, rather glib, simple conclusion that yes it's the fall of communism, yes it's the fall of Eastern Europe, yes it's the fall of the Warsaw Pact, may cover you but it won't fully explain what's going on'.[1]

The events in East Germany and throughout Eastern Europe in 1989 apparently marked the collapse of the Cold War. Old certainties and assumptions – economic, political or military – became null and void. The question remains, then, whether western public discourse has met the challenge of interpreting revolutionary change (Halliday et al, 1992; McLaughlin, 1993, 1999). John Simpson, one of the few reporters to cover all the East European revolutions, thinks that this places an onus of responsibility on the reporter when trying to make sense of such events:

[When] the Berlin Wall came down and then the revolution in Czechoslovakia and then...in Romania...it makes you look at it very carefully because you know that there'll be controversy about these things for the rest of your life, so therefore you want to be absolutely certain of what you think the truth is and the reality is because people will be arguing about it for a long time and asking about it...but I just knew that that was a time when you knew history was being made...And I'm just profoundly glad, grateful that I was able to be there.[2]

Admiral William Crowe, 'Cold Warrior' and Chair of the US Joint Chiefs of Staff, summed up the loss of Cold War certainty and its implications for US national security interests: 'This is a time of very uncertain strategic transition. The future's not what it used to be.'[3] Indeed, the West's response to the end of the Cold War was hardly revolutionary or epoch-making. Many of the institutions and organisations set up to manage the conflict are still in existence – the UN, NATO, the European Union – and they have come under considerable strain in the face of continuing economic problems and an array of global crises. The news presenter, Jeremy Paxman, remarked that it took 'something of a leap of imagination to realise that there are some people – politicians, industrialists and, above all, generals – who've been watching the scenes in Berlin with a feeling other than joy in their hearts because the events of the last few days raise enormous potential questions' (BBC2, *Newsnight*, 10 November 1989). He might have added western journalists to his list of suspects because it was clear that there was no persistent, ideological framework of interpretation to replace the Cold War paradigm for reporting world events. John Simpson has argued that even in the midst of uncertainty, the role of television journalism was simply to 'reflect reality':

1989, like 1956 and 1968, was a year when the entire world changed direction and we're still living through the consequences of that: wars, upheavals, the collapse of old systems and old certainties. And until new certainties replace them, the real world will be a place of violence and conflict and our television screens will have to reflect that.[4]

The East European ' revolutions' were, as Noam Chomsky might say, 'the right story' of freedom and democracy in 1989. There was also a 'wrong story' of freedom and democracy that year and the international news media ignored it: an outburst of 'people power' and democracy in Brazil and Chile in clear defiance of the US just as it prepared to run roughshod over Panama. Elections in Chile on 14

December and in Brazil on 17 December 1989 confounded the legacy of fascism and totalitarianism that had plagued the countries of South America for over a century but which the US fostered and supported in pursuit of its political and economic interests. There was no live media coverage of these events, no media celebrations and ecstatic front-page headlines. As Lawrence Weschler argues, this had serious implications for our understanding of connected events on both continents:

> [Our] media's failure adequately to cover developments...in Chile and Brazil badly skews our understanding of what is happening in the world in general and in Eastern Europe in particular. This is true not only retrospectively – Eastern Europe is not the only place in the world these days trying to struggle out from under decades of often violent and terribly constricting superpower domination – but also prospectively: the sorts of economic dilemmas eastern Europeans seem likely to face in the decades ahead as they attempt the transition to a wide-open free market – an acute polarisation of wealth, the inescapable consequences of their crushing national debts, the surrender of their national sovereignty over key economic decisions to such monitoring organisations as the International Monetary Fund – are precisely the sort that Latin Americans have been struggling with for several decades. Indeed, these two sets of concerns...were very much at the forefront of the campaigns in Chile and Brazil the past several months, though, again, they went largely unreported in the American media. (1990, p.26)

So how do journalists make sense of the various post-Cold War crises in Bosnia or Somalia? The story of the East European Revolutions seemed at first to fit the framework: people, nations, breaking free from communist tyranny to embrace the freedom and democracy of the West. Subsequent events confounded that. The *Daily Telegraph* glanced back at the four years since the East European revolutions and remarked that 'the economic consequences of Western victory in the Cold War have brought chaos, not a new order, to Eastern Europe' (*Sunday Telegraph*, 19 December 1993). And just as Poland and Hungary voted for some form of socialism in their general election of 1993, even the *Guardian* slipped back into the old Cold War hype and hysteria with the remarkable headline: 'RED TIDE SWEEPS EASTERN EUROPE' (21 September 1993). The concept of a 'New

World Order' was a convenient propaganda cover for global policing in the immediate aftermath of the Cold War.

The certainty for journalism throughout the Cold War was the bipolar world of East and West, communism and capitalism, because it provided a framework of interpretation – a way of seeing the world and of reporting international relations – that conformed to pre-dictable patterns and narrative outcomes. Pierre Bourdieu's idea of 'master patterns', by which he means 'an infinite number of individual patterns directly applicable to specific situations are generated' is useful here (1972, p.192). The problem is that while such master patterns help us to sustain thought, they may also take the place of thought. While they should help us to master reality with minimum effort, 'they may also encourage those who rely on them not to bother to refer to reality'(ibid). This is a crucial point when we come to consider the role of the western media during the Cold War – they constructed their Cold War imagery both through *and* within one such 'master pattern' or interpretative framework. If we accept this, we have to make a distinction between the actual framework, the 'deep structures' of thought and action, and the instrumental 'enemy image' which served to rationalise it. It would be wrong to argue that they are one and the same. The Cold War was characterised by alternating periods of hostility and *détente* and these determined the functional utility of the enemy image. But periods of *détente* did not signify crisis in the fundamental ideologi-cal framework. That remained constant throughout the conflict.

THE COLD WAR AND THE ENEMY IMAGE

The western news media presented the Cold War as a stand-off between two superpowers with sole responsibility for danger or trouble lying squarely with the Soviet Union, 'the evil empire'. As George Gerbner argues, the enemy image, 'has deep institutional sources and broad social consequences. It projects the fears of a system by dramatising and exaggerating the dangers that seem to lurk around every corner. It works to unify its subjects and mobilises them for action' (1991, p.31). At its worst, the framework restricted thought and action. It was as much part of what Edward Thompson (1982) called 'the deep structure of the Cold War' as the nuclear arms race, because it helped dehumanise the 'other side' out of existence. The sources of the Cold War enemy image are rooted in the West's response to the October Revolution in 1917. Walter Lippmann and Charles Mertz carried out a content analysis of the *New York Times'* coverage of the revolution and found it hostile and propagandist. For the *New York Times*, they wrote, the Bolsheviks were 'both cadaver and world-wide menace' (Chomsky,1989, p.26). Most journalists, and indeed their newspapers, were ignorant of the causes and circumstances of the revolution and revolutionary politics, and they failed to report developments with any depth of analysis or insight. Some were even compromised by their involvement in the subversive activities of western intelligence. Whilst the majority of European and American newspapers were reporting, mostly from outside Russia, that the Bolsheviks were doomed to fail and were without popular support, Arthur Ransome of the London *Daily News* wrote: 'It is folly to deny the actual fact that the Bolsheviks do hold a majority of the politically active population'(Knightley, 1982, p.133). The *New York Times* was the worst offender and a look at its coverage over a period of time reveals how ludicrous it had become. In the period of two years since the October Revolution, the paper reported four times that Lenin and Trotsky had made plans to flee Russia, three times that they had actually fled the country; three times that Lenin had been imprisoned, once that Lenin planned to retire, and once that he had been assassinated (ibid).

The revolution's first great test was the Russian Civil War and the allied intervention in 1918. Western reporting on the allied intervention was heavily censored and only reports sympathetic to or in the interests of the counter-revolution were allowed. Most reports in the West, whether about Bolshevik thinking and strategy, or about the course of the intervention, relied on sources close to western governments or exiled Russian groups hostile to the revolution. Arthur Ransome eventually disowned such sources, especially the British secret services, to report on a much more objective level that the allied attitude to the revolution was wrong and that it only bred Bolshevik suspicions about the real intention of the allies (ibid, p.135). With few exceptions, coverage relied on anti-Bolshevik hysteria based on rumours and black propaganda. Reporting fell into the same pattern of falsehood and exaggeration that emerged in coverage of the First World War and the Russian Revolution. Defeats of the western alliance were reported as victories while low morale and poor discipline in the allied armies were not reported at all. The Red Army on the other hand was reported to be near collapse and defeat even as it was rolling back the allied intervention (ibid, p.142).

Only a few journalists such as the radical American reporter John Reed, and Morgan Philips Price of the *Manchester Guardian*, distinguished themselves with comprehensive and intelligent coverage. Philips Price reported events at the centre of Bolshevik power, providing insights into how the Russian revolution was faring in face of the western intervention. His reports were structured not around rumour and propaganda but first-hand observations and interviews with the leadership (ibid, p.139). Both Philips Price and John Reed served their readers with first-hand, immediate and non-judgemental accounts of a revolution in the making.

By contrast popular fiction in books, on television and in the cinema promoted images of the superpowers in simplistic binary opposition of good and evil: Uncle Sam versus Ivan the Terrible, the Eagle versus the Bear (an image used in a Pentagon video on the arms race), the Promised Land versus the Evil Empire. In the Soviet Union the images were reversed. The West represented the kind of economic and social inequalities that the revolution sought to overthrow. The shortcomings of the revolution were minimised with persistent reference to capitalist exploitation and western imperialism. Throughout the new Cold War of the 1980s, each side was commonly depicted peering at the other over the Berlin Wall with fear and suspicion (McNair, 1988; Dennis et al, 1991). Such portrayals were prevalent throughout the Cold War but, put in an historical context, they had a universal utility that could be applied to any external threat for the containment of the domestic populace (Chomsky,1989, p.28; see also Gitlin, 1980; Parenti, 1993).

The most negative and virulent images prevailed over relatively short periods of crisis in US–Russian/Soviet relations. A longer, historical perspective on how each side defined the other points to a more dynamic process of political and cultural conflict and struggle on all fronts of the Cold War. While the new Cold War of the 1980s saw the picture at its blackest extreme, other periods of Cold War and *détente* witnessed mixed images and shifting perceptions. The propaganda was successful in concealing a history of more 'normalised' relations between the US and Russia as competing 'great powers', periods when they engaged in much more open economic, political and cultural exchange. Everette Dennis et al (1991) work within a broad historical and comparative framework to examine changes in how the US and Russia/Soviet Union saw each other from the nineteenth century. For example, while condemning the inequalities of American capitalism, Leninist journalism would also praise its productive forces, its technological advances and its great engineering feats (Zassoursky, 1991; Mickiewicz, 1991). Among the

American media, images of stupid and violent Russians would mix with stories of Soviet–American cooperation and friendship, especially during the Second World War when the alliance with the Soviet Union was so crucial (Gerbner,1991; Lukosiunas, 1991; Richter,1991; Zassoursky, 1991).

It is not always down to the media. In some cases, the Soviet Union was its 'own worst enemy' when it came to putting its case across to western publics. McNair (1988) considers some of the constraints faced by western correspondents when reporting *from* the Soviet Union during the new Cold War and, conversely, the failure or inability of the Soviet authorities to shape or influence western news coverage of Cold War issues. This helped shape 'enemy images' of the Soviet Union as much as the West's own political and cultural prejudices. The KAL incident in 1983 is a good example of this. Soviet fighter planes shot down a Korean airliner over a sensitive and restricted area of Soviet airspace, believing it to be an American spy plane. A total of 269 passengers and crew were killed provoking outrage in the West. According to the US, it was proof of Soviet policy to shoot down any aircraft that strayed into Soviet airspace without first asking questions. The Soviets stuck to their spy plane theory but in the early, crucial stages of the controversy, they played to the wrong audience in the wrong way. They seemed more concerned with presenting their version to their own people rather than competing with the US in persuading western publics that they had a credible defence. Thus, US propaganda played unopposed to more sceptical European opinion until it finally began to collapse under the weight of its own contradictions and in face of more convincing evidence from Soviet and independent sources. By then however it was of academic interest; the western media had lost interest in the story (McNair, 1988, pp.80ff, pp.95ff). In the next section, we will see ways in which the enemy image informed media coverage of the most crucial and persistent theme of the Cold War: arms control and the nuclear debate.

Reporting Nuclear Disarmament and the Peace Movement

Several research studies show how it was possible to understand the nuclear debate in the media on a number of levels: as a propaganda battle between the superpowers (GUMG, 1985; McNair 1988; Hallin and Mancini, 1989), or between Conservatives and Labour in the 1983 and 1987 general elections in Britain (McNair, 1988). We can also look at the contribution to the debate of the peace movement and how it was reported within the broad Cold War propaganda framework (Aubrey, 1982; GUMG, 1985; McNair, 1988). To get some idea of the parameters of the framework, it might be useful to offer an example of how the nuclear debate was *not* reported.

At the height of the new Cold War and the anti-Cruise missile demonstrations in the West, the *New Left Review* published *Exterminism and Cold War* (1982), an international collection of essays that set out a socialist critique of the nuclear arms race. They addressed the problem from four points of enquiry:

1. 'the social nature and basis of..."exterminism" – the apparent drive of industrial civilisation towards its own self-destruction in the post-war arms race'
2. 'the respective roles and responsibilities of the two [superpowers]'
3. 'the relative importance of the distinct major theatres of the Cold War – the Far East, Europe, and the Third World'
4. 'the whole nexus of problems posed by the quest for a realistic way out of the looming dangers of "Exterminism and Cold War"' (1982, p.xi).

The mainstream media, by contrast, offered the narrowest possible interpretation. They reported that the nuclear weapon was a defensive deterrent against the Soviet threat of invasion, domination, or even nuclear annihilation. Andrew Wilson, defence correspondent with the *Observer*, noted the culture of fascination with nuclear weapons and weapons technology among defence correspondents in general. As with all lobby correspondents, journalists on the defence beat came into regular contact with officials in the 'defence community' and in many instances forged lasting friendships. They became immersed in a defence culture that, as Wilson argues, 'provided the essential framework within which to pursue peace-time planning for operations involving the death of millions' (1982, p.37).

Coverage of the nuclear debate was underwritten by strict adherence to the rules of a crude numbers game (GUMG, 1985; McNair, 1988). The debate became so abstract and quantitative that it distracted from an underlying, qualitative concept of 'first use' or the 'pre-emptive strike'. This assumed that a limited nuclear war could be fought and won by such 'overwhelming force' that the enemy would never have a chance to retaliate. As long as the public understood that the goal of arms control was to ensure 'nuclear parity' between East and West – each side having a rough equivalence of nuclear weapons – they would not think too much about what the weapons were designed for or about the capability of a particular missile over and above its counterpart on the other side. Unless of course there was an alternative view, another source of information and argument such as the peace movement.

The peace movement in Britain was a broad umbrella grouping of intellectuals, politicians, the Greenham Common women and the Campaign for Nuclear Disarmament (CND), most of whom were labelled as 'extremist' or 'unpatriotic'. Other religious or establishment figures were labelled 'naive' and 'idealistic', or 'hysterical' and 'mad' (Sabey, 1982, p.55). A television news reporter described them as 'at best misguided, at worst dangerous and subversive' (McNair, 1988, p.178). Ministry of Defence propaganda linked the peace movement to the extreme left and claimed that CND was directly funded by the Soviet Union with the aim of undermining western security policy. Indeed, to express any kind of opposition and dissent against the 'nuclear deterrent' was to go against the interests of 'national security'. For example, in order to discredit a big disarmament protest in October 1981, sections of the media framed it as a domestic security threat in that it would tie up scarce police resources and leave Britain vulnerable to attack not from the Soviet Union but the IRA. As a *News of the World* columnist complained: 'at a time when the risk of IRA attack is high, why allow people like the CND to hold a massive demonstration? Yesterday's march tied up more than 1,000 policemen. No wonder the bombers keep getting away with it.' The *Sunday Telegraph* reported that 'Thousands of police, including helicopter patrols, kept watch amid fears that the demonstration could provide cover for another IRA bomb outrage' (Sabey, 1982, p.60). Similar labelling was applied to the much more narrowly-based, middle-class, middle-aged nuclear freeze movement in the US (Entman and Rojecki, 1993; Gitlin, 1980).

Another significant feature of coverage at this time was the prevailing structures of access in the media. These were such that voices supporting the official view were able to dominate media coverage and define the issues from their perspective. Although alternative viewpoints did filter through, these were usually framed negatively. Whereas spokespersons for the official perspective were interviewed at length and without serious inquiry, representatives of the peace movement were subjected to close scrutiny and repeated interruptions.

Official propaganda also extended to public relations stunts by senior politicians which attracted significant media coverage (GUMG, 1985; McNair, 1988). One notable example was Easter 1983 when then Secretary of Defence Michael Heseltine staged a visit to the Berlin Wall as peace marches took place all over Britain. The intent was clear: to draw a counterpoint between the West's defence of freedom and the peace movement's attempt to undermine the means of maintaining that defence, the nuclear deterrent. At around the same period, Prime Minister Margaret Thatcher declared that the women holding hands around the military base in Greenham Common would be far better off holding hands around the Berlin Wall.

McNair points out another tactic which the British government adopted towards the peace movement and which had considerable success: that was to simply ignore the peace movement in the hope that the media would lose interest. A demonstration in 1984 against the Trident nuclear submarine system in Barrow-in-Furness was attended by 20,000 people yet ITN only gave it a summary item lasting a few seconds. BBC did not report it all (1988, p.179). The Glasgow University Media Group concluded that the implicit, damning assumption underpinning news coverage of the peace movement was, 'It won't change anything' (GUMG, 1985, p. 234).

In the next section, we will see what happened from 1985 when Mikhail Gorbachev came to power in the Soviet Union, heralding a new era of perestroika and glasnost, a programme of economic and social reform that began to impact upon the image of the enemy. The 'enemy' began to influence and shape its image to its own advantage by using western-style news management strategies such as timing stories for maximum media exposure or creating 'exclusive' or 'controversial' media events.

The Impact of Glasnost and Perestroika on the Enemy Image

Perestroika, or 'reconstruction', referred to the idea that the problems of the Soviet economy, the gap for example between supply and demand, could only be solved by a radical rethink of economic policy. Glasnost, or 'openness', refers to a new period of liberalism in Soviet life and culture in which criticism and debate were allowed as long as they were constructive, and as long as people suggested better alternatives for making the revolution work for the betterment of all the people. Glasnost was the means by which the public could be mobilised into supporting the programme of reforms proposed under perestroika, and projecting a more positive image to the world was a vital part of the task. Not least among these changes was the transformation of the Soviet leader from Evil Emperor to Nice Guy. In the image-conscious West, Mikhail Gorbachev achieved 'superstar' status. Compared to his predecessors, he was young, photogenic and charismatic. But, as he toured the capitals of the West to popular acclaim, he became a propaganda liability for the West. Take, for example, his performance vis-a-vis Ronald Reagan during the Moscow Superpower Summit in May 1988. One of the highlights of the summit in this respect was his joint walkabout with Ronald Reagan round Red Square. Here is how BBC News and ITN compared the two men:

> *Newscaster*: Mr Gorbachev saw the chance to win a few hearts and grabbed it with both hands [TAKES A CHILD IN HIS ARMS]. All Mr Reagan managed was a handshake. Like before, and more so here in Moscow, Mr Gorbachev is tending to out stage Mr Reagan. He's a lot quicker with the repartee although Mr Reagan still scores the odd point [REAGAN PUTS AN ARM ROUND GORBACHEV'S SHOULDER]. (*Newsnight*, 31 May 1988)

> *Reporter*: For all the world it looked like the two superpower leaders were campaigning together on a joint ticket, Mr Gorbachev producing a small boy from the crowd and bearing him aloft for a handshake with the President in true American election style. Mr Reagan appeared so taken with the moment that he threw his arm around the Soviet leader's shoulders. (ITN, 17.45, 31 May 1988)

On the last day, Gorbachev held a long news conference, speaking to the western media on all issues, sometimes without notes and even stopping to reorganise the seating arrangements in order to surmount the failure of the simultaneous-translation facility. The event contrasted with a poorly attended news conference at the American Embassy, where Ronald Reagan appeared to struggle with the issues and was criticised for selecting favoured US journalists for questions. The comparison was highlighted in some sections of the British news media. In Gorbachev, the BBC observed 'a man in control: quick-witted, dynamic, formidable' (*Newsnight*, BBC2, 22.30, 1 June 1988). ITN described his performance as 'an extraordinary tour de force without a note' (ITN, 13.00, 1 June 1988). The *Guardian* reported that 'Gorbachev was masterful and...Reagan was genially feeble, even by his own modest standards.' The *Independent* judged Reagan's conference 'deeply embarrassing' and 'a flop', although a more sympathetic account in *The Times* concluded that his 'rambling answers, inconclusive sentences, hesitations, and apparent difficulty in grasping the point of many questions' were due to fatigue.[5] Gorbachev's popularity and credibility rating in Europe was rising as Reagan's was flagging: the American leadership role was under symbolic assault. This was especially significant at a time when NATO planners were arguing for 'modernisation' of the alliance's nuclear forces in Western Europe to defend against the Soviet threat.

The Soviets also showed they had learned some useful lessons in western-style news management. When in Moscow for the superpower summit, President Reagan was scheduled to meet dissidents at the American embassy. But the Kremlin announced a major news conference with the famous dissident, Andrei Sakharov, to take place a few days later, on 3 June 1988. At the same time, they set up an interview for the western news media with controversial Soviet politician, Boris Yeltsin. That evening, the main news bulletins were dominated by the dramatic attack Yeltsin made on conservative members of the Politburo. It was reported as an exciting, sensational departure from the normal conduct of Soviet politics, and as a story in its own right. Yeltsin, unknown to western publics at the time, came across as a colourful personality with an interesting story to tell. His 'struggle for the people against the system' engrossed journalists and 'experts' on the Soviet Union alike. In marked contrast, Reagan's meeting with Soviet dissidents was only mentioned in a general round-up of the main summit events of the day and seemed rather routine set against the dramatic news of Sakharov's press conference and Yeltsin's exclusive interview.

The West could legitimise its stance on nuclear weapons, and its response to the peace movement, as long as the Cold War prevailed but change to *détente* undermined the tactic considerably. The solution was to project 'evil' and 'instability' from unseen meta-physical forces to what was visible. Gorbachev was a 'nice guy', yes, and the Soviet people no doubt wanted peace and friendship with the West but the West had to be careful. The Soviet empire was not quite evil any longer but it had a long way to go before it could be trusted on western principles of human rights. It was also undergoing unprecedented social and economic reforms with glasnost and perestroika. That brought its own instabilities, hence the oft-quoted truism that an empire is at its most dangerous when it is reforming itself from within. For an illustration of how this rhetoric worked, we turn again to the Moscow Summit. It was originally arranged to mark the ratification of the INF Treaty, concluded in Washington the previous year to reduce and eventually eradicate their stocks of intermediate or medium-range nuclear forces. The next logical step was further progress in talks for a long-range strategic arms treaty (START), which, if agreed, would have profound implications for superpower relations and the entire basis of the Cold War. However, talks in Geneva had ground to a halt over the US refusal to include its sea-launched missiles in the negotiations. For the US, talk about START was out. So what did the media report? At events like superpower summits, disputes over complex issues in arms control could be eclipsed by other distracting themes. For example, the impasse over START at the Moscow Summit was explained with wider reference to human rights, and to the future of Gorbachev and his reform proposals.

In advance of the Moscow summit, the American news management strategy was to tap into the powerful ideological connotations that the concept of human rights carried and which easily filtered through to routine Cold War news. Thus, Ronald Reagan set the US agenda for the meeting when he stopped over in Helsinki to give a speech commemorating the Helsinki Accords of 1975. Although human rights protocols formed only a part of the Accords, Reagan focused on them exclusively. He accused the Soviet Union of failing to live up to them since signing.

On the basis of his speech, and his plan for an unofficial meeting with Soviet dissidents in Moscow, the western news media dubbed the occasion 'The Human Rights Summit' before it had even started. 'Human rights is his theme', said the BBC headline (13.00, 27 May 1988); 'President Reagan...has put human rights at the top of the agenda', announced ITN (13.00, 27 May 1988). Reagan was successful in framing wider issues within the human rights theme. BBC reported his view that 'international security cannot be separated from human rights' (18.00, 27 May 1988). In contrast, the Soviet position was reported as a negative, ritual response to the preferred American agenda, not as an equally valid contending viewpoint. *Channel Four News* reported that the Soviets could only 'respond predictably' with 'ritual denunciations of the speech' (27 May 1988). Accounts of internal Soviet affairs were framed in a similar way. For example, some reports on glasnost and perestroika focused on their destabilising influence over Soviet politics and their impact on western assumptions about Soviet society. This in turn undermined the certainty and predictability of East–West relations and the Cold War system. As one reporter put it, 'It was simpler for NATO when the Bear was always growling. The question now is how should the West react?' (*Newsnight*, 31 May 1988).

Ever alert to deception from any quarter, western think-tanks and media pundits fulfilled their designated role as watchdogs for national security. Zassoursky refers to timely publications like *The Soviet Propaganda Machine* and *Mesmerized By The Bear: The Soviet Strategy of Deception* (Zassoursky, 1991, p.18). Caspar Weinberger, a 'Cold Warrior' with regular access to British television news, told *Channel Four News* that the Soviets were simply using new tactics, public relations, for their old unchanging strategy of 'world domination' and that it was important for the West to 'keep [its] guard up' (2 June 1988); there was no suggestion here that the West might also use public relations for its own strategy of world domination. On a similar note, *New York Times* columnist A.M. Rosenthal urged American leaders to be cautious about Gorbachev, 'a man who is still the dictator of the most powerful totalitarian nation in the world' (Chang, 1991, p.70). These were the principal western justifications for its non-response to Soviet initiatives on arms control.

NEWS IN A POST-COLD WAR ERA: A CRISIS IN THE JOURNALISTIC FRAMEWORK

The dominant news framework, then, was as much an ideological construct as the Cold War itself. So long as the conduct and pattern of international relations and international crises seemed to conform to the dominant assumptions underpinning the Cold War – on all fronts and in all battlegrounds – then the Cold War news paradigm was a successful means of puzzle-solving, of making sense of international conflict. And while images of the Soviet Union altered according to the intensity of hostilities, or in response to the propaganda strategies of either side, the Cold War framework remained intact. Even during *détente*, the superpowers were still perceived as no more than 'Friendly Enemies' (Hallin and Mancini, 1989). But once the Cold War system slid into crisis and collapsed, then so did its explanatory framework. It was no longer adequate for intellectual analysis or for journalistic reportage but academics, politicians and journalists seemed to find, if only for a brief spell, an ideal replacement: the 'New World Order'.

The term 'New World Order' has been used to signify a conceptual world view in the post-Cold War era. Yet it is a highly problematical intellectual framework and journalists who adopted it found that it failed to explain the global crises and conflicts that have taken place in the period. In a special feature for the *Independent on Sunday*, Cal McCrystal argued that, 'Despite the end of the Cold War and promises of a "New World Order", we are continually reminded that war remains a bad habit' with around thirty 'substantial' conflicts around the globe.[6] In fact, only a few years after the Wall, journalists were already thinking in terms of a 'New World Disorder' that, as Hugo Young wrote, 'touches its presumptive masters as well as its undoubted victims'.[7] The *Observer* commented on 'A world crying out for order', arguing that the idea of 'the New World Order was not just over optimistic: it was stupidly misleading. Order was always the last thing that was going to be achieved.'[8] Certainly, from the perspective of the so-called 'developing world', the post-Cold War era already stands as a disastrous time. Panama, Iraq, Somalia and Haiti are just some examples of what western peace-keeping and peace-enforcement can do for the powerless in the name of global law and order. For them, little or nothing has changed (Chomsky, 1993, 1994; Mowlana et al, 1992; Peters, 1992).

The notion of a 'New World Disorder' has also been cited as reason for the big powers to exercise their military muscle and boost the defence budget. This was the most dominant of the two broad world views to emerge from media debate about the post-Cold War order. It emphasised the need for the West to keep its existing security structures intact, to keep its guard up. In an uncertain world, instability was the new enemy and it came in a variety of forms. For example, *Newsnight* pointed out the dangers of nuclear weapons falling into the hands of a 'Middle Eastern despot' or a 'deranged Soviet colonel' (BBC2, 8 November 1991). There was also the 'war on drugs', nationalism in the former Soviet republic and the threat of Islamic fundamentalism.

There was an alternative view around, that of a transformed security, economic and political order in the world, based on the Helsinki process and tied in with the United Nations. The existing military alliances would atrophy and no one power would assume the task of global policing. This view was pushed by the Soviets in the run-up to German unification but it was never taken seriously by western governments for whom the preservation of the status quo – a US-led Atlantic Alliance – was paramount. And it was never taken very seriously by television news media who continued to approach security issues from the dominant perspective. On the eve of the Malta Summit, December 1989, Gorbachev and Bush made their way to Malta with contrasting opening gambits that provided the news media with the desired imagery. Gorbachev stopped off for an almost messianic state visit to Italy where he was pictured swamped by huge crowds of adoring fans in Rome and Milan, but his PR master-stroke was stepping onto the hallowed anti-communist ground of the Vatican for an 'historic' reconciliation with the Pope. Bush sent out a different message. As he landed on the American aircraft carrier *Forrestal* in the Mediterranean, fighter planes were taking off from a base in the Pacific to help quash another attempted insurrection in the Philippines. The point was not lost on the British news:

[PLANES TAKING OFF FROM AND LANDING ON THE FORRESTAL]
On the eve of the Malta Summit, *a display of American military might.* Just hours after ordering his pilots to support government troops in the Philippines, George Bush reviewed US air-power in the Mediterranean...America's action in the Philippines was the first major military intervention ordered by President Bush and has bolstered his reputation as a decision-maker. It follows criticism that he failed to help the recent coup attempt against Panama's General Noriega and that he's responded weakly to upheavals in Eastern Europe. Now, just before his meeting with Mr Gorbachev, *Mr Bush has a new, bolder image.* (ITN, 22.00, 1 December 1989)

This has the ring of a washing-powder advertisement. Bush is presented as the 'greenhorn' President still overwhelmed by his new responsibility as American leader and in need of a new image as a bold, hands-on decision-maker. Yet Noam Chomsky chronicles Bush's past record as a national security apparatchik in successive administrations since the 1970s, culminating in his post as director of the CIA, and shows that he had little to learn about projecting American power around the world (1992b, pp.59ff). Far from needing 'a new, bolder image', Bush was very much an 'old brand' US President. Still, it is a useful public relations strategy and a persistent one as media coverage of recent American interventions show. Two weeks after the Malta Summit, Bush was trying out his 'new, bolder image' again: invading Panama, capturing its leader, General Manuel Noriega, an old friend from way back, and installing his new man with a quick oath of allegiance to God and America. As Noam Chomsky has demonstrated, the American media response to the operation itself was very favourable, whatever their complaints about being corralled away from the action (1992a). In Britain a *Newsnight* report on the operation began, 'So the George Bush "wimp factor" disappeared with one big bang in Panama' (20 December 1989). This after all was the US's 'backyard' and the American media pulled out all the stops to manufacture the crisis, caricature and demonise General Noriega, minimise civilian casualties, and distract public attention away from the real geopolitical objectives of the operation (Chomsky, 1992a, pp.144ff).

Forty-five years of Cold War propaganda and ideology was not simply put back in the box by glasnost and perestroika. When it came to reporting the Soviet Union's response to the invasion some familiar propaganda reflexes helped absorb the impact of international condemnation. For example, a BBC journalist recalled Gorbachev's state visit to Cuba earlier that year. 'The reformist Gorbachev and old-style Communist Fidel Castro have little in common these days', he said. 'At least they didn't until the US invasion of Panama. The reaction by both has been a leap back to Cold War rhetoric' (BBC1, 21.00, 20 December 1989). Yet this and other reports did not seem to see the bigger picture which was that the Soviet Union and Cuba were but just two voices among the United Nations clamour to condemn the invasion.

Far from criticising the American leadership role in marshalling the Gulf War effort at the expense of the UN, the British media largely endorsed it as proof positive that the US was in an ideal position to direct the New World Order. As American warships headed for the Gulf not to 'free Kuwait' at that stage but to 'defend Saudi Arabia', ITN noted that 'America is once again adopting the role of policeman of the world' (ITN, 22.00, 8 August 1990). But in the first stages of the crisis, it was reported that the option of 'Taking on a war-machine as enormous as Iraq has already, in effect, been ruled out by the defence ministries of the western world', and that 'Foreign Office sources indicate that any military action is now out of the question' (BBC1, 21.00, 2 August 1990). A report on *Channel Four News* concluded that despite western involvement in the Iran–Iraq War, 'Any new conflict would be unwinnable' (2 August

1990). Nonetheless, news items were very clear that a solution could only come from the West led by the US. BBC's John Simpson thought it 'impossible to think that there could be an Arab solution...but if there's to be a solution rather than a compromise it'll come mostly from the West' (BBC1, 21.00, 8 August 1990).

By the end of November, the US was talking of 'freeing Kuwait' even if that meant all-out war. To this end it launched a propaganda campaign to forge a military alliance of western and Arab powers, and overcome divisions in western public opinion over the doubling of its forces in the Gulf (MacArthur, 1992). There was much criticism of the way the US hijacked the UN to forge his western–Arab coalition against Saddam Hussein in the early stages of the crisis but history shows such criticism to be misplaced. Bush simply revived the original and principal purpose of the United Nations: as an agency of enforcement with a hierarchy of leadership and very clear parameters of conduct in the global arena. President Franklin D. Roosevelt set out the blueprint in 1943 when he determined that 'there should be four policemen in the world – the US, Great Britain, Russia, and China...The rest of the world would disarm...As soon as any of the other nations was caught arming they would be threatened first with quarantine and if quarantine did not work they would be bombed.'[9] It was a model of the 'New World Order' that did not translate very well into the grand, idealistic rhetoric of the UN Charter but it was clearly invoked through George Bush's ideas in a speech on the Gulf crisis. He promised that by the time the US dealt with Saddam Hussein, they:

> will have taught a dangerous dictator and *any* tyrant tempted to follow in his footsteps that the US has a new credibility, and that what we say goes, and that there is no place for lawless aggression in the Persian Gulf and in this New World Order that we seek to create. And we mean it! And [Saddam Hussein] will understand that when the day is done![10]

When Bush announced the beginning of war, he invoked the New World Order again, this time with the racist undertones that informed much of his bellicose rhetoric against Saddam Hussein. 'We have before us', he said, 'the opportunity to forge for ourselves and for future generations a New World Order, a world where the rule of law, *not the law of the jungle*, governs the conduct of nations' (17 January 1991). Some weeks later, the British Foreign Secretary,

Douglas Hurd, endorsed the rhetoric when he told an audience: 'In the late twentieth century nations must be able to conduct affairs by a code more worthy of rational human beings than the law of the jungle.'[11]

On American media coverage of the Gulf crisis, Edward Said remarks that 'the central media failing [was] an unquestioning acceptance of American power', and argues that 'public rhetoric...[was] simply undeterred, uncomplicated by any considerations of detail, realism, or cause and effect' in respect to the crisis at hand. The news media simply fulfilled their designated role as they had done so well in their coverage of Vietnam, Grenada and Panama. When the crisis in the Gulf finally gave way to war, Said was just finishing his new work, *Culture and Imperialism*, and he remembers how he looked again at what he had written:

> Here was a new chapter of the imperial story, with the [US] now at the centre of the world stage instead of France and Britain. And as culture in the form of various narratives of Western ascendancy had shaped the nineteenth-century imperial dynamic, so it was the media that now played the same role.[12]

Eqbal Ahmad reflected on how the twentieth century has been 'most remarkable for its simultaneous capacity to promise hope and deliver disappointments', and has ended as it began with 'renewed hopes of a just and peaceable world order...being overwhelmed by politicians and warriors whose political minds remain rooted in the past'. He warned that, 'We are being lied to; and we must not be deceived. What we are actually witnessing is a display of imperialism relieved of the limits imposed by superpower rivalry and nuclear deterrence' (1992).

The UN sanctions that were effective in November were no longer effective in January.[13] Diplomacy and negotiations via the UN had become 'unhelpful'. By contrast, Bush's military build-up in the Gulf was read as 'going the extra mile for peace', and his bellicose rhetoric as extraordinary diplomacy. A worldwide coalition stood behind the world's only superpower against a pariah state whose leader could not see reason. War had become 'inevitable' (Philo and McLaughlin, 1995). Some journalists appreciated the wider geopolitical implications of this for US military power in the world. David Dimbleby remarked to the American Ambassador to Britain that the bombing 'suggests that America's ability to react militarily has really become quite extraordinary, despite all the critics beforehand who said it will never work out like that' (BBC1, 10.00, 18 January 1991).

There was nothing in any of this of a 'US decline' resulting from 'imperial overstretch' (Kennedy, 1989). After the war, Bush declared to the nation: 'It's a proud day for America and, by God!, we've kicked Vietnam syndrome once and for all!'[14] At a US Army victory cabaret, a senior officer told the troops that the Iraqis 'never had a chance'. Their whole problem, he thought, was their complete ignorance of US military power, 'the lethality, the speed and the vigour of execution that resided in our equipment and in our leadership'. The snag for the US: 'We knew we were good – we didn't know *how* good.'[15]

Bush's successor, President Bill Clinton, also suffered a credibility gap when he eased into office in 1993. The election campaign smears concerning his past still lingered in the public mind and as he prepared to take office from Bush, the crisis in Somalia provided his first major test of leadership. Throughout 1992, television images from Somalia of thousands of starving people in the midst of civil war had brought home to the West the legacy of Cold War, superpower rivalry in the 'Third World'. The superpowers had gone but much of their fire power remained in the hands of rival factions who fought to fill the power vacuum. The images also served as an uncomfortable reminder to all that, as in Bosnia, the concept of a New World Order was conditional only upon the furtherance of western interests. The outgoing President Bush and President-elect, Bill Clinton, announced their intention to send in the troops to help the aid agencies distribute food around the country without hindrance or intimidation from the various armed factions. Thus 'Operation Restore Hope' was presented as a mission of mercy rather than an old-fashioned, geopolitical, Cold War-style invasion. And it would do the image of either President no harm at all.

Yet, according to a *Los Angeles Times* report, there was another aspect to the story that the media in the US, and it seems in Britain, did not include in their coverage: oil. It was oil which motivated the US to launch such a large-scale military operation at a time when it shied away from comparable commitments elsewhere. In what might have been better named 'Operation Restore Oil', the *LA Times* obtained documents that revealed that 'nearly two-thirds of Somalia was allocated to the American oil giants Conoco, Amoco, Chevron and Phillips in the final years before Somalia's pro-US President Siad Barre was overthrown...in January 1991'. This land had the potential to 'yield significant amounts of oil and natural gas if the US-led military mission can restore peace to [Somalia]'. There is also evidence that the oil company Conoco closely cooperated with the US forces in their 'humanitarian effort' and even leased one of its properties in Mogadishu to serve as a temporary US embassy. The *LA Times* report revealed that the close tie between the US military and the oil companies 'has left many Somalis and foreign development experts deeply troubled...leading many to liken the...operation to a miniature version of Operation Desert Storm'.[16] I looked at several samples of British television news coverage of the story but found no references to links with oil or any other major western interests. However, coverage certainly bore similarities with that of Panama and the Gulf War.

The major US media were alerted in advance to the exact place on a beach near Mogadishu where the huge military landing would take place on 9 December 1992. The day before, the BBC reported that it would be 'an invasion by arrangement, not a dawn raid' and called it 'a humanitarian mission but with muscle' (21.00, 8 December 1992). And the *News At Ten* predicted that 'the gun-men will find out what they're really up against, with the eyes of the world watching' (ITN, 8 December 1992). As in coverage of Panama and the Gulf War, the show of military might and technology seemed to freeze the critical impulses of the news media in Britain as they launched into the story with gung-ho headlines such as 'Hundreds of American marines storm Mogadishu' (BBC1, 13.00, 9 December 1992), forgetting, it seemed, that this was supposed to be a 'humanitarian' mission of mercy, not *The Sands of Iwo Jima*. This ITN report captures perfectly the tone and mood of coverage in the first critical hours of the operation:

[FILM, AMERICAN LANDINGS]
D-Day in Somalia. Outlined against the moon-lit Indian Ocean, the spearhead force hit the beaches. Giant hovercraft disgorged the American marines of Team Tiger...Out at sea, the warships...Overhead, wave upon wave of helicopters thundered in carrying yet more troops to secure the airport and the docks. The UN peace keepers who've been holding the fort here just looked on as this huge operation unfolded around them. (12.30, 9 December 1992)

A US Marines' commander told reporters that, 'Our objective here is to come in and display maximum force, to let everyone know that we mean business.' How the warring parties in Somalia received this is unknown but the commander certainly impressed ITN who reported that 'The Somalis have been left in no doubt that these US marines mean business' (12.30, 9 December 1992), and on how 'The Americans show who's in charge in Somalia' (22.00, 9 December 1992). But within a year, the Americans were still in Somalia and they looked anything but 'in charge'. As 'Operation Restore Hope' slowly fell apart, the British media took a more critical view, not only of the humanitarian mission but the entire western intervention. The close policing of the media that was so evident in Grenada, Panama and the Gulf appeared to be missing in Somalia in spite of the heavy PR campaign that heralded the arrival of American troops.The crucial point of departure came in June when 23 Pakistani soldiers were killed in a gun-battle with the forces of Somali 'warlord' General Aideed. The UN responded with an assault on Aideed's head-quarters on 12 June. At first news reports reported reasons for the attack straightforwardly. The BBC headlines declared how:

> United Nations forces attack the Somali capital in retaliation for the killing of 23 Pakistani peace keepers. Four arms dumps are destroyed, 200 prisoners taken in an attempt to disarm criminal elements. (21.50, 12 June 1993)

With no sense of irony the reporter summed it up as 'all part of the UN's latest efforts to bring peace to Somalia'. He described it as 'a military success, albeit against a much weaker enemy' and concluded that 'the real test for the UN now is to win the hearts and minds of the Somali people while keeping up this hard line approach' (ibid). The next day, however, the tone of the coverage changed when Pakistani troops shot dead 20 unarmed Somali protesters. BBC News reported that 'Anger among Somalis over the actions of the [UN] is rapidly turning to fury [and]...is losing the UN the sympathy it cannot do without' (BBC1, 18.20, 13 June 1993). ITN showed pictures of wounded civilians being treated in a makeshift operating theatre and reported how 'Somali people are finding it harder and harder to understand the purpose of a humanitarian mission which has turned into a military offensive....Peace-keeping in Somalia has taken on a new and deadly meaning' (ITN, 23.15, 13 June 1993). Another BBC item showed American helicopter gunships targeting missiles at mortar batteries in Mogadishu. The reporter said it was part of 'the UN policy of destroying weapons here', but reported that 'they're doing it during the day and over busy streets filled with innocent civilians'. He remarked that 'For many Somalis, hatred for the UN now overwhelms any animosity against General Aideed.' The item refers to Aideed's comparison of the UN's deeds with those of a dictator and concludes that 'The sight of French soldiers...planting explosives to destroy a radio station that broadcasts against the [UN] does lend force to the comparison' (21.00, 14 June 1993).

As the last American troops withdrew from Somalia on 25 March 1994, ITN broadcast a strongly worded report from Bill Neeley that they were getting out 'before good intentions paved the road to hell' yet its own assessment of the operation would suggest that was too late. The report recalled that 'When US troops came, there was no government – there is no government now', and that 'what began with a near farcical night-landing under TV lights soon degenerated into an undeclared war'. The American commander told the news media how he prayed that 'the Somali people would raise themselves out of this turmoil and anarchy and build some kind of society based on love instead of...the gun'. ITN's reporter exploded the commander's pious sentiments with the bombshell that 'the US has just given weapons worth £20 million to the Somali police to subdue the clans that America could not subdue' (22.00, 25 March 1994).

The picture of Somalia that came across in the news media, then, was of a country in chaos, its people starving and ruled by warring factions. Its only hope, it seemed, was western aid and military intervention. The country had become a test-bed for imposition of the 'new world order' President Bush promised during the Gulf Crisis in 1990. However, there were other countries in Africa that experienced total disorder and civil war but which did not figure in western plans for this 'New World Order'; in contrast with Somalia, Rwanda and Sierra Leone were conspicuous by the absence of global policing.

'Don't Tread on Us'

Bill Clinton also chose to bomb Iraq twice and threaten North Korea over their alleged nuclear weapons programmes and their apparent reluctance to allow inspection by the International Atomic Energy Agency. These foreign policy options were designed to help to project his image as a 'new, bolder' US President and again the news media were ready to oblige. For example, when Clinton ordered the first bombing raids on Iraq in January 1993, a BBC reporter noted that 'passing the torch from Bush to Clinton is a time when both men want to show they are not going to be pushed about, so there's a certain amount of domestic and world public relations involved in all this' (BBC1, 21.00, 13 January 1993).[17] A second strike followed in June 1993, this time on the grounds that Iraq had plotted to assassinate ex-President George Bush. Suspects had been arrested and their trial was still in progress in Kuwait when the US decided its own investigation was proof enough to justify another Cruise missile bombardment on the capital. The US President told the world that, 'From the first days of our revolution, America's security has depended on the clarity of this message: don't tread on us!' While he justified the bombing as self-defence under the terms of Article 51 of the UN Charter, he warned Iraq not to do likewise. And he emphatically denied that the bombing had anything to do with image. ITN's newscaster took this up with his Washington correspondent:

> *Newscaster*: Any suggestion that he might have done it to sharpen up his image?
> *Reporter*: Well, he was asked that question today and as you might expect specifically denied it. But officials are not denying that it does give him a boost in those areas where he's seen to be weakest. He's not seen as being a decisive leader or as being a strong military commander. But there was no dithering, no public agonising about this and his statement, 'Don't tread on us', was seen as a very strong, almost Reaganesque warning. (ITN, 22.00, 28 June 1993)

The BBC reported on Clinton's visit two weeks later to South Korea or, to be more precise, on his day 'in and around the demilitarised zone' dressed in military fatigues and threatening North Korea with 'annihilation'. The contradiction of military posturing in a demilitarised zone was apparently lost on the reporter but he was quick to see it was 'clearly designed to sharpen (Clinton's) military image' (BBC1, 22.05, 11 July 1993).

CONCLUDING REMARKS

The New World Order rhetoric, therefore, simply has not stood the test of time, logic or American foreign policy goals and, for their part, journalists reporting on wars and conflicts in the Balkans or in parts of Africa, for example, have struggled to find a new framework. Kate Adie (BBC News) talks about the need in the Bosnian war to find some certainty among this confusion for the sake of the viewers and their engagement with the story:

> At home, viewers like to identify with one side – Who are the good guys? Who are the bad guys? – and when you are trying to report on something like Yugoslavia where everybody is up to something – nobody's being totally good, nobody's being totally bad – then you lose out with viewers. It's not that viewers are simplistic. It is just that in understanding any complex problem people wish to look for what is right and what is wrong, what is good and what is bad, and if it's not clear then people begin to lose either sympathy or interest.[18]

This is a remarkable statement for a reporter to make since few if any wars present us with clear-cut choices between good and evil. To make such fine moral distinctions for the sake of viewer interest or sympathy seems to reduce war to the status of a spectator sport. Yet, Phil Davison of the *Independent* says that too many journalists in Bosnia took sides in the war on a purely emotional level, a reaction he thinks was wholly unjustified.[19] Misha Glenny argues that to do so with little or no objective knowledge of the conflict, its root causes and history, was tantamount to 'fanning the flames of conflict in the Balkans'.[20]

In the absence of any clear framework for interpreting , explaining and reporting conflict around the world, the war reporter has tended to see things from a very narrow interpretive basis. The Big Themes of East versus West, Totalitarianism versus Freedom and Democracy do not seem to do adequate justice to explanations of 'genocide' (Rwanda, 1994) or 'ethnic cleansing' (Croatia, Bosnia or Kosovo). In a profession defined by institutional routines and procedures, journalists in these contexts have sometimes muddied the ethical waters and tried to see things from more individualistic, personalised perspectives, and even become part of the story they are meant to report.

8 War, Objectivity and the Journalism of Attachment

In launching their mission to vanquish 'evil' in Bosnia or Rwanda, [reporters] are using other people's life and death conflicts to work out their own existential angst, turning the world's war zones into private battlegrounds where troubled journalists can fight for their own souls by playing the role of crusader.

Mick Hume, editor of the now defunct *Living Marxism* (LM) magazine, in *Whose War is it Anyway?*, 1997

I try for the truth and sometimes the truth's a good story and sometimes it isn't, and actually that's all that matters.

Maggie O'Kane, *Guardian*[1]

Journalism has a long history but it was not until the nineteenth century that objectivity informed its practice and legitimation as a neutral medium of information, even in the midst of battle. William Howard Russell knew whose side he was on when he reported on the Crimean War and the Indian Mutiny (1858) but in the American Civil War he posed as a neutral observer, 'a dangerous role in any civil war where impartial comment will always look like hostility to the protagonists' (Hankinson, 1982, p.154). He professed himself 'a free agent', keeping an open mind on the conflict, vowing to 'ascertain and tell the truth [without] fear, favour or affection', and declaring that he had 'no theories to uphold, no prejudices to subserve, no interests to advance, no instructions to fulfil'. Yet for all his professed neutrality, his political sympathies were very much inclined against slavery and therefore against the Confederacy (ibid, p.156). The 'miserable parent' of the 'luckless tribe' would look with much interest at the debate that rages today when reporters go to report a civil conflict, a debate about objectivity and impartiality in situations where it is impossible to demarcate the moral dividing lines between 'right' and 'wrong', 'good' and 'bad'.

In an article called 'Truth is Our Currency', the former reporter Martin Bell states a journalistic heresy. 'I was trained in a tradition of objective and dispassionate journalism', he says. 'I believed in it once. I don't believe in it anymore.' He sees objective reporting as a sort of 'bystander journalism' that ill-equips the reporter for 'the challenges of the times and insists that he still believes in impartiality and he still believes in facts. But he wonders about the meaning of objectivity, whether it really exists. For him, the very act of reporting is essentially subjective. Objective, dispassionate journalism has its place but not in the midst of some brutal war or human calamity. It is still possible in the reporting of domestic politics and it is a statutory requirement for television news but it is inadequate to meet the needs of the good war reporter' (1998, pp.102–3). Bell is by no means alone when he rejects 'bystander journalism'. Veteran ITN reporter Michael Nicholson argues that it misses the real stories, the real headlines:

All the great journalists that I've admired...were people who weren't afraid to show their emotions, afraid to show their humanity. There's this line isn't there that the reporter should stand on the sidelines...They should be a spectator trying to objectively report a story without trying to get emotionally involved. Well I've always said...that you've got to get as close to a story as you can and sometimes that means becoming a casualty yourself, a physical casualty or, as I was in Sarajevo, an emotional casualty. But I see nothing wrong with that. How many newspaper reporters get the front page splash because they're actually in a place and have written it as they saw it as a human being, a person? Not as a spectator reporter but, you know, 'I had blood splashed on my hands', 'I cradled a baby who was...', you know. They're the stories that make the front page, that grab people...One of the things about Sarajevo was that it was one of the few instances...in which you were very much part of the scene because you couldn't get out of the place. You were under siege yourself. You weren't on a hill watching a town under siege being shelled, you were were in that city being shelled, sharing the anguish and despair of people, and therefore...how could you be objective? No, I don't believe in this so-called objectivity. You can still report the facts. You can still be as close to the truth as any person can be and still show a commitment, an emotional anguish. I don't see them to be contradictory.[3]

Nicholson reported the story of the Bosnian War for the British company ITN but decided to cross the line to become personally involved when he came across 200 orphans outside Sarajevo. Nicholson helped organise a rescue mission to save the children from the relentless Bosnian Serb bombardment of the city from the hills around. One of them was nine-year-old Natasha Mihaljcic whom Nicholson ended up taking home to adopt as his daughter. Nicholson wrote of the difficulty of staying detached and objective as he looked around at the children and has no regrets about getting involved (1993). It became a big media story in itself and seemed to make sense of a war that few in the West could or wanted to make sense of; it was eventually fictionalised in the 1999 movie, *Welcome to Sarajevo*.

Martin Bell proposes an alternative journalism, a journalism of attachment 'that cares as well as knows'. It does not take sides any more than aid agencies but it 'is aware of the moral ground on which it operates'. For him, reporting a conflict like Bosnia according to the traditional norms of objective journalism removes any sort of moral content from the story and leaves only an empty spectacle. Journalists should ask questions of their own role beyond self-promotion or professional neutrality. They need to ask themselves can and do they want to make a difference in a turbulent world? And what difference should that be? Should journalists be objective in reporting war? Is it possible? Does it really exist? Bell's advocacy for a more subjective, partisan approach to reporting attracted considerable criticism from within and without journalism and we will look at some of these criticisms later. First, though, it is important to examine briefly the whole notion of objectivity in journalism, its historical origins and development, and its contemporary crisis within the profession in relation to war reporting.

'THE FACTS BELONG TO HISTORY': OBJECTIVITY AND ITS ORIGINS

There are many fascinating instances of journalism of war correspondents crossing the line between correspondent and warrior and actually taking part in the fighting or setting themselves up as military or political advisers. During the Mexican War (1846–48), newspaper reporter and owner George Wilkins Kendall rode with the Texas Rangers as both journalist and combatant. This dual role and the intelligence he drew from it gave him a decisive edge over his competitors (Lande, 1996, p.51), but from a military point of view it set an unhealthy precedent for military–press relations in wartime. Lieutenant-General Lord Chelmsford, commander of British forces in the Anglo-Zulu War of 1879, complained bitterly about correspondents who were 'always ready without sufficient data for their guidance to express their opinions on every conceivable military subject *ex cathedra*' (Laband and Knight, 1996, p.v). During the Sioux Uprising in the US, in 1890, the *Chicago Inter Ocean* sympathised with the plight of the US Army command in its dealing with the press. It admitted that 'the war correspondent ever was the most warlike personage [and] there is the stuff that makes a good brigadier in most good war correspondents'(Kolbenschlag, 1990, p.41). As if to prove the point, the *Nebraska State Journal* valorised its reporter, William Kelley, as 'champion Indian fighter among war correspondents' after he picked up a rifle from a dead union soldier and killed two Sioux braves (ibid, p.69). In the Spanish–American War (1898), journalists spied for the US Army and Navy, took part in combat operations, assumed quasi-officer roles and even hoisted the first flags to claim Cuba as part of the US (Brown, 1967, p.vii). Richard Harding Davis was one of the most famous reporters of the war and saw no conflict of interest between reporting war as a professional journalist and fighting it as a patriotic citizen. Much in the style of George Kendall, he rode with Theodore Roosevelt's Rough Riders as both journalist and buccaneer and paid tribute to other American journalists for their part in the war, mostly for their 'reconnoitring, scouting, and fighting' (Lande, 1996, p.165).

With the retreat of the German Army in Europe in the Second World War, armed journalists accepted surrenders in what Richard Johnston called 'a manhunt with notebooks and cameras' (Collier, 1989, p.193). Evelyn Irons of the London *Evening Standard*, for example, arrived in a small Bavarian village with three other reporters – all armed with revolvers – and apparently forced its surrender (ibid). Ernest Hemingway packed a brace of pistols in breach both of army rules and of the Geneva Conventions: journalists had the honorary rank of captain and they could dress accordingly, but unless they actually enlisted they were still civilian and could not carry a weapon. Peter Arnett recalls his pistol-packing days reporting the Vietnam War when 'it was tempting to play soldier. In the early years I carried a large revolver that I lovingly polished while relishing the approval of the GIs I was covering. I never did fire that pistol...and eventually threw it away while running for dear life...during a Vietcong rocket attack' (1996). Journalists such as CBS contract reporter Kurt Lohbeck were roundly criticised from within their profession for associating themselves so closely with the Mujahideen rebels in the Soviet–Afghan war from 1979 (Williams Walsh, 1990). It was difficult to tell what Lohbeck's relationship actually was with a rebel faction led by Abdul Haq. It soon became obvious that he was helping them with their PR, building up useful western media contacts, but there were suspicions he was also helping them make contact with arms dealers. Lohbeck had a rather murky career as a political lobbyist and journalist but CBS were happy to hire him without vetting him because he came cheap and he boasted knowledge of the region and contacts with the Mujahideen. As Williams Walsh argues, keeping a staff reporter in the region would cost the network anything up to US$200,000 per year (ibid, p.28). Lohbeck always claimed he was a reporter, not 'a player' but all the evidence suggests that he was 'a partisan in a holy war' (ibid, p.36).

The Spanish Civil War (1936–39) was a conflict of stark ideological and political positions which seemed blurred and contentious in previous wars, and which presaged not only an imminent world war but the Cold War to follow. The correspondents who went to report it were marked out by their partisanship in a conflict which seemed to demand loyalty and commitment to one side or the other. Reporting on the Republican side were Claude Cockburn, Arthur Koestler, Ernest Hemingway, Herbert Matthews and Martha Gellhorn, 'at her happiest striding out alone on a journalist's cause' such as Spain (Shakespeare, 1998, p.225). Kim Philby reported for *The Times* on the Nationalist side, but was also working as a Soviet spy (Knightley, 1982, p.178). Herbert Matthews seemed to speak for most of the foreign correspondents in Spain at that time when he wrote:

> All of us who lived the Spanish Civil War felt deeply emotional about it...I always felt the falseness and hypocrisy of those who claimed to be unbiased, and the foolish, if not rank stupidity of editors and readers who demand objectivity or impartiality of correspondents writing about the war...(In) condemning bias one rejects the only factors which really matter – honesty, understanding and thoroughness. A reader has the right to ask for all the facts; he has no right to ask that a journalist or historian agree with him (ibid, p.179).

However, Knightley argues that some correspondents forgot about the importance of facts altogether and became nothing more than propaganda mouthpieces for one side or the other. It is alleged , for example, that Arthur Koestler, of the *London News Chronicle*, and Claude Cockburn, of *The Week* and the *Daily Worker*, mixed propaganda with fact and were not averse to inventing stories to further the Republican cause which they championed with great passion as communists first and reporters second. Knightley objects not so much to their partisanship as to the assumption that newspaper readers had no right to the truth if the truth damaged the cause of right against wrong (ibid, p.181). Holme argues that with so much propaganda issuing forth from Spain, it was 'the straightforward news reporting' by correspondents such as Hugh Christopher Holme (*Reuters*), Noel Monks (*Daily Express*) and George Steer (*The Times*) that provoked the greatest emotional responses to outrages such as the bombing of Guernica (1995, p.47).

There were early attempts to enter some notion of objectivity into war reporting. An early pioneer of the approach was James Gordon Bennett, publisher of the *New York Herald*, who put the emphasis of coverage on reporting and gathering facts and information rather than propagandising. This, he thought, distinguished the *Herald* in its coverage of such events as the Canadian Revolution in 1837. The political sympathies of his reporters were their own, he said, but 'their facts belong to history' (Bjork, 1994, p.857). James R. Gilmore, in his introduction to the collected letters of Charles Page, the famous American Civil War reporter, wrote that 'in the thick of the fight, where sabres clash, and minieballs whistle', or from a vantage point of 'a friendly tree, or on some commanding hill', the reporter could observe events first hand and achieve ultimate objectivity where even historians failed, dependent as they were on secondary sources. The reporter had only to 'be cool, truthful, and intrepid' to provide the readers with 'a living photograph of the tremendous conflict' (Page, 1898, p.vii). This comparison between journalists and historians is a persistent theme in discussions of objectivity. Like history, objectivity in journalism can be discussed in terms of either pure method or, as Pierre Vilar puts it, an 'attitude of clarity'. Vilar was writing about the method and the practice of history but it could just as well apply to journalism.'Can one be objective in writing contemporary history?', he asked:

Differences among historians are to be found in their attitudes. There is a dishonest attitude: to call oneself objective, while knowing oneself to be partisan; there is the blind attitude: to be partisan while believing oneself to be objective; and then there is the attitude of clarity: to state one's position, while believing firmly that thorough analysis is the best way to buttress that position. It is pejorative to say of a work of history that it is a plea for a cause. Yet a good plea made by a good lawyer and for a worthy cause can become a model to the historian. (Southworth, 1977, p.xvi)

British historian E.H. Carr wrote extensively on this question of objectivity in the writing of history and his observations are very relevant to the problem as it applies to journalism. In his classic book, *What is History?* (1986), he considers Collingwood's philosophy of history as a model of development. This includes a number of principal axioms: that 'the facts of history never come to us "pure" [but] are always refracted through the mind of the recorder' so we must question the historian's position as much as the facts he or she presents (ibid, p.16); that the historian requires 'imaginative understanding for the minds of the people with whom [one] is dealing' as opposed to 'sympathy' which implies partiality (ibid, p.18); that 'we can view the past, and achieve our understanding of the past, only through the eyes of the present'; that the very vocabulary we use to describe the great events of the past – 'democracy, empire, war, revolution' – have undeniable contemporary resonance from which we cannot escape (ibid, p.19). 'The function of the past', in the Collingwood view of history, 'is neither to love the past nor to emancipate [oneself] from the past, but to master and understand it as the key to to the understanding of the present' (ibid, p.20).

However, Carr sees several dangers in adopting such a view. It encourages the belief that the historian does not require objectivity at all, that it is all subjective interpretation: ergo, 'history is what the historian makes' of it. This is 'a purely pragmatic [Nietzschean] view of the facts,…that the criterion of a right interpretation is its suitability to some present purpose?' In other words, 'the facts of history are nothing, interpretation is everything' (ibid, pp.20ff). Carr believed the contrary, that objectivity was possible in history and that to call an historian objective meant two things: first, that one 'has a capacity to rise above the limited vision of [one's] own situation in society and in history', and secondly that one 'has the capacity to project [one's] vision into the future in such a way as to give [one] a more profound and more lasting insight into the past than can be attained by those...whose outlook is entirely bounded by their own immediate situation...The historian of the past can make an approach towards objectivity only as he approaches towards the understanding of the future'(ibid, pp.117–18).

These arguments have obvious relevance for journalism but the exact details of *how* objectivity informed its practice are still contested. There are several developments however in the fields of economics, philosophy, science, and technology that might at least offer us some clearer idea. For example, in philosophy, theories of realism and positivism suggested the possibility of an objective, reportable universe. The rapid development of photography appeared to support the belief in one's ability, as Dan Schiller says, 'to represent reality – to depict, apparently without human inter-vention , an entire world of referents [that] bolstered the apparently universal recognition of [photography] as a supreme standard of accuracy and truth' (McNair, 1994, p.27). It has been suggested that objectivity finds its origins in the particular requirements of the new telegraph press agencies in the US such as Associated Press. These agencies had diverse clientele so their information had to be 'neutral' if it was to be universally marketable. None of this evidence is conclusive but it does point to a more compelling historical con-juncture: the growth of a new commercial press in the midst of increasing rates of mass literacy and mass consumerism. By the 1920s and 1930s, belief in the ideal of objectivity came to be seen as 'naive empiricism'. It was damaged by journalism's susceptibility to First World War propaganda and faced serious challenge with the rise of fascist dictatorships in Europe. These developments, and the emergence of public relations as a new form of commercial com-munication, completely undermined the naive faith in facts and led many to believe that objectivity or neutrality in any field of human discourse was unattainable. Suddenly, there was no such thing as fact but only subjective interpretation. But Walter Lippmann always believed young journalists should be taught the value of objectivity as a discipline of mind and a means towards an end, not an end in itself. 'The study of error...', he wrote, 'serves as a stimulating intro-duction to the study of truth. As our minds become more deeply aware of their own subjectivism, we find a zest in the objective method that is not otherwise there' (1992, p.174). For Lippmann, the principles of the objective method should be taught not as dull academic discipline, but 'as victories over the superstitions of the mind [so that] the exhilaration of the chase and of the conquest may carry the pupil over the hard transition from his own self-bound experience to the phase where his curiosity has matured and his reason has acquired passion' (ibid). David Halberstam understood from Lippmann, whom he admired, that 'journalism [is] not just facts and bulletins, journalism must explain things, journalism must embrace ideas' (1979, p.372).

OBJECTIVITY UNDER FIRE

Objectivity has come under serious critique from academics (GUMG, 1976; Lichtenberg, 1996; Streckfuss, 1990) as well as from journalists such as Martin Bell. A whole body of literature suggests that the news media do not simply report and reflect our social world but that they more or less play an active part in shaping, even constructing it; that they represent sectional interests rather than society as a whole (see GUMG, 1976; Parenti, 1993). When these sort of criticisms are levelled at journalists, their traditional defence is objectivity. According to Michael Schudson (1978), objectivity is based on the assumption that a series of 'facts' or truth claims about the world can be validated by the rules and procedures of a professional community. The distortions and biases, the subjective value judgements of the individual or of particular interest groups, are filtered out so that among journalists at any rate, 'The belief in objectivity is a faith in "facts", a distrust of "values", and a commitment to their segregation' (ibid, p.6). Tuchman refers to this method as 'a strategic ritual' protecting journalists from the risks of their trade, a mechanism of defence against any attempts to impugn professional integrity. For Tuchman, objectivity is not an ideal; it is simply a means of protecting the journalist from getting the story wrong (1972, pp. 661ff). The Russian reporter Andrei Babitsky has said that, 'Strange as it may seem, a war correspondent is often good at what he does because of a certain detachment. I mean, a journalist is not an academic. He is a *dilettante* by definition.'[3]

Radical critiques measure journalistic claims to objectivity against analyses of how the news media produce and represent their version of reality according to sectional interests. Bias is not in the eye of the beholder but is structured within the entire news process; the news sees and constructs reality according to a dominant or institutional ideology (GUMG, 1976). 'What passes for objectivity', argues Michael

Parenti, 'is the acceptance of a social reality shaped by the dominant forces of society – without any critical examination of that reality's hidden agendas, its class interests, and its ideological biases' (1993, p.52). It is the difference respectively between the journalist as the professional, institutionalised reporter and the journalist as the partial eyewitness and writer. John Pilger points to the transparency of this ideology of professionalism, especially in a public service broadcaster like the BBC whose coverage of domestic and foreign crises has demonstrated its true agenda and its true allegiances:

> These people waffle on about objectivity as if by joining that institution or any institution they suddenly rise to this Nirvana where they can consider all points of view and produce something in five minutes. It's nonsense and it's made into nonsense because the moment there's any kind of pressure on the establishment you find reporters coming clean, as they did after the Falklands. They were very truculent: 'These were our people, our side. And now we'll get back to being objective.' It's the same with the term 'balance'. I mean censorship for me always works by omission. That's the most virulent censorship and what we have is an enormous imbalance one way,...the accredited point of view, the sort of consensus point of view which has nothing to do with objectivity, nothing to do with impartiality and very little to do with the truth.[4]

The pressure to pursue objectivity in reporting has had serious consequences for the journalist as writer. James Cameron, a reporter often cited by foreign correspondents today as their inspiration, thought that 'objectivity in some circumstances is both meaningless and impossible'. He could not see 'how a reporter attempting to define a situation involving some sort of ethical conflict can do it with sufficient demonstrable neutrality to fulfil some arbitrary concept of "objectivity" '. This was not the acid test for Cameron who 'always tended to argue that objectivity was of less importance than the truth, and that the reporter whose technique was informed by no opinion lacked a very serious dimension' (1967, p.72). Mark Pedelty studied the American press corps in El Salvador during some of the worst years of its civil war. He was interested in how the American journalists saw their approach to their job in a different light to local, Salvadoran journalists. The Americans insisted they 'report' news as fact; the Salvadorans talked in terms of 'making' news. The Americans talked about 'objectivity', while the Salvador-ans thought the highest aspiration was 'honesty' (1995, pp.226–7). As Pedelty argues, the ethic of honest journalism comes between objective journalism and propaganda. 'Objective journalists deny their subjectivities, rather than acknowledge them and critically challenge them. They reduce complexities, rather than explain them. They evade contradiction, rather than letting the reader in on the inevitable doubts and difficulties encountered in any act of discovery' (ibid, p.227).

Theodore Glasser fears that objectivity has 'stripped journalists of their creativity and their imagination; it has robbed [them] of their passion and their perspective'. Objectivity has 'transformed journalism into something more technical than intellectual; it has turned the art of story-telling into the technique of report-writing'. But most regrettably, he says, objectivity has 'denied journalists their citizenship; as disinterested observers, as impartial reporters, jour-nalists are expected to be morally disengaged and politically inactive'. The implications of this are quite profound. In order for journalism to be creative, imaginative, in order for it to be passionate and opinionated, in order to inject into it some level of intellectual or moral engagement, some level of political activism, then the task, as Glasser puts it, is to 'liberate journalism from the burden of objec-tivity' (Glasser, 1992, p.181). It is very doubtful that mainstream journalism would see things that way and Glasser admits as much himself. In his view, and this is very close to Tuchman and others, objectivity, like many practices in journalism, is not so much a philo-sophical ideal as a function of efficient news gathering, a commercial imperative.

WAR AND THE NEW JOURNALISM

There is, however, an alternative journalism, one that subverts the whole notion of objectivity as a professional canon, what some call the New Journalism. It includes journalists-cum-novelists such as Norman Mailer, Truman Capote, Tom Wolfe, Joan Didion and Hunter S. Thompson. More a trend than a movement, the 'New Journalism' emerged in the 1960s as a rebellion against the practices of conventional journalism. It is journalism as art, the writer's moral vision and personal perspective always to the fore. The techniques of factual journalism (the use of the passive voice, the chronicling of events, the use of interviews) are blended with those of fiction (the authorial point of view or first person narrative, the use of style and

imagination). Wakefield (1974) argues that such writing is imaginative, 'not because the author has distorted the facts, but because (she)
he has presented them in a full, rather than a naked manner,
brought out the sights, sounds, and feel surrounding these facts and
connected them by comparison with other facts of history, society,
and literature in an artistic manner that does not diminish but gives
greater depth and dimension to the facts' (ibid, p.41). New
Journalism, therefore, rejects the notion of objectivity altogether and
embraces *subjectivity* in its representation of reality and, as Hollowell
puts it, '[serves] the function of fiction' by illuminating 'the ethical
dilemmas of our time' (1977, p.11).

Compare, for example, the ways in which Joan Didion and
Ryszard Kapuscinski write about fear. Didion reflects on fear as the
'mechanism of terror' that in part explains the degree to which right-
wing death squads subjugated El Salvador in the 1980s. Her book
Salvador opens with her first impressions of the country as she takes
a taxi from the airport:

> Terror is the given of the place. Black-and-white police cars cruise
> in pairs, each with the barrel of a rifle extruding from an open
> window. Roadblocks materialize at random, soldiers fanning out
> from trucks and taking positions, fingers always on triggers, safeties
> clicking on and off. Aim is taken as if to pass the time. Every
> morning *El Diario de Hoy* and *La Prensa* carry cautionary stories...A
> mother and her two sons hacked to death in their beds by eight
> *desconocidos*, unknown men...the unidentified body of a young
> man, strangled, found on the shoulder of a road...the unidentified
> bodies of three young men, found on another road, their faces
> partially destroyed by bayonets, one face carved to represent a
> cross...The dead and pieces of the dead turn up in El Salvador
> everywhere, every day, as taken for granted as in a nightmare, or
> a horror movie...Bodies turn up in the brush of vacant lots, in the
> garbage thrown down ravines in the richest districts, in public rest
> rooms, in bus stations. (1983, pp.14–15, p.19)

Fear, in Didion's account of El Salvador, is a reign of terror, a 'given
of the place'. Kapuscinski sees it differently. His book *Shah of Shahs*
is an anatomy of the overthrow of the Shah of Iran by the revolution
in 1979. He is interested in the underlying impulses and dynamics
that make a revolution and reveals fear as a voracious monster that
must be slain if revolution is possible:

Fear: a predatory, voracious animal living inside us. It does not let us forget it's there. It keeps eating at us and twisting our guts. It demands food all the time, and we see that it gets the choicest delicacies. Its preferred fare is dismal gossip, bad news, panicky thoughts, nightmare images. From a thousand pieces of gossip, portents, ideas, we always cull the worst ones – the ones that fear likes best. Anything to satisfy the monster and set it at ease...All books about all revolutions begin with a chapter that describes the decay of tottering authority or the misery and sufferings of the people. They should begin with a psychological chapter, one that shows how a harassed, terrified man suddenly breaks his terror, stops being afraid. This unusual process, sometimes accomplished in an instant like a shock or a lustration, demands illuminating. Man gets rid of fear and feels free. Without that there would be no revolution. (1982, pp.110–11)

In Didion, fear defeats; in Kapuscinski, fear is defeated. Both, however, reject the constraints of the 'disciplined' and 'objective' report and seek truth and revelation in the subjective, the meditative. Taken several steps further, the Russian journalist, Atom Borovik, seeks his truth about the war in Afghanistan in the surreal:

One time I woke from a nightmare in a cold sweat. In my dream I'd seen a field strewn with corpses. Even awake, I could smell the vivid violetlike odor of carrion. In the morning, I learned that my refrigerator was broken. It was shaking feverishly (it was afraid too, the bastard) in a gigantic pool of blood. The blood was still oozing out of the freezer, which my predecessor had packed tight with meat. Despite all my efforts to scrape the linoleum clean, the large bloodstain had remained on the floor ever since. Every time I saw the bloodstain it reminded me of the dream, as did the war itself – a running, real-life nightmare. To find out about the meaning of my nightmare, I once borrowed a dictionary of dreams from an acquaintance, but apparently no one else had ever dreamed such vileness. (1990, p.110)

It is Kapuscinski, however, who reveals the deeper, broader picture, and like all great writers has forged his own unique style. He does not assume absolute truth or prescribe a moral course but, as James Aucoin puts it, he takes you there, shows you an incomplete picture and then challenges you to find the missing pieces. He implicitly passes responsibility on to the reader (Aucoin, 2001, p.15). It is not conventional, objective journalism, and it is not journalism of attachment, but it is better jounalism for that.

Hunter S. Thompson, a chief exponent of the New Journalism, once noted that 'The only thing [he] ever saw that came close to Objective Journalism was a close-circuit TV set-up that watched shoplifters in the General Store at Woody Creek, Colorado.' The war zones of the world are a long way from Woody Creek, yet the issues of 'objectivity' and 'attachment', and the dilemmas they present to the war correspondent, have drawn some bitter exchanges of fire on the Home Front.

'A TWISTED SORT OF THERAPY': THE JOURNALISM OF ATTACHMENT CRITIQUE

The most sustained critique of the journalism of attachment has come from Mick Hume, editor of the now defunct *LM* (formerly *Living Marxism*) magazine. His pamphlet *Whose War Is It Anyway?* (1997) is strongly argued and, while his own political position is not entirely clear, it is a coherent and significant contribution to the debate. Hume sees the trend of personalised, crusading reporting as a 'menace to good journalism – and to those whose lives it invades'. It neglects the historical and political context of the conflict it reports and portrays it instead as merely a metaphysical struggle between good and evil. Journalists who adhere to this kind of reporting set themselves up – intentionally or by default – as judge and jury. Their mission is not to explain and contextualise but to promulgate the morally correct line and this, says Hume, obscures and undermines their role as impartial and objective reporters. Hume is adamant. 'The journalism of attachment', he says, 'is self-righteous. Worse, it is repressive. Those who fall the wrong side of the line the press corps draws between Good and Evil...can expect to be on the receiving end of more than a bad press' (ibid, p.4).

Robert Fisk, special Middle East correspondent for the *Independent*, also suspects the ideological impulses of reporting steeped in moral outrage and says it is not what he understands by 'journalism':

> I can remember...in the Gulf, one of my colleagues, a normally very sensible, rational guy...became a bit odd. He said, 'We've got to smash Saddam. It's the only way to do it. The Arabs are with us.' He was cheerleading in print. It was a very serious problem and it happened in the Kosovo war. [One of the] reporters came in

talking about 'Here in Djakovice you can see evil and you can smell evil.' To which my reply is if a guy is talking like that either he needs a holiday or he should go into holy orders. This is ridiculous. This is not journalism, you know...[it] is the sort of journalism I'm totally against. There's another reporter who I have a lot of respect for but he's always looking into his own heart: 'Behind me, unimaginable horrors are taking place in our time.' Big problem.[5]

Mick Hume argues that there is nothing wrong with taking sides in a conflict.The problem is the tendency of reporters to mix emotion with the reporting of facts. When the facts are suppressed, when they do not fit the moral framework reporters have constructed for themselves, then the reader, the viewer, the listener, is the loser. 'There is a difference', he says, 'between taking sides and taking liberties with the facts in order to promote your favoured cause. There is a difference between expressing an opinion and presenting your personal passions and prejudices as objective reporting. And there is a difference between reporting from the midst of a conflict and writing as if you were the one at war, so that journalists and their feelings become the news' (1997, p.5). Martin Bell and reporters who share his general view would insist that objectivity is still possible even if the reporter adopts a moral standpoint on the rights and wrongs of a conflict. Mick Hume and others argue that this is an untenable position. Stephen Ward wonders how it can inform reporting of conflicts like Northern Ireland or Bosnia (1998, p.124). It allows for no grey areas, no doubts, no scepticism, no questions. What happens when certain facts fail to fit the moral framework? What then? What happens when the 'bad guys' tell the truth? Or when the 'good guys' tell lies?

The Bosnian War was reported as a titanic battle between good and evil in which journalists in general adopted a sustained anti-Serb narrative. Atrocity stories were reported with scant regard for their veracity – no checking, no official confirmations or denials, just the rush to instant judgement. Roy Gutman reported for *Newsday* on Serbian death camps, only later admitting that he neglected to check the story out in his rush to tell the world 'the truth' (Hume, 1997, p.9). Hume gives several examples of the Journalism of Attachment in action when reporting the war in Bosnia. The Sarajevo market place massacre of February 1994 was blamed on Bosnian Serbs despite a UN investigation that pointed to

Bosnian Muslim involvement, a possible attempt to attract worldwide sympathy and provoke a tough military response against the Serbs. Or the Bosnian Serb, tried and convicted for war crimes, who was nonetheless allowed to tell his confession to the world's media; this was spun as testament to what the Serbs were capable of in Bosnia but much of it was unverified and based on half truths and exaggerations. In stories like these, Hume argues, 'The reporters and their editors imposed their own external agenda in deciding which facts did and did not qualify as news' (ibid, p.11). Maggie O'Kane filed up to 50 reports on the war in Bosnia yet only one of those tried to explain the Serbian position in the conflict. 'In retrospect', she says, 'I could have seen more of the Serbian side...but you gravitate to where the bigger story is. We were all in Sarajevo writing human interest stories' (ibid, p.13). But O'Kane is unapologetic in her basic ethical approach to the Bosnia story and she draws a clear line between professional objectivity and telling the truth; the two in her view, and that of many of her colleagues, are not always the same:

> I think the highest thing we can achieve is the truth. The truth is not objective sometimes [and] actually there's nothing very objective about a pogrom and a sweeping policy of ethnic cleansing across an entire country. It's very brutal, it's very calculated and it's very one-sided...I think the interesting thing about objectivity is that the people who wave those banners are usually either people who've got something to hide as in the case of the Serbs who were criticising journalistic coverage and saying we weren't objective and were biased, that's one category. Secondly, often political establishment figures who were uncomfortable with the reporting and therefore attacked journalists for lacking objectivity...so you have to ask where are they coming from?...I sort of feel that I try for the truth and sometimes the truth's a good story and sometimes it isn't and actually that's all that matters.[6]

Alex Thomson is of a similar view regarding his reporting of Kosovo in 1999. He is clear and unapologetic in his dismissal of objectivity in situations where it invalidates difficult or inconvenient truths or where it lends spurious legitimacy to torture, rape or ethnic cleansing:

I made no attempt to be objective in my reporting about the Serb pogrom which was being conducted in Kosovo. I was there, I saw the build-up to it. I'd seen what the Serbs did in Croatia, I'd seen what they did in Bosnia, and I saw the same individuals, the same generals, the same senior commanders controlling things in Kosovo. And I saw the refugees. Did I see the refugees?! In Kukes, in northern Albania, in northern Macedonia, day after day after day on those mountainsides, coming out and telling the same stories...What is objectivity in that situation? What *is* objectivity?!...Do we mean by objectivity that there is essentially a kind of middle ground of explanation which can legitimately explain why these people are being raped and tortured and burned out of their houses? That's bullshit. You just tell people what's happening. You let them make their own moral judgement about it.There was no doubt this war [Kosovo] was being fought for the best of intentions. It's the only war I've ever supported that has seen my government fight. I'm more than happy to support what happened, not in my work – it's not my business and it's irrelevant anyway – but in my own personal feelings...I was overjoyed when they started bombing Novi Sad and wasting the Serb's infrastructure – absolutely overjoyed.[7]

CNN's Christiane Amanpour thinks that in a story like the genocide in Rwanda, reporters should certainly be fair but that does *not* mean treating the perpetrators on an equal basis with their victims or 'insisting on drawing a balance when no balance exists'. She attacks today's 'culture of moral equivalence [where]... journalism seems uncomfortable with identifying a victim and aggressor'. In Bosnia, for example, 'Britain and France kept insisting both sides in that conflict were equally guilty. They were not. That has been recognized in retrospect, but in the meantime it caused international inaction and unnecessary loss of life, not to mention a sense of political impotence on the part of the west.'[8]

But for Mick Hume, journalists who stake out the high moral ground in this way do it not for the sake of the innocent victims of some conflict but to fill a vacuum of moral certainty in their own life, their work or in the society in which they originate. These journalists, he says, set themselves on 'a moral mission on behalf of a demoralised society'. War reporting becomes for them 'a twisted sort of therapy', a discovery of a sense of purpose for themselves and their audience. It appears to fill a need in journalists to rediscover some value in a profession fatally compromised by cynicism and the profit motive. So journalists becomes part of the story in which they write or talk about themselves and each other in endless feature articles and documentaries (1997, pp.17–21), such as Max Ophul's 1995 film, *The Troubles We've Seen*. In the movies the journalist is usually seen as hard-boiled and cynical but the foreign correspondent is depicted as the hero, risking life and limb to get the story, but also getting involved in the story too.[9]

This mode of reporting became the norm for covering conflicts elsewhere in the world, especially in Africa where, Hume argues, 'western journalists could give even freer rein to their prejudices and force the facts into their preconceived framework'. So the massacre of Tutus by Hutus in Rwanda was reported all over the world but when the mainly Tutu Rwandan Patriotic Front came to power and sought their revenge on Hutu refugees in Zaire, their attacks were hardly reported at all (1997, p.12; see also Gowing, 1998).

When we looked back at the reporting of the Crimean War, we saw two types of reporting: one that was concerned with the strategy and tactics of battle and which was associated with William Russell, and the other that focused on the human stories of war as exemplified by Edwin Godkin. The journalism of attachment tends to lean towards the latter which some say is influenced by the number of women journalists reporting war and conflicts these days. It is assumed that unlike their male colleagues, women journalists are keen to get beyond the obsession with military hardware and report the human costs of war: suffering, loss and bereavement, displacement and upheaval. But it is wrong to see the prominence of the female war correspondent as a relatively new phenomenon (see Elwood-Akers, 1988; Sebba, 1994; Wagner, 1989). And it is certainly wrong to suggest that there is a strict gender difference in style between men and women reporters. Some women journalists see they have advantages over their male colleagues. Jan Goodwin, for example, reported on the Afghan resistance to the Russian occupation during the 1980s and felt 'that as a woman, I was able to see a different side of guerrillas from the one that is normally shown to journalists – with me the freedom fighters could allow themselves to be vulnerable. And I in turn came to respect and care for these men' (1987, p.xviii). One has to wonder if the image of the caring woman journalist helping vulnerable 'freedom fighters' get in touch with their feelings in the mountain wilderness of Afghanistan does anything for the efforts of most women journalists to struggle for and win credibility in a still male-dominated occupation.

A better exemplar of the qualities of the female war correspondent might be the crisis in East Timor in 1999. When Indonesia agreed to end its illegal 25-year occupation of the country and allow a free referendum on independence, it promised to withdraw its troops; with their tacit support, however, pro-Indonesian militia set about a campaign of terror and intimidation against the majority of the population who wanted independence. They also lashed out at the United Nations and the assembled media, laying siege to the UN compound in the capital Dili. The UN eventually announced its intention to withdraw its western staff and advised the journalists to do likewise. Three of them refused, choosing to stay with the local staff inside. Victoria Brittain thought it no accident that all three journalists were women. The Dutch freelance journalist and photographer Irene Slegt became, says Brittain, 'the voice to the outside world of 1,500 desperate Timorese who had taken refuge in the compound and faced certain death if the UN plans to abandon them had been carried out'. A friend of Slegt described her as 'the kind of woman who's prepared to feel an emotional sympathy for the people she's working among, where a man would override that in the interests of common sense'. With her were Minka Nijhuis, a writer, and *Sunday Times* correspondent, Marie Colvin.[10] This presents quite a black and white picture that excludes the possibility of a man acting on emotion or sympathy, and a woman acting on common sense. Brittain says that 'of course there are plenty of careerist women for whom common sense comes first but I think that most people who are on a sharp career track tend to be men, and women are much more likely not to be so interested in that':

[The] kind of choices that Irene's made, you know to go after these unfashionable stories – East Timor turned out to be an unfashionable one – but she spent 20 years working on these kinds of unfashionable stories. And she's a good example of the kind of woman who's not a journalist because she wants to make a big career or a big name or big money. She's a journalist because she wants to find out what makes the world tick and communicate that to other people and I think that's why I identify with her because that's what I have tried to do. Men, particularly younger men, they want to be big or they wouldn't go into journalism in the first place. They'd become primary school teachers.[11]

As Brittain wrote at the time, the gender gap is thrown into sharp relief in the 'intensity of war [when] even outsiders find themselves uncomfortably revealed, shorn of the props and mannerisms which allow most people, men in particular, to mask themselves most of the time'. Men respond to fear with bravado, she argued, and male war correspondents are no different: 'they become obsessed with weapons and start identifying with the military as role models, in the hope of feeling stronger and braver themselves'.[12] The response of the woman correspondent to the extremes of the war correspondent, says Brittain, 'is to identify with the people whose intimate lives are shattered. Irene Slegt [had] no hesitation in saying about women journalists what many of us would hesitate to put into words: "We are more courageous...you see men losing it quicker" .' For young male correspondents coming up and taking on assignments in this war zone or that, 'the shape of journalism now is very much about your ego, your starring and general you-ness'. Male correspondents 'don't make great companions in difficult situations...whereas there's something about women,...not that they're just sort of soft or anything. They're just able to be more attuned to what else is going on in the situation.' This is particularly the case with television which is why Brittain stopped doing TV news and prefers print journalism. She 'couldn't stand the way it deformed what you were trying to see'. Television by its very nature, with its stand-ups to camera, projects the journalist and makes her very visible where maybe she prefers anonymity:

> You know, you became the story whereas, particularly where you're doing very difficult things like civil wars, the kind of stories that I do a lot in Africa, obviously you stand out for a kick off because you are white but beyond that you want to be as invisible as possible and I think most male journalists find that a bit difficult. They don't want to be invisible. The whole reason they're a journalist is because they want a picture byline on the front page. I just think that's a shame and it makes the work that much more difficult.[13]

The image of the macho male correspondent and his soldier fantasies was caricatured by *Guardian* cartoonist Steve Bell, just after Nato's Kosovo campaign. Lucan Hardnose, with his crew-cut and combat jacket, is a Kosovo correspondent and we follow his adventures, note-book in hand and a red rose between his teeth, 'living in the love of the common people with KFOR, North of Pristina' or riding a KFOR tank in full battle dress to the adulation of a liberated people: 'Every journalist should sit on a tank and feel what it is like to be loved, to be *really* loved', he writes. 'It's humbling, it's bloody, bloody humbling!' (*Guardian*, 22 June 1999, see overleaf). Like all caricatures this works as an exaggeration of reality but it would be unfair to use it against the many male correspondents and cameramen who take risks not for their own greater glory but for a story they care about. Maggie O'Kane praises the courage of women such as Slegt and Colvin but in Dili they were just doing their jobs as writers and correspondents rather than striking out for the sisterhood. While they stayed under siege in the compound with many frightened people, a number of male correspondents were taking risks to report what was happening outside on the streets and on the island. The news cameraman Max Stahl was taking great risks by going into the forest and getting pictures of people being forced by the militias into West Timor. He was lucky to survive and collect well-deserved plaudits for his pictures but another journalist, Sanders Thoenes of the *Financial Times*, was shot dead by the militia and dumped in an alleyway.[14]

However, Mark Urban sees the journalism of attachment as part of the cultural *Zeitgeist*, a cultural condition 'in which victimhood is everything in these conflicts and where it's almost impossible in the reporting of somewhere like Bosnia or Kosovo for someone with a gun in their hand to be a hero in the way that it was, even in the early days of the Northern Ireland conflict or the Falklands'. Much of what passes for war reporting now 'is simply about how high you can crank the emotion-ometer'. But this, says Urban, does not come down to a 'feminisation of news values'. Rather, it is 'a view of conflict in which you simply concentrate on the civilian victims and you only interview the military protagonists through a heavy filter of cultural bias or aggressive...innuendo [which] is utterly self-defeating'.[15]

Martin Bell argues that reporters and aid workers would take their inspiration from officers of the British Army, such as his friend Colonel Bob Stewart, and find leadership and courage in themselves (Hume, 1997, p.21). But this assumption, that viewers and readers need to be led by the reporter through a minefield of moral distinctions, between good guys and bad guys, good victims and bad victims, to be told whose side to take, is exactly what bothers critics such as Stephen Ward who cautions against such moral leadership

in 'a pluralistic society with few common standards' (1998, p.124). It is simply not what the reporter is there to do, says John Simpson, who is 'getting increasingly tired of all of this crap. It's "look at me journalism". It's not the purpose of being there. I don't think the BBC is that kind of organisation and I don't really want to impose those kinds of views and attitudes on to people.' He explains that his approach is rooted in the tradition of BBC public service journalism that focuses not on the story-teller but on telling the story. Viewers want to know about events on the ground in Beijing or Belgrade, not what John Simpson is thinking or feeling about those events because what he feels just gets in the way of their understanding and is 'of no value or of no interest to anybody'.[16] This, he thinks, is all the more essential when reporting complex events on which it is possible to take more than one perspective. People should be able to appreciate the complexity and not have their opinions directed or their minds made up for them:

> Nowadays you might say there's only one view that you could take about the Tiananmen Square massacre and that probably is true. But as I found when I was there, there was more than one view you could take about the bombing of Belgrade. I think that one of the strengths of my position there was that I wasn't trying to tell people what to think and I wasn't trying to whip up feelings, and I wasn't telling people how I felt when I saw people dying or being killed. I was able simply to explain what was going on. Sometimes that was terrible and it was indeed – the death, the horrible death of people right in front of my eyes. I don't feel the requirement to rant on how I personally felt about it and the effect it had on my life because I didn't think that was what anybody else was interested in.[17]

Robert Fisk recalls an old saying: 'You cannot bribe or twist, thank God, the British journalist but seeing what he'll do unbribed there's no occasion to.'[18] The journalism of attachment is said to encourage voluntary and moral self-censorship. Systematic censorship and control were largely absent from the Bosnian War because, says Mick Hume, it simply was not required. Nothing the international media said undermined the general propaganda framework as promoted in the West or threatened anyone's security. And there was no need to control the movements of reporters because they rarely if ever ventured behind Serb lines to get the story there. He concludes that those 'who pursue the Journalism of Attachment...are playing a dangerous game for high stakes. The language of evil, genocide, and Holocaust can exact a high price from the accused. Such a substitution of emotion and histrionics for rational and critical analysis must also prove a major set-back for standards of journalism' (1997, p.27). For Hume, there must be reporters out there who will take a stand for a journalism that takes a balanced view of a conflict, that is informed and that checks the facts and carefully sources the evidence.

Lindsey Hilsum remarks that after reporting on the mass killings in Rwanda in 1994, she read something of Primo Levi's work that she found herself disagreeing with:

> He said to understand is to justify and I don't think [that is always true]. The job of a journalist is to try and understand, not to understand emotionally, but to understand historically. And so I am not objective about the fact that a government had a policy of trying to exterminate all the Tutsis and all the moderate Hutus in Rwanda. That was a terrible, wicked thing to do. But my job as a journalist is to try and understand how this situation came about and to understand why those Hutus in those villages picked up their machetes and slaughtered people. It's not my job to stand there saying, 'This is appalling, this is terrible, I've never seen anything so awful in my life.' My job is to try and get beyond that...Now some people will then say I am justifying it because I try and understand what was going on in the minds of those people who did that...But that's not the case at all, it's my job.[19]

Hilsum tells how she 'crossed the line to commitment' one day in 1997 when she testified at the United Nations International Criminal Tribunal for Rwanda (ICTR). She was called by the prosecution to support the case that what happened in Rwanda in 1994 'constituted crimes against humanity and genocide' (1997, p.29). Some journalists have taken similar action. Ed Vulliamy and Martin Bell have testified to the International Criminal Tribunal for the Former Yugoslavia (ICTFY); others have refused on the grounds that it is not for journalists to get involved in the story they report and that to testify against possible sources and contacts would be to erode a fundamental principle of journalism and destroy the credibility and effectiveness of the journalist. Who would talk to the journalist again if they thought it might prejudice their position? But Hilsum argues that 'the normal rules of journalistic ethics are overwhelmed by murder' on the scale perpetrated in Rwanda. She was one of the very few western journalist actually there when it was all happening so she felt it was her 'moral duty to use [her] unique position to influence the historical record in the court' (ibid, p.30). She argues further for the 'need to find a balance between the practical and ethical demands of reporting, and our responsibility as citizens – or human beings – in the face of extreme mass crimes' (ibid, p.32).

Robert Fisk opposes crusading journalism but thinks 'that when a journalist sees something which is outrageous, to write as if it's just a road accident, or an earthquake or an act of God over which he has no opinions or no feelings as a human being, then there's not much point being a writer let alone a journalist'.[20] Radical Australian journalist Wilfred Burchett rejected 'the commonly enough held opinion that journalists should remain aloof from politics, not join parties or accept the discipline that membership implies. Journalists are members of human society with the same rights and duties and social responsibilities as everyone else, including those of political options' (1980, p.328). For Burchett, journalism was about conscience and his obligations to his readers. He believed that he had in his working life achieved 'a sort of journalistic Nirvana' resistant to political, institutional or commercial pressure or interference:

> This demanded freedom from any discipline except that of getting the facts on important issues back to the sort of people likely to act – often at great self-sacrifice – on the information they received...Over the years, and in many countries, I had a circle of readers who did not buy papers for the stock market reports or strip cartoons, but for facts on vital issues affecting their lives and their consciences. In keeping both eyes and both ears open during my forty years's reporting from the world's hotspots, I had become more and more conscious of my responsibilities to my readers. The point of departure is a great faith in ordinary human beings and the sane and decent way they behave when they have the true facts of the case. (ibid, p.328)

'HONEST JOURNALISM' AND THE 'ATTITUDE OF CLARITY'

In the age of satellite and cable, of instant deadlines, instant news, says Martin Bell, journalists are under ever-increasing pressure to get the story out. Sometimes this has resulted in bad practice – unchecked facts and sources, on the spot judgements and analyses.

But in general, the presence of reporters perhaps ensures that wars are not as brutal and terrible as they might otherwise be, making war crimes harder to commit, the guilt harder to deny, the sentence harder to escape (1998, p.104). Looking back on his idea of the journalism of attachment and the debate it provoked, Martin Bell stands by it in principle but insists it was 'widely misunderstood'. The 'journalism of attachment', he says:

is not a licence for campaigning journalism, to which I am opposed...I'm very suspicious, and I've seen it happen, when people go into foreign countries, and war zones...knowing what they're going to find and lo and behold they find it. I never belonged to that. I would in retrospect wish I had emphasised more the part of my doctrine which says that the facts are sacred. It's just that I don't believe that journalists should act as if they had no influence because they do. They affect the events that they are reflecting; there's no question of that. They do have a moral responsibility which I think is increasingly accepted. And I wasn't so much prescribing a new journalism as describing a changed journalism; it changed in the 30 something years I was doing it and I was describing what I believed to be best practice at the time I was leaving it in 1997.[21]

Bell tells an anecdote from Bosnia which he believes to be true. A journalist visits a sniper position in or around Sarajevo: possibly Serb, possibly Muslim, possibly Croat. The sniper tells him he has two civilians in his sights. 'Which of them do you want me to shoot?', he asks. The journalist turns to leave and the sniper fires twice. 'That is a pity', he calls after him. 'You could have saved one of their lives' (1997, p.9).

The journalist, then, is in an impossible position: damned if he acts, damned if he doesn't. Martin Bell did not deserve the opprobrium that was heaped upon his head in the wake of his 'heresy'. He was after all the BBC journalist exemplar, public service to the bone. But it is clear that he touched a nerve. Intentionally or not, he stirred up a debate about the proper role of the journalist in the war zone that tapped into wider cultural anxieties about the clash between the public and the private, the collective and the individual. To reprise Vilar, the best any honest journalist can do is adopt an 'attitude of clarity: [stating] one's position, while believing firmly that thorough analysis is the best way to buttress that position' (Southworth, 1977, p.xvi). The problem for critics of the journalism of attachment is that reporters are not accountable for the words they speak in the same way as democratically elected politicians or international organisations such as the United Nations. It is not simply an issue of conscience, they argue, but the wider consequences of the decision to get emotionally or morally involved in the story. Burns argues that journalists cannot lay claim to 'providing the highest standards of objective and balanced reporting while still presenting themselves as impartial arbiters pressing for action' (1996, p.98). Yet one could argue from this discussion that the journalists he refers to do not actually make any claims to provide 'the highest standards of objectivity' but instead make a choice based on a very different ethic: individual conscience, or 'honest journalism' as Mark Pedelty encountered it in El Salvador (1995). During a short sojourn in Vietnam, *LA Times* correspondent Jacques Leslie came to see objectivity as impossible, 'a refuge for the meek, who'd rather omit what was least tangible, which is surely where truth lies'. He, too, takes 'honesty' as the ultimate standard the reporter should attain, 'which meant facing the truth, following it down its own path, not sculpting an idealized image of it, all clean and sparkling with bogus ideology. I knew no objective journalists but I knew some honest ones'(1995, p.169).

When Richard Dimbleby witnessed the liberation of the Belsen death camp he struggled in his report for BBC radio to humanly convey the absolutely unspeakable. What judgement would we make of him today if we listened to him report: 'What must have taken place in this camp is unimaginable but until we get a statement from the allies, it is impossible to verify'? But Dimbleby dispensed with objectivity and reported what he saw as a human being. His bosses in London not only refused to believe his report but they were reluctant to even broadcast in full until forced to by political pressure. Perhaps they were waiting for a balancing view from the Nazis?

That was in 1945. In August 1992, Ed Vulliamy of the *Guardian* and an ITN news team arrived to report on conditions in Trnopolje prison camp, in Bosnia, and started a chain of events that made them the focus of the story long after the war had ended. The defining image of the story was that of Fikret Alic, a prisoner whose emaciated figure behind the barbed wire became the symbol of the war in Bosnia (Vulliamy, 1993, p.5). Vulliamy's report and ITN's footage were reported around the world – one newspaper headlined it, 'Belsen '92'

– and he remembers the sheer inanity of repeating his story for the hundreth time on some TV station or other in America.[22]

Subsequently, however, a report by German journalist Thomas Deichmann appeared in *LM* magazine ('The Picture that Fooled the World', February 1997), charging that the ITN pictures were misleading: the pictures of Alic and his fellow inmates, he alleged, were taken from inside a barbed wire enclosure, with the prisoners standing on the outside. ITN's lawyers had already demanded in the previous month that the offending edition be withheld from publication and pulped. The request was refused and ITN filed a libel suit against *LM* ('The Mag that ITN Wants to Gag'), edited by Mick Hume and published by Inform Inc. Unusually for a libel case, the court put the burden of proof on the defendants: *LM* found itself having to not only prove the circumstances of the ITN film report but also the intent of the news crew. The magazine argued that this would require 'a time machine and a mind reader' to achieve. Deichmann in his article had given the ITN crew the benefit of the doubt as to their intentions but argued that the effect of the world publicity and the treatment of the story by other sections of the media was to crank up public hysteria about another 'Holocaust' in the heart of Europe. Although the ITN reporters expressed concerns privately about such an effect, they made no attempt to set the record straight publicly about the exact circumstances of their film report. The court ordered *LM* to pay ITN £375,000 in libel damages, forcing its closure. Mick Hume called it 'a disgrace to democracy and a menace to good journalism' (2000, p.40) whereas ITN executive Stuart Purvis declared it 'a victory for frontline journalism over pundit journalism' (ibid, p.42).

CONCLUDING REMARKS

There is no doubt that however aggrieved it felt about Deichmann's charges, ITN used excessive force to make its case. In some ways its victory in the courts was a rather pyrrhic one and made it look like the bully in the media playground. But the case crystallises some of the issues raised in this chapter about the professional, political and personal pressures that prevail upon the journalist in the modern war zone. Journalists such as Ed Vulliamy, Maggie O'Kane, Mike Nicholson and Martin Bell would argue that the war in Bosnia was nothing like any they had ever reported before and required a response that went beyond professional requirements for neutrality and objectivity. 'I am one of those reporters', writes Vulliamy, 'who cannot see this [war] as "just another story" from which I must remain detached and in which I must be neutral. I think that if I did require myself to be neutral, I would not understand the war. I would not understand why people are suffering in the inimitable way that they are, nor the lies that are being told and why, and I would not be able to judge or measure the grotesque inertia of what likes to pompously call itself "The International Community" in its abdication of its responsibilities' (1993, p.6).

Vulliamy and others saw people suffering terribly in Bosnia and crossed the line to take a stand with them and demand action from the 'international community', from NATO or the UN or the EU. But Mick Hume, John Simpson, Nik Gowing and others argue that in a three-sided war like Bosnia, whose side do you take when it is clear that each protagonist is acutely sensitive to the value of the international media and of harnessing world opinion in favour of their cause? Peter Arnett tells how he made contact with Chechen rebels in the first Chechen war and found their morale buoyant in spite of their isolation and their hopeless military position. 'We have the support of the government of the international media', they told him, 'and you are one of its ambassadors' (1996). The problem with diplomatic immunity, of course, is that it can always be cancelled. The story should serve as a reminder to reporters everywhere of the delicate balancing act they must perform between 'caring as well as knowing' and becoming 'ambassadors', witting or unwitting, for the next big cause. War correspondents are not diplomats or politicians and they are certainly not part of any government. The following chapter looks at what happens when some forget this in their reporting of 'humanitarian crises' and call for something to be done.

9   'Something Must Be Done' Journalism

We want the news but [if] you can do anything in diplomacy, in a military way, or through political intrigue, which I gather is a favourite pastime of yours, you are to forget the Times and serve the cause which is more important to me even to exclusive news dispatches.

Lord Northcliffe to Stanley Washburn, correspondent for *The Times* on the Russian front during the First World War, in Washburn, *On the Russian Front in WWI*, 1982

We are in an age of government-by-news cycle.

Christiane Amanpour, CNN[1]

In 1993, British Foreign Secretary, Douglas Hurd, delivered a speech to the Traveller's Club, in London, in which he criticised media coverage of foreign affairs, particularly the founder members of the 'something must be done' school of journalism who took up positions and called for western intervention in Bosnia and various other wars and humanitarian crises. He argued that their posturing was inconsistent for there were equally devastating conflicts in the world which they totally ignored. Even if the West had intervened in Bosnia, they would be criticising that too.[2] It was a self-serving attack on Hurd's part; media coverage was shedding light on what was essentially a non-policy on the war in Bosnia. Nevertheless, his comments pointed to an apparently new trend among reporters and the media organisations they worked for to get involved in the politics of the story they were supposed to simply report. Yet when a reporter or newspaper or television documentary brings home to us the need for intervention in some conflict or crisis involving the suffering of countless civilians then we should not be so surprised. As we saw in the last chapter, the committed reporter, the partisan journalist, is not a new figure in the cultural landscape but part of a tradition of journalism. One could call William Howard Russell a founder of the 'something must be done' school for his reports on the appalling conditions suffered by the troops at the Crimean front. Janaurius MacGahan would also qualify as a founding member; in 1876, he reported on Turkish atrocities in southern Bulgaria and his series of dispatches resulted in Russia going to war against Turkey on 29 April 1877. One could add to the school the reporters of the Spanish Civil War who called for western intervention to stop the rise of fascism in Europe. And what of the reporters of two world wars who willingly campaigned to bring about American intervention in those conflicts? We may criticise, take issue, perhaps even expose inconsistencies and contradictions in what journalists might have said and done in serious humanitarian crises, but we should also consider what might have happened had there been no journalists present or willing to report them. Some recent cases highlight the point.

Television pictures of thousands of refugees stranded on a wet, windswept hillside in northern Iraq, in April 1991, marked the first time many in the West had ever heard of the Kurds. The pictures became emblematic of the Gulf War; just as the images of 'smart weapons' seemed to say something about the superiority of military technology in the West – war it seems at the flick of a joystick – images of helpless and abandoned refugees seemed to bring home to people the contradictions of the war and undermine the purity of western realpolitik. Martin Shaw (1996) sees the Kurdish crisis as possibly the clearest-cut example of how intense media pressure can in some way affect foreign policy. Yet, in the case of the Kurds at any rate, the western alliance was simply put on the spot: it had encouraged the revolt in the first place only to then stand back and allow Saddam Hussein to crush it. It was now being held accountable and responsible for the terrible consequences. 'The Allies', argues Nik Gowing, 'had thought about only fighting a war to get the Iraqis out of Kuwait, not what happened next. They didn't envisage the Kurds spilling over from Northern Iraq to southern Turkey and so that's why there was no policy; there was a policy vacuum, policy panic.'[3] It is less clear whether that set a precedent for subsequent crises such as Bosnia, Rwanda or Somalia. These featured some of the vital components determining decisive media influence. In Bosnia (1992–95) and Rwanda (1994), there were plenty of pictures of atrocities and human suffering on a wide scale but they provoked limited international action. The massacre in Rwanda in 1994, mainly of the Tutu population, was truly horrific and much reported and written about. However, other waves of mass killings of Hutus by Tutus in Burundi in 1993 and again in 1996 in the former Zaire barely made the international news agenda (Gourevitch, 1998; Gowing, 1998). Not only that but none of these crises reached the critical mass that would invoke concerted international intervention. In Somalia in 1993, by contrast, pictures of dead US Rangers being dragged through the streets of the capital, Mogadishu, provoked public outrage in America and, apparently, the subsequent withdrawal of US troops from UNAMOG, the United Nations Aid Mission in Mogadishu. However, Gowing suggests that a policy reversal was already under way and that those video pictures simply hastened the inevitable.[4] So when we talk about the media's influence over foreign policy-making and humanitarian intervention we must address the question with reference to factors such as media attention, media influence and information management.

MEDIA ATTENTION

After the official end of the Gulf War in 1991, reports reached the West that the Iraqi army was putting down armed revolts from Shia and Kurdish minorities. The West had originally fomented these revolts in order to destabilise the Iraqi war effort but it was now happy to see them defeated if only to ensure that Iraq remained intact and governed by a non-Islamic regime. In a twist of irony familiar to critics of western policy gymnastics, Saddam Hussein was still their man in Baghdad. The uprisings, and the refugee crises that flowed from their suppression, attracted unwelcome attention from some sections of the western media. In Britain, the BBC, ITN, the *Guardian* and the *Daily Mirror* persisted with difficult questions about western policy motives. However, the principal point of pressure was for immediate action to relieve the refugees with aid and supplies, and the establishment of protection zones in the north and south of the country in order to prevent Iraqi military incursions. The fate of the Shia Moslem and Kurdish peoples in the south-east of the country, on the border with Iran, was less well publicised. So how did two very similar human tragedies come to be treated so differently by the media? Why did the Kurdish crisis in the north attract such extensive and apparently effective media coverage while the Shia and Kurdish revolts in the south, just as disastrous for those people, receive little or no coverage? Shaw checklists a number of possible reasons. One variable was timing. The fate of the Shias in the south was simply airbrushed out of the picture of a New World Order in which, as George Bush proclaimed without irony, there would be 'no more law of the jungle'; the Kurdish crisis on the other hand came to a head just as postwar euphoria in the West was being displaced with a feeling that the job had not been done, that the West should have assassinated, or at least overthrown, Saddam Hussein. Shaw also points out that for all their hi-tech, portable communications technology, the international media found it easier to reach the Kurds in the north-east from the western-friendly Turkey than they could the Shias and Kurds in the south-east from the much less friendly Iran (1996, pp.156ff). We could also factor in the inherent news value of the story. The television images of thousands of miserable people on a rain swept, muddy mountainside without food, shelter or medical supplies were instant, dramatic and shocking. In a BBC report from April 1991, Charles Wheeler stood braced against the elements in a makeshift refugee camp and delivered a simple indictment of western inaction:

> If you spend more than five or ten minutes in this weather then no matter how many clothes you're wearing, you're soaked and you're wet and you're miserable. And these people have been here two weeks...There's a big green plain here – it's a valley, a high valley. It should be possible to drop tents, to drop food from aircraft...What these people cannot understand is why they're still sitting here and why so little aid is coming from outside.[5]

Of the various factors governing the extent of media power to influence foreign policy and intervention, it is the attention span of the western media, and indeed western governments, that appears to provoke most debate. A significant cross section of media, political and diplomatic opinion sees media attention as random and arbitrary. Nik Gowing reflects on his former job as Diplomatic Editor for *Channel Four News*,[6] on how he would sit at a bank of TV monitors taking satellite feeds of armed conflicts from around the world. He says that 'there are times when I begin to think of all this conflict coverage as supermarket war video...Editorially we can pick and choose – just like walking down the shelves of breakfast cereal. One day Nagorno Karabakh. The next day, Tajikistan. Perhaps Georgia or Afghanistan. Then a bit of Angola, Liberia, or Yemen and perhaps Algeria if we're lucky' (1996, p.81). In his Traveller's Club speech, Douglas Hurd pointed to this very characteristic of international news coverage, alluding to Walter Lippman's metaphor of media coverage being like a searchlight:

The searchlight of media coverage [of international conflicts] is not the even and regular sweep of a lighthouse. It is patchy, dwelling on some rocks only briefly, on others at length. It is determined partly by editorial guidance but also by practical questions...It is inevitably selective. In that selectiveness the media are actors as well as spectators in foreign affairs.[7]

In direct response to Hurd, John Simpson concedes the point about 'the random nature of the media's approach to the world', especially television which he parodies as 'a very curious beast [with] huge muscles, distinctly poor eyesight and a disturbingly short attention-span'. It is the very fact of drawing public attention to what was happening in places like Sarajevo that most likely bothered politicians and diplomats.[8] Furthermore, the perception that media attention to conflicts and crises around the world is fickle and arbitrary ignores some explicit agenda-setting criteria at work in news selection. There is a direct and obvious inverse relationship between media attention to such conflicts and western interest and involvement in them. At the time of the Gulf War and the Kurdish crisis in 1991, the media neglected the crisis and collapse of the Soviet Union, especially the unrest in the Baltic States and the war between two other breakaway republics, Armenia and Azerbaijan. There was little or no coverage either of conflicts in South East Asia, Africa and South America. Minear et al argue that such conflicts only attract coverage sporadically, 'at moments of high violence, calamitous suffering or political crisis' (1996, p.49). In Europe, Slovenia and Croatia's break from the Yugoslav federation presaged the dangerous and explosive conflicts to come in the Balkans, yet media attention at that stage was, to say the least, minimal. Misha Glenny, a specialist correspondent with BBC World Service at the time, predicted that the area was a powderkeg ready to explode. He was nicknamed 'Misha Gloomy' by some of his colleagues and advised by news executives to tone down his doom-laden prophecies.[9] Other long-standing conflicts continued as major international news stories because of continued and direct western interest. The Middle East conflict, involving Israel and the Palestinians in particular, was still high on the international agenda. It had moved from a focal point of Lebanon in the 1980s to Israel in the 1990s, where young radical Palestinians had launched an uprising or *intifada* against the Israeli occupation of their land, an uprising that threatened to destabilise the seeds of a peace process between the PLO and Israel. Indeed, the involvement of many of Israel's Arab enemies in the western alliance against Iraq in the Gulf War added a new dimension to the Arab–Israeli conflict and served to hold media attention to efforts towards its resolution (see Wolfsfeld, 1997).

The criterion of western intervention may be economically driven, too. In an ever more competitive international market, media companies streamline to compete and survive. Streamlining, though, means rationalising resources: the difference in other words between what they would like to cover and what they say they can afford to cover. Quantitative evidence suggests that this rationalisation has affected television news in the US more severely than in Britain. In the US, total foreign news coverage on nightly peaktime network TV news has declined by half from 3733 minutes in 1989 to 1838 minutes in 1996 at ABC; and from 3351 to 1175 during the same period at NBC (Utley, 1998, p.84). Television news in Britain by comparison seems to have maintained a reasonable level of foreign news coverage over 25 years from 1975–99; at least in quantitative terms. Indeed, the BBC's *Nine O'Clock News* doubled its foreign news coverage in that period (Barnett et al, 2000). However, there are other less obvious, qualitative effects of rationalisation. Nik Gowing points to the growing tendency among commercial media to dispense with the correspondent on the ground and rely instead on news agency pictures to which they add their own less reliable copy. 'The bottom line', he thinks, 'is that having a named recognised journalist on location increasingly carries a high marginal cost that many news organisations will not pay' (1997, p.23). Broadcasters remain officially committed to a consistent level of correspondent-led news reporting from the world's conflict zones but the reality is that they are just as subject to market forces as their competitors among the press. On a more controversial note, Gowing identifies a cynical view within the profession that there exists a prestige factor determining which conflicts the media cover and when. This is all about pitching for the end of year round of media awards, cherry-picking the stories most likely to attract the key nominations, which in themselves make ideal promotional fodder. Conflicts occurring in this period then stand a better chance of attracting a few choice 'bang bang' or 'death and destruction' stories (ibid).

It is difficult, then, to pinpoint a single factor that attracts media attention to one conflict and not another but it seems that the direct involvement of major powers is significant. Yet even the most intensive and sustained media coverage of a conflict or crisis like Rwanda or Bosnia does not necessarily translate into influence or determine foreign policy decision-making and outcomes. Again, it is necessary to consider a range of policy variables and contexts.

MEDIA INFLUENCE ON POLICY-MAKING

How did media coverage influence western decision-making in a crisis like that in Iraq in April 1991? Daniel Schorr chronicles the sequence of factors that led the US to do a complete policy U-turn and take direct military measures to relieve the human suffering and protect the refugees. He is quite forthright in his claim for media influence in the Kurdish crisis:

> Score one for the power of the media, especially television, as a policy-making force. Coverage of the massacre and exodus of the Kurds generated public pressures that were instrumental in slowing the hasty American military withdrawal from Iraq and forcing a return to help guard and care for the victims of Saddam Hussein's vengeance. (1995, p.53)

Official American response was slow at first and media attention minimal until American television picked up a BBC News report on the crisis in which a woman asks: 'Why did George Bush do nothing?' The initial official response was one of reticence. Bush expressed sympathy for the plight of the Kurds but refused to accept ultimate American responsibility or obligation to act. The US and its allies, he insisted, had done the job they set out to do in the Gulf War – liberate Kuwait, not intervene in internal Iraqi affairs. That Bush and John Major called on the Kurds and Shias to revolt in the first place was beside the point (ibid, p.55). The coverage of BBC and ITN (along with the *Guardian* and the *Mirror)* was more vivid and sustained than anything the American news media managed at that juncture. John Major soon took decisive action and proposed a protected area, a no-fly zone to the Iraqi military and airforce. The US soon followed suit, anxious to avoid the creeping sense that it was being callous and uncaring about the plight of the Kurdish refugees but by then Bush's stratospheric postwar approval rating of 92 per cent had taken a nose dive by 12 points in a *Newsweek* opinion poll, a drop attributed in part to his mishandling of the crisis (ibid, p.56).

Eventually, on 12 April, Bush announced 'Operation Provide Comfort', a relief operation that would involve US military commitment. He appeared to acknowledge the role of the media in effecting this dramatic policy U-turn when he remarked at a news conference that: 'No one can see pictures or hear the accounts of this human suffering – men, women and, most painful of all, innocent children, and not be deeply moved'. Schorr concludes in much the same vein as Shaw, that the Kurdish crisis was unique in terms of media influence: 'It is rare in American history that television, which is most often manipulated to *support* a policy, creates an unofficial plebiscite that forces a *change* in policy.' It raised some debate among the media themselves. Walter Goodman, *New York Times* TV critic, asked: 'Should American policy be driven by scenes that happen to be accessible to cameras and that make the most impact on the screen?' (ibid, p.57). But, Schorr argues, this question overlooks the impact of dramatic pictures of human suffering on the American psyche in a situation in which they felt some sense of responsibility. In other words, the pictures from the mountains of northern Iraq had context for those who watched and responded to them. 'It was that combination', says Schorr, 'that overwhelmed governmental passivity' (ibid).

At first glance, then, the Kurdish crisis seems to be a neat case study of the way the media can affect international policy-making, even reversing previously stated policy aims and outcomes. It was 'TV's finest hour', says Martin Shaw. 'The same media which had been so thoroughly managed in the Gulf campaign were gloriously liberated in its aftermath.'[10] However, closer scrutiny suggests that the crisis may simply have happened in the right place at the right time, that it provoked a short-term response by an embarrassed western alliance anxious to avert a public relations disaster in the aftermath of its triumph in the Gulf War. There was no radical reversal of geopolitical strategy as a result of news coverage; the response was purely palliative as it was in the humanitarian crisis created by the war in Bosnia in the years to follow. And ultimately, the lot of the Kurdish people of northern Iraq has barely improved since 1991; like most Iraqi citizens, especially children, they are suffering the worst effects of the present internationally imposed sanctions regime. With the exception of John Pilger and Maggie O'Kane there have been few media calls for something to be done about the country's soaring infant mortality rate due to the sanctions regime the West continues to impose on spurious and unjustified grounds. O'Kane thinks it is 'the huge untold story of the last decade, that it's going on and that it's caused so much bloody misery and nobody's interested'.[11] But, as Pilger argues, there is a public out there that is engaged and interested and refuses to conform to the glib assumption of 'compassion fatigue'. Pilger's most recent film, *Paying the Price: Killing the Children of Iraq*, (ITV 2001), has helped raise public awareness of the issue and keeps it alive. Public reaction cannot be measured by ratings but by the degree of debate such films attract, the letters received, the telephone calls logged.[12]

The Kurdish crisis presents important precedents when identifying and assessing media influence on western policy on the Bosnian war. Nothing seemed clear cut in the media coverage of Bosnia – if anything it was hit and miss, rather like the policy-making itself. The conflict was of course longer and more complex than the Gulf War. The western powers were not directly involved: they avoided taking sides or engaging in sustained strategic military action. Indeed that was the last thing they wanted, the assumption being that once in there it would be difficult to extract themselves. When they did become involved, it was under the auspices of the United Nations, NATO and the EU, and with the help of other international human rights organisations and aid agencies. Intervention, says Mark Urban, is contingent upon effective consensus building abroad:

> I'm always most comfortable [when] all the things are there on the fruit machine, all the prerequisites are there and the legal one is fantastically important...That was not there in Kosovo. Certainly Tony Blair in his speeches was tempted to try and invent new principles of international law. Well that's fine, you can invent new principles that can evolve...but it does have to be by consensus...if you're going to have values-based intervention...otherwise what you find is you will never have UN authority behind it. Therefore it will be seen as America throwing its weight around, the West throwing its weight around...So I'm not a Do Nothing merchant but I do think as we have seen in Bosnia it took a long time for an international consensus to build.[13]

One could also argue that time was just what was needed to stall and procrastinate – anything to avoid troop commitment. When the US wanted to secure its vested interests in the Panama Canal Zone, in 1989, it did not take weeks out to painstakingly build a consensus. It simply ordered in the troops, overthrew the government and installed one that would not get awkward and insist on the terms of the Panama Canal Treaty ceding the zone back to Panama in 1999. The consensus followed afterwards when all agreed there was not much that could be done about it.

Media coverage of Bosnia was quite slow to establish itself at first but when it did focus it was quite clearly in the direction of the Bosnian Muslim population. There were repeated calls from journalists for 'something to be done' to relieve the sieges of Sarajevo and Srbrenica but very little response from western governments. Martin Bell, who covered the Bosnian war for the BBC, took a very personal view of what the West should do to stop the Serbian bombardments of Sarajevo and Srbrenica:

> I didn't have a political intention [in Bosnia]. I wasn't consciously trying to change the non-policy of my government but I did hope that just showing these pictures [of death and injury] in my country would have an effect, that eventually people would say, 'This is unconscionable what we're not doing.'[14]

There have been American studies into the relationship between the media, foreign policy and public opinion on the war in Bosnia that suggests some dissonance between, on one hand, the knowledge people had of the conflict and on the other the level of interest they had in its resolution and indeed the support they gave for particular measures proposed over others. 'As a result', say Bennett et al, 'mobilising elites into clear coalitions has been difficult [and] leaders may be reluctant to whip up public frenzy without a clear consensus at the top and a good idea of the shape public opinion will take' (1997, pp.102–3). That really is a do nothing charter. It is not clear what the authors mean when they use the phrase 'whip up public frenzy' – perhaps it is unfortunate hyperbole? – but one would have thought that good leadership means energising the opinion-making process with clear and accurate information for informed public discussion. Otherwise it is much too easy and convenient for 'elites' to abdicate their responsibilities on the basis that there is no public support for intervention. Elite politicians credit the media with a remarkable degree of power in relation to the policy-making process. Former US Secretary of State James Baker claims that 'vital national interest now is sometimes determined by what is covered on television' so that although, for example, reform in Russia is more vital to American interests than what is going on in the Balkans, the media story is the Balkans and that, he says, 'puts added burden on policy makers' (1996, pp.7–8). Of course, in regards to some conflict situations, it may well be that doing nothing may be the best policy but that, too, requires the communication of a clear rationale to the public so that it might become interested and informed, engaged in healthy democratic debate. As witnessed in the Persian Gulf War, western leaders are very quick to act unilaterally and at will, as in the Gulf, and then build consensus around that; they may even launch sophisticated and expensive propaganda campaigns to meet that end or exert due force upon dissident members of the international community. Other research, by Richard Sobel for example, suggests that the American press was so attuned to elite, ultra conservative opinion on Bosnia that they 'misrepresented the range and circumstances of public approval for intervention in Bosnia'. Furthermore, says Sobel, public opinion poll after poll showed strong public support for multilateral intervention but weak government action; yet the media neglected to factor that support into their policy debates about Bosnia (1998, pp.28–9). To borrow from Brecht, if the public sphere is not conforming to the right opinions, construct a new public sphere.

'Real time TV pictures', says Nik Gowing, 'compress response times in a crisis. They put pressure on choice and priorities in crisis management.They slow responses. They shape the policy agenda but do not dictate responses. They highlight policy dilemmas but do not resolve them' (1996, p.83). He points to the inability of policy makers to control journalists with censorship and propaganda in the way they could with the Gulf War, and to their frustration with media demands for action. However, he suspects that in fact media pressure provides a plausible excuse not to become embroiled in future conflicts unless they can guarantee some public relations capital: a short-term, successful commitment with minimum casualties. Policy-makers, says Gowing, will always deny that real time TV coverage directly impacts upon their work yet they still express anxieties about it (ibid, pp.85ff). As a television journalist, Gowing has made a valuable and welcome contribution to this most complex debate but if there is one lacuna in his research agenda then that is the issue of policy-making versus public response. It is valid to argue on available evidence that television does not affect long-term response but the intriguing question is what happens if television short-circuits the policy-making nexus and taps into a groundswell of public support for intervention that policy-makers cannot spin and control or that they wish not to consider?

Looking back, Martin Bell is now somewhat more circumspect in his assessment of how much influence instant news really has:

It depends on different cases. Sometimes the effect is no more than cosmetic, that some action will be taken or apparently decisive action like the establishment of the UN safe areas in Bosnia, with everyone saying we're doing something when in fact actually it didn't mean very much because they weren't willing to go to the wall to defend those safe areas, notably in Srbrenica. But I think...if a government has no fixed or settled policy on something and really doesn't know what to do then that vacuum will be filled by public opinion because we will clamour for action of a certain sort and that in turn will be triggered usually by television pictures.[15]

Other reporters see it in terms of news value and compassion fatigue and, as Michael Nicholson would argue, this suits the policy-makers:

The occasional spectacular changes things but I'm afraid that if they don't reach the spectacular status then it's just the drip, drip drip of nightly reports...I think we would con ourselves as television people to think that we change events but I think the politicians are canny enough to know that as long as it's kept fairly low-key people will sooner or later get tired of it and they won't need to do much about it...I don't think the British public were too outraged by what was going on in Kosovo. I actually didn't think they cared too much about it. I think they were *very* upset by what happened in Bosnia.[16]

Lindsey Hilsum, Diplomatic Editor for *Channel Four News*, talks about a clear difference in outlook between British and American journalists in how they see their role and their power to effect changes in policy direction. She explains it in terms of cultural difference:

Obviously [coverage] does matter and we are to some extent being disingenuous when we say [otherwise], and it's probably partly because of being British. I mean if you ask American journalists whether there is much more tradition of the media having impact and power...they would not be so diffident about it as we. It's partly a cultural and a tradition thing... So I think that we know it does have an impact but the point is that we can't say what impact it has and we can't designate what impact it has.[17]

Christiane Amanpour of CNN concedes a significant 'CNN factor' at work in terms of pressure and impact on policy-making but she is not sure this is always positive: 'Often politicians are caught flat-footed on being forced to react to an event immediately, without taking the time to study and make considered, better informed responses. We are in an age of government-by-news cycle.'[18]

These differences among journalists about how they see their role, the extent to which they feel they are 'effective communicators', seem to confirm Gowing's core argument: that media effects on policy, even when focused and linked to geopolitical interests, are never more than short term. The various piecemeal responses to media pressure – such as the establishment of protection areas or no-fly zones – were not policy responses but merely palliative measures to relieve urgent need. They had no long-term effect of ending the war or bringing about direct, western military intervention. Policy-making goes much deeper than that. It goes right to the heart of diplomacy, realpolitik, self-interest. In their study of American press coverage of Iran and US foreign policy, Dorman and Farhang (1987) argue for some form of media influence but place it very firmly in a nexus of policy variables. Even at that, they talk about an 'affective influence' rather than a determining one in which the press play a more normative, democratic role, keeping the public informed and holding US policy-makers to account. This they argue is 'too intangible to be easily quantified and too complex to be comprehended in isolation from other sources of influence' (p.229). As Gowing points out in the case of Bosnia, some policy-makers would argue that short-term, palliative responses actually distorted the war, even prolonged it. He believes that 'real time television coverage of such regional conflicts and crises will create emotions but ultimately make no difference to the fundamental calculations in foreign policy making' (1996, p.84). Such 'fundamental calculations' would include the flow of information, and the extent and efficacy of information management.

INFORMATION AND INFORMATION MANAGEMENT

Gowing looks at the ways in which the various parties to the second Rwandan crisis in 1996 – the warring factions themselves, the international aid agencies and news media – handled information. It was a complex conflict in which the war zone was virtually shut down to the outside world. This served to distort public understanding of the nature of the crisis, its cost in human lives and the military action taken to counter it. Gowing argues that the crisis was an indictment of those who profess themselves competent information handlers and disseminators 'in the new real time environment created by the latest satellite, communication and information technology' (1998, p.5). Journalists complain of not having time to do their job and gather some hard news. As Gowing notes, 'the more immediate the real time journalism, the greater the inaccuracy and therefore the lower the credibility' (ibid, p.36).

Gowing is particularly scathing in his criticism of humanitarian agencies and non-governmental organisations (NGOs) which, he thinks, emerged from the crisis with little credit. Their reporting of what was happening was often inaccurate and unreliable, sometimes completely wrong. Crucially, 'They were caught out by the issue of information and how to handle it well' (ibid). By way of contrast, the political and military strategies employed by regional govern-ments in Central Africa, and their handling of information and intelligence, were of a higher level than that of the aid agencies and the media, belying the stereotypical view of the conflict as one between 'rag tag rebels' and 'tin pot governments'. Minear et al (1996) record a similar sophistication in the regime in Haiti that had overthrown Aristide as elected leader in 1993 provoking an American invasion in 1994 and the reinstatement of Aristide. The coup regime while it lasted showed itself very knowledgeable and 'manipulative of media and policy processes in the US' in comparison with the much more amateurish efforts of the pro-Aristide lobby (p.60).

As for the international media and their reporting of what happened in Rwanda, Gowing suggests that they rethink the reflex to fit every crisis in Africa since 1993 into the case of Somalia, i.e. as a humanitarian disaster. Indeed, their reporting from Rwanda in 1996 suggests a failure to learn even from the mistakes of covering the first Rwanda crisis in 1994. Part of the problem lies in the practice of assigning inexperienced journalists to report complex regional conflicts, a problem exacerbated by hiring local stringers who have themselves one bias or another towards parties to the conflict (1998, p.13). These reporters continued to frame it as an ethnic or tribal war (ibid, p.38), rather than report it for what it actually was – a complex, regional conflict (ibid, p.43). Not only that but they relied too heavily on humanitarian agencies as reliable, 'official' sources, failing to see that these sources competed with each other for media attention by generating their own self-serving information and news angles (ibid, p.23; see also Minear et al, 1996). A backlash of sorts eventually followed but by then, as so often in conflict reporting, it was too late. A Canadian government report recommended that the media be less naive in future dealings with these organisations (Gowing, 1998, p.24). Minear et al see another, more positive and 'affective' role the media can play in these 'complex emergencies' and crises. Like Gowing, they appreciate the complexity of the government policy nexus and argue that this sometimes exposes internal conflicts over strategies and agendas which 'expose a gap in governmental competence that the media may highlight and help remedy' (1996, p.17).

CONCLUDING REMARKS

The arguments about the impact or effect of 'real time' news coverage on foreign policy-making are, like the wider, endless, debate about media effects on society, subject to a host of qualifications that only serve to frustrate and obscure sensible argument. Even where some type of media effect is demonstrable, it may be neither replicable in every situation nor fundamental in terms of long-term policy objectives (Gowing, 1996; Livingston, 1997). Foreign policy, after all, is politics, not philanthropy. As we have seen, coverage of some of the worst incidents of the Bosnian war – the marketplace massacre in Sarajevo or the siege of Srebrenica – provoked tough talking from NATO about what would happen to the Serbs if they continued their actions but, crucially, it did not change the western policy of non-intervention. On the other hand, television pictures of dead US Rangers being dragged through the streets of Mogadishu, in Somalia, revulsed public opinion, leading to the most definitive policy decision possible: complete withdrawal of American forces. Nik Gowing says the effect of that footage was limited to speeding up a policy outcome that was already determined at the centre; the negative television coverage was a pretext rather than determinant.[19] Nonetheless, it was still a policy humiliation for the Clinton administration and it shaped and influenced the UN's attitude to what happened a year later in Rwanda, in Central Africa. According to an edition of *Panorama* (BBC, 1997; see also Gourevitch, 1998) the UN ignored on the ground warnings that orchestrated massacres were being perpetrated by the majority Hutus against the minority Tutu population. One of the key factors influencing this policy was the experience of Somalia and the negative world TV coverage it generated. As Steven Livingston suggests, 'The grand, interesting, and often heated debate about the "CNN effect" will continue to fail us unless we distil it into its constituent parts. That means speaking more precisely about the effects relative to specific policies' (1997, p.15).

But the crucial and controversial argument must rest with the journalists and the essential distinction again between the personal and the professional. Is it proper for journalists to witness a war or some humanitarian crisis, report on the blood and the gore to some symbolic backdrop of horror and human degradation, and then with great emotion and passion single out the guilty party and call for them to to be bombed? Most of the journalists I interviewed for this book said it was impossible to be objective in such situations and some of them make no apologies for calling for military force where that seems necessary, but I sensed in their responses and in the many newspaper and journal articles, the books and memoirs, and the television chat shows and documentaries, in which their viewpoints are sought after, that they do not fully appreciate the many dangers inherent in emotionalism. Let us say, for sake of argument, that it was right and proper for journalists to take a stand and call for military intervention in Bosnia and Kosovo. But had they gone to Algeria or Chechnya or Sierra Leone, they would also have witnessed terrible scenes and perhaps call for intervention but they did not. Why? Because no one is going to call for NATO to bomb Moscow until it pulls out of Chechnya and behaves like a proper member of the 'international community'; and no one is going to call for Henry Kissinger to be brought to trial for war crimes no matter how powerful Christopher Hitchens argues the case. Calls for intervention can be made in any number of conflicts but sound does not carry in a vacuum. For Nik Gowing the acid test is this: how strong is the policy and how strong is the spin? The ability to control information and manipulate media coverage is all:

Now if there's strong spin or strong manipulation of the media that means there's a strong policy. They have decided how far they will go in a crisis...They will have made their decision how far they want to go, how minimalist they want to be, how much they want to give an impression of action...So we only really have an effect if some kind of profound event, like the Kurds in southern Turkey at the end of the Gulf War in February 1991, like Srbrenica in April

1993, when there's no policy and everyone panicked and said, 'Oh shit, we've got to do something!' But good spinning means good policy, even if it's not the right policy to stop it; good spinning means the government feel they've got it within their hands.[20]

There is also an insular ethnocentrism about the 'something must be done school' of journalism, an assumption that uncivilised things such as civil war, genocide, and ethnic cleansing, happen 'out there' to 'them', never in America or Canada or Britain. The assumption of 'distant violence' is that the reporter can leave it behind and move on. Michael Ignatieff uses the analogy of the bush fire that moves ever closer and ever faster to the edge of town and 'while it may consume the roofs of our neighbours, the sparks will never leap to our own. Yet the fire keeps drawing closer.' Ignatieff grabs for his copy of Conrad's *Heart of Darkness* as a warning to us that it is no longer confined to 'the remotest jungles of the European imagination [but is] barely two hours' journey from our homes' (1995, p.38). More specifically, if a journalist appeared on television one day to report that an 'ethnic minority' has for the last year been terrorised in their own homes by petrol bombs, pipe bombs, shootings and intimidation by right-wing militias preaching a fiery blend of nationalism and religious fundamentalism, we might expect him or her to file from Serbia or Kosovo or somewhere else in the Balkans, not Belfast, Northern Ireland, a place Margaret Thatcher once said was 'as British as Finchley'. We might also expect the journalist to take a stand, to care as well as know, and to call for something to be done. But it would never happen in Northern Ireland where the rules of journalism are inexplicably 'different' and somehow more 'complicated'.

Part IV

Conclusions

10   Conclusion

The terrorist attacks on America on 11 September 2001 horrified the western world and commanded saturation media attention. As if to convince us that this was really happening, pictures of the passenger planes slamming into the World Trade Center towers in New York City were endlessly replayed on television and displayed frame by frame in newspaper photo supplements. A BBC News bulletin opened with footage of the second plane hitting the south tower: 'the face of war in the twenty-first century', said the news anchor; a war politicians and commentators said would be like no other. If this is so, then what will that mean for the war correspondent?

In some senses there seems little to distinguish the war correspondents of today from William Howard Russell but history shows that through the major conflicts spanning the last two centuries, their role has changed dramatically. Successive new technologies, new methods of military censorship and control, have redefined the job to an extent that undermines their professional integrity and effectiveness. From the moment Russell set foot in Russia to cover the Crimean War for *The Times*, thousands of journalists have joined his luckless tribe to report wars around the world and to even 'make a difference' – changing military or diplomatic strategy, revealing the horrors of Srebrenica or Grozny, or even appealing for 'humanitarian' intervention. Ask what motivates them, what drives them on, and they will talk about their fascination with the story of war, with travelling to exotic and dangerous places in pursuit of that 'front row seat in the making of history'.[1] They know the risks but they shrug them off with fatalistic acceptance and sometimes they become media stories themselves. As the first bombs fell on Afghanistan (7 October 2001), the *Independent* carried a special feature report on the conditions experienced by journalists who were not even in the country a week but were already missing their home comforts: 'Reporters live on bread, onions and water from gutter'; 'Foreign correspondents are down to one lavatory per 45 people'; luxury, no doubt, by Afghan standards of living.[2] The capture by the Taliban of *Sunday Express* reporter Yvonne Ridley became a story alarmingly bigger than even the war itself. When the reporter was finally released, looking rather tense among her Taliban escorts, she told the gathering media pack that she was well treated. Next day the *Daily Express* splashed its front-page, 'world exclusive' on Ridley's 'Taliban Hell' in which she lay captive in a 'filthy, rat-infested prison cell', 'went on hunger strike' and 'fought with vicious guards'. She even 'risked death to keep secret diary for *Express* readers' (9 October 2001). This in turn became a major media story, not least in the *Daily Express* which ghost-wrote it and billed it as a 'world exclusive'; ironic in the sense that no other newspaper in the world would have left one of its reporters so exposed, especially one totally unprepared and inexperienced to operate in what must have been one of the most volatile and dangerous parts of the world.[3] At the same time as Ridley was fighting her one-woman war against the Taliban, the BBC's 'Chief News Correspondent', Kate Adie, was being pilloried by the tabloids for allegedly revealing embargoed information about the Prime Minister's itinerary in the Middle East. In fact, she committed no such breach but merely confirmed a leading question from her news anchor about Blair's next stop. Amid furious complaints from 10 Downing Street, the BBC failed to protect her from the flak even in the wake of a full front-page headline from the *Sun*, 'Sack Kate Adie' (10 October 2001). In response, Adie threatened libel action against the *Sun* and suggested that the original breach of security, such that it was, lay with 10 Downing Street for the way in which they briefed the media. However, some critics also suspected sinister spinning going on in government circles. It seemed all too convenient that the row helped deflect public attention away from difficult domestic stories.[4] Adie might take comfort in the words of Charles Page, writing in 1898, that the war correspondent 'will inevitably write things that will offend somebody. Somebody will say harsh things of you, and perhaps seek you out to destroy you. Never mind. Such is...the misery of correspondents' (1898, p.146).

As different wars this century have introduced new technologies of killing, so too have the media introduced or used new technologies to report the killing. The battles and drama of the Spanish--American war of 1898 electrified the newly literate masses courtesy of the first organised, commercial use of the telegraph; the Boer War in 1900 was brought to the British public by photography and news reels; the Second World War was the ultimate radio war; and Korea and Vietnam were hailed as the first television wars. The Gulf War was also a television war but cable and satellite technology brought the added illusion of 24-hour news coverage, live and uncensored. America's war against Afghanistan in October 2001 heralded a new byline, 'Live via video-phone'. The technology is new and the picture quality is poor but, as Charles Arthur argues, the impact lies in the apparent immediacy and verité of the images.[5] Yet, arguably, the biggest political impact in this latest war has been made by familiar media technology. Al-Jazeera, the Qatari satellite TV company, scooped the major international media with the first images of bombing attacks on Kabul. More sensationally, it broadcast uncensored an instant video rebuttal by Osama bin Laden (7 October 2001). The video was mocked by western commentators but it made an immediate impact because it was so perfectly timed, playing to heightened emotions in the Middle East – the widely felt resentment, even anger, against the West – and it amplified the sense of fear and anxiety in the US of more attacks. It was also a propaganda coup against the US's bombs and food strategy. Up until then, the West was happy to use Al-Jazeera in its propaganda campaign to construct a grand pan-Arab coalition in support of the 'war against terrorism'. George Bush, Colin Powell and Tony Blair all gave it interviews but within days of the war, and with the most astonishing arrogance, they were fretting about the station's impact on public opinion in the Middle East and calling for it to be censored or silenced altogether. The British made a clumsy attempt to 'advise' their broad-casters about the pitfalls of using material such as the bin Laden video: it might contain secret codes instructing terrorist cells in the West to take revenge for the bombing of Afghanistan.

So what of the future? In the new digital era, can we still talk about 'mass communication', 'mass propaganda' or 'the mass audience'? Are we likely to see the development of propaganda that, like adver-tising, addresses discreet target audiences – 'surgically precise' propaganda, perhaps? And can we still talk about '*broad*-casting' as the pre-eminent, most efficient means of instantaneous commun-ication? Probably but, in the age of the world wide web, only just. The war in Serbia/Kosovo in 1999 demonstrated the potential of the web and email for offering a diversity of sources of latest news about the conflict to a new public of internet users (Fleming, 2001). Digital technology, so goes the hype, will mean greater choice of program-ming and create hundreds of fragmented, niche audiences whose value to advertisers will be determined by differentiated incomes and lifestyles rather than narrowly fixed social categories (McLaughlin, 2001). Caryn James of the *New York Times* writes that the diversity of news sources available to the American public in the 'war against terrorism' both rattles and compels the major television networks. They express unease at the threat these represent to their monopoly yet at the same time they are quite happy to use the same material to fill the information vacuum.[6] It is a fitting irony, then, that the only pictures of the war in Afghanistan they can find are credited to Al-Jazeera, complete with captions and graphics in Arabic.

The 1990s drew to a close with NATO's brief but intensive bombing campaign against Serbia over Kosovo. Its briefings and videos dazzled the western media pack into blind compliance and made the NATO spokesman, Jamie Shea, famous for 15 weeks. Shea has not been seen since the bombs started falling on Afghanistan. It is not NATO's war, after all, but America's, and it is clear that the global crisis following 11 September prompted a full-scale propaganda campaign to prepare uncertain western publics for a very different type of war. There was no doubt that it would not be another Gulf or another Kosovo and that applied to military–media relations as much as anything else. For as this book has shown, military methods of censoring and restricting journalists in the war zone have developed with one eye on the lessons of the past and another on the exigencies of the present. In spite of the lessons of Vietnam – the so-called 'Vietnam Syndrome' – there has been a discernible, gradual shift away from coercive approaches to the control of journalists in the war zone to something more subtle and persuasive. The military brought journalists on side, co-opting them into the propaganda war effort, and it is clear that the journalists have responded so positively that they have become too dependent on the briefings. It is worth recalling again the judgement of Henry Nevinson on the performance of his colleagues in France during the First World War: how they 'lived chirping together like little birds in a nest', feeding on what crumbs of information the military fed them (Farrar, 1998, p.227).

Still, as I have argued in this book, there were quite a number of journalists who were prepared to stand back and ask questions of the material and information the briefers were feeding them which I think was significant and important to acknowledge. But the media response to the first few weeks of bombing of Afghanistan has been less encouraging. On 20 October, the Americans sent their special forces into the country in a blaze of propaganda. The Pentagon released dramatic video footage of night time operations by small teams of 'special forces' against a 'command and control centre' near

Kandahar, a Taliban stronghold used until recently by the Taliban's spiritual leader, Mullah Omar, but presumably, if the Pentagon's propaganda was to be believed, already destroyed by intensive aerial bombing (perhaps it was missed in the fog of war?). The television stations loved the video and seemed to be reading from the same press release. A reporter for ITN declared that a small team stormed the centre 'with virtually no resistance ' from the Taliban – probably because the compound was lightly defended – while the BBC reported that the team destroyed a small cache of weapons left at the scene: some small arms and a rocket launcher. The military must have been delighted at the media's uncritical and euphoric reception of what was plainly a heavily contrived propaganda operation. However aware they might be, off-record, of their place in the propaganda war, journalists still go a long way towards endorsing it with their straight reporting of official briefings on prime time news. David Smith, Washington correspondent for *Channel Four News*, emphasised *twice* in his two-way with London that the message the Pentagon conveyed in their video was 'clear':

> *Let's be very clear* here – the message is in those pictures...Here we are, watching American ground troops...go to war. And I thought one of the most significant messages of all came from Richard Myers [Chairman, Joint US Chiefs of Staff] when he was saying quite simply...that what these operations show us overnight is that we can deploy,we can manoeuvre, we can infiltrate without interference at our time and place of choosing. *The message is clear.* First, to American people, 'You're watching the boys going into action, the best and the bravest, the Rangers, the men who were at Normandy. And don't necessarily fear the worst of a ground war.' But more importantly, I suppose, to the Taliban, that the Americans are going in after them...and the fact that they went after a compound that had been used until a few weeks ago by Mullah Omar, the Taliban leader, says it all. (19.00, 20 October 2001; emphasis added)

It is possible that direct censorship and control may be unnecessary in Afghanistan and in the wider 'war against terrorism', that the powers that be can rely on a culture of inhibition, self-censorship and thought-control in the wake of the attacks on the US. The 'war against terrorism', said George Bush and so many other politicians and commentators, would be like no other war before it. Yet, as the first bombs fell on Afghanistan, BBC *News 24* quoted an American source that this was 'not so much World War Three as Cold War Two' (7 October 2001). In other words, back to the good old days when we had proper bad guys to aim nuclear rockets at and spies under every bed. As I argued in Chapter 7 of this book, the Cold War provided journalists, among a host of other intellectuals, with a framework of political, economic and moral certainties and when it unravelled then so did the ideological framework that underpinned it. When Iraq invaded Kuwait in 1990, US President George Bush toured the Middle East trying to forge a grand coalition of nations, western and Middle Eastern, to force Iraq out of the oil-rich kingdom. He talked about a 'New World Order' and an end to 'the law of the jungle'. But the grand coalition barely survived the Gulf War in 1991 and the interminable conflict between Israel and the Palestinians. It broke down completely amid successive humanitarian crises around the world, especially in Somalia, Rwanda, and Sierra Leone. And it was made a mockery of when George W. Bush Jr and his administration tore up successive treaties on trade, the environment, nuclear weapons proliferation and international justice. The terrible events of 11 September turned all that upside down. Suddenly, the US felt vulnerable; suddenly, it depended on its friends and neighbours around the world. It was forced to make new friends out of old enemies and make compromises and deals like it never had to before. It finally repaid its long-standing contributions arrears to the United Nations, an organisation it always resented, and it talked once again about an independent Palestinian state with Jerusalem as its capital. Instead of 'New World Order', we had 'New World Terror'. It was no more than the resurrection of Cold War rhetoric: if you are not for us you are against us, to understand is to justify, to explain is to excuse. The concept of bipolarity has come back to haunt us: East versus West, Them and Us, the Clash of Civilisations, War of the Worlds.[7] In a widely syndicated article, Francis Fukuyama insisted that such a conflict would not invalidate his famous 'end of history' thesis but prove it because his argument was always that the liberal capitalist state was the ultimate and unsurpassable point of human progress.[8] Those who refused to join with the US in its war against terrorism would discover that much in their eventual defeat. This presumably included the dissenters and the sceptics who dared to differ or to ask us to look at the conflict from the point of view of the hundreds of millions of people who live in central Asia and who wonder why

American airplanes are dropping bombs and peanut butter on Afghanistan with the message, 'Resistance is futile'?

But to say or even think such things is to somehow insult the memory of the people who lost their lives in the US on 11 September. Is it possible that we are entering a prolonged era of conflict managed by propaganda and thought control? What now of the journalism of attachment, the journalism that 'cares as well as knows'? And will we see the day when journalists such as Robert Fisk and John Pilger or writers such as Harold Pinter, are hauled before a parliamentary committee and asked if they are, were, or ever have been 'moral perfectionists'? The existence of a robust public arena is as important in war time as it is in peace time because it is a major feature distinguishing democracy from totalitarianism. If we seek to condemn and marginalise those who challenge the certainties of the anti-terrorist consensus, if we censor or inhibit the independent correspondent, the dissident journalist, the peacenik writer because we do not like what they say or think, then who will form the line of intellectual defence in the next propaganda war?

'I never planned to get into this business', says Maggie O'Kane of the *Guardian*, 'and I probably won't plan to get out of it...but there may be a point when you become very fearful that perhaps you can't go on doing the job very well'.[9] Professionally, Martin Bell sees himself as 'a footnote' in the history of war reporting (Gowing, 1995). These are salutary epitaphs for the war correspondent in such uncertain times for the challenge remains the same: to report a conflict as objectively and accurately as possible without undue risk to self and without compromise to professional integrity.

Appendix 1
Recommendations to News Organisations for Journalists' Safety[1]

Recommendations to news organisations for journalists' safety:

- 'Preservation of human life and safety is paramount. Staff and freelancers should be made aware that unwarranted risks in pursuit of a story are unacceptable and must be strongly discouraged. Assignments to war zones or hostile environments must be voluntary and should only involve experienced news-gathering practitioners.'
- 'All staff and freelancers asked to work in hostile environments must have access to appropriate safety training and retraining. Employers are encouraged to make this mandatory.'
- 'Employers must provide efficient safety equipment to all staff and freelancers assigned to hazardous locations, including personal-issue kevlar vests or jackets, protective headgear and properly protected vehicles, if necessary.'
- 'All staff and freelancers should be afforded personal insurance while working in hostile areas, including coverage against death and personal injury.'
- 'Employers should provide and encourage the use of voluntary and confidential counselling for staff and freelancers returning from hostile areas, or after the coverage of distressing events. (This is likely to require some training of media managers in the recognition of the symptoms of post-traumatic stress disorder).'
- 'Media companies and their representatives are neutral observers; they don't carry firearms in the course of their work.'
- 'Media groups should work together to establish a data bank of safety information, including the exchange of up-to-date safety assessments of hostile and dangerous areas.'

Appendix 2
Surviving Hostile Regions²

AKE is the first company to design and deliver a course specifically for journalists.

Length: Courses are 1 to 5 days. The length and content of the courses are specifically tailored to type of business, area of operation and support available.

Cost of course: US$1,400.

Number of participants: Around 500 journalists have attended the course.

Staff: The course is taught by former British Special Air Service (SAS) personnel.

The three principles of the course: the awareness, anticipation, avoidance of unnecessary danger.

Types of courses: specialist training, team building, security, medical.

Specialist training includes a course called Surviving Hostile Regions. This course trains journalists for surviving hostile regions and environments: weather, disease and war.

The Surviving Hostile Regions syllabus:

  weapons and effects
  casualty assessment
  weapon types (small arms)
  airway clearance
  weapons employment
  cardio-pulmonary resuscitation
  control of bleeding

heavy weapons
treatment of burns
target awareness
fractures theory
military–media relations
map-reading techniques
venomous animals
personal protection
common diseases
mines and booby traps
climatic conditions
self-sufficiency
public disorder
the trauma casualty
hostage survival
planning
exercise

The company's website allows participants to register online and purchase equipment such as individual trauma belt packs and medical-team belt kits.

It is located in Hereford, UK, but also offers courses in the United States.

Company website: http://www.ake.co.uk

Company telephone: 44-14-32-26-711111

Appendix 3
MoD Green Book Rules for Media Reporting

THE MINISTRY OF DEFENCE (MOD) GREEN BOOK (GUIDELINES
FOR THE BRITISH MEDIA REPORTING THE GULF WAR)

Restricted Subjects (at the discretion of the Joint Information Bureau,
Riyadh):

- composition of the force and the locations of ships, units and
  aircraft
- details of military movements
- operational orders
- plans or intentions
- casualties
- organisations
- place names
- tactical details, e.g. defensive positions, camouflage methods,
  weapon capabilities or deployments
- names or numbers of ships, aircraft, or military units
- names of individual service men

Appendix 4
US Military Ground Rules for Media Reporting of the Persian Gulf War

The following information was restricted because its release could 'jeopardize operations and endanger lives':

1. 'Specific numerical information on troop strength'
2. 'Details of future military plans, operations or strikes, including postponed or cancelled operations'
3. 'Information, photography or imagery that would reveal specific location of military forces or show the level of security at military bases or encampments'
4. 'Rules of engagement details'
5. 'Information on intelligence collection activities, including targets, methods, and results'
6. 'Specific information on friendly force troop movements tactical deployments, and dispositions that would jeopardize operational security or lives'
7. 'Identification of mission aircraft points of origin'
8. 'Information on the effectiveness or ineffectiveness of enemy camouflage, cover, deception, targeting, direct or indirect fire, intelligence collection, or security measures'
9. 'Specific identifying information on missing or downed aircraft or ships while search and rescue operations are planned or under way'
10. 'Special operations forces' methods, unique equipment or tactics'
11. 'Specific operating methods and tactics'
12. 'Information on operational or support vulnerabilities that could be used against US forces such as details of major battle damage or major personnel losses' (Hughes, 1992, pp.460ff)

Notes

CHAPTER 1: INTRODUCTION

1. BBC2, *Arena*, 'Ryszard Kapuscinski: Your Man Who Is There', 29 January 1988; see also Kapuscinski (1982, 1983, 2001)
2. Telephone interview with the author, 4 February 2000

CHAPTER 2: THE WAR CORRESPONDENT

1. Lindsey Hilsum, Diplomatic Editor, Channel Four News; interview with the author, London, 26 October 1999
2. Nik Gowing, Diplomatic Editor, BBC World; interview with with the author, London, 29 November 1999
3. Mark Laity, interview with the author, London, 18 November 1999. Laity is now a press officer at NATO HQ, Brussels
4. BBC2, *Late Show*, 'Tales from the Gulf', 19 July 1991
5. Interview with the author, London, 29 November 1999
6. Interview with the author, Surrey, 25 October 1999
7. Ibid
8. *Observer*, 28 May 2000
9. Channel Four, *True Stories*, 'Babitsky's War', 2000
10. *Channel Four News*, 14 June 1999
11. IPI, *Deathwatch 1999*
12. Ibid
13. Ibid
14. Telephone interview with the author, 2 February 2000
15. *Independent*, 24 April, 1999
16. Telephone interview with the author, 29 February 2000
17. Interview with the author, London 26 October 1999
18. Interview with the author, Surrey, 25 October 1999
19. Telephone interview with the author, 29 February 2000
20. BBC2, *Late Show*, 'Tales from Sarajevo', 1994
21. Interview with the author, London, 29 November 1999
22. Email correspondence with the author, 5 December 1999
23. Telephone interview with the author, 9 December 1999
24. Telephone interview with the author, 29 February 2000
25. Interview with the author, Surrey, 25 October 1999
26. Interview with the author, London, 25 Ocoitober 1999
27. Telephone interview with the author, 4 February 2000
28. Interview with the author, London, 27 October 1999
29. Interview with the author, Belfast, 18 Ocotober 1999
30. Ibid
31. Telephone interview with the author 2 November 1999
32. Interview with the author, London, 29 November 1999

33. Interview with the author, London, 29 November 1999
34. Telephone interview with the author, 2 November 1999
35. Interview with the author, Belfast, 18 Ocotober 1999
36. Telephone interview with the author, 4 February 2000
37. Telephone interview with the author, 9 December 1999
38. Interview with the author, London, 18 November 1999
39. Interview with the author, London, 27 October 1999
40. Interview with the author, London 26 October 1999
41. Telephone interview with the author, 4 February 2000
42. Telephone interview with author, 2 November 1999
43. Telephone interview with the author, 29 February 2000
44. Interview with the author, London, 29 November 1999
45. Interview with the author, Surrey, 25 October 1999
46. Interview with the author, London, 29 November 1999

CHAPTER 3: FROM TELEGRAPH TO SATELLITE: THE IMPACT OF MEDIA TECHNOLOGY ON WAR REPORTING

1. BBC2, *Late Show*, 'Tales from the Gulf', 19 July 1991
2. Telephone interview with the author, 29 February 2000
3. Interview with the author, London, 29 November 1999
4. Interview with the author, London, 26 October 1999
5. Interview with the author, London, 29 November 1999
6. Ibid
7. Ibid
8. Telephone interview with the author, 9 December 1999
9. Ibid

CHAPTER 4: JOURNALISTS IN THE WAR ZONE: FROM CRIMEA TO KOREA

1. Relations between reporters and Montgomery were so good that the BBC's War Reporting unit presented the General with a puppy he promptly called Hitler. BBC reporter Frank Gillard recalls that Hitler did not survive the war, having been run over by a tank in the final push against Germany in Europe; BBC2, *What Did You Do In The War Auntie?*, 1995.

CHAPTER 5: JOURNALISTS AND THE MILITARY SINCE VIETNAM

1. Telephone interview with the author, 4 February 2000
2. Email correspondence with the author, 22 August 2001
3. Ibid
4. Interview with the author, Surrey, 25 October 1999
5. Interview with the author, Belfast, 18 October, 1999
6. BBC2 *Late Show*, 'Tales from the Gulf', 19 July 1991
7. Telephone interview with the author, 29 February 2000
8. Interview with the author, Belfast, 18 October, 1999
9. 'Tales from the Gulf'
10. Interview with the author, London, 27 October 1999

11. Interview with the author, London, 25 October 1999
12. Interview with the author, Surrey, 25 October 1999
13. Interview with the author, London, 25 October 1999
14. Interview with the author, Surrey, 25 October 1999

CHAPTER 6: LESSONS LEARNED? THE MEDIA, THE MILITARY AND THE KOSOVO CRISIS

1. Interview with the author, London, 18 November 1999. Mark Laity has since left the BBC to take up a new post as assistant press secretary to Jamie Shea at NATO Headquarters in Brussels.
2. Interview with the author, Belfast, 18 October 1999
3. The analysis in this section is based on a sample of British and American television news programmes from 16–20 December 1998: BBC News at 13.00hrs, 18.00, 21.00 and BBC2 *Newsnight* at 22.30; ITN bulletins at 12.30, 18.30, 23.00, and *Channel Four News* at 19.00; the sample of American programmes comprised of CNN and NBC bulletins at 17.00 on each day of the sample period.
4. The analysis is based on a sample of British and American television news programmes from 12–19 April 1999: BBC News at 13.00, 18.00, 21.00 and BBC2 *Newsnight* at 22.30; ITN bulletins at 12.30, 18.30, 23.00, and *Channel Four News* at 19.00; the sample of American programmes comprised of CNN and NBC bulletins at 17.00 on each day of the sample period.
5. Interview with the author, London, 1 December 1999
6. Telephone interview with the author, 2 February 2000
7. Interview with the author, London, 1 December 1999
8. Telephone interview with the author, 29 February 2000
9. Telephone interview with the author, 2 February 2000
10. Ibid
11. Interview with the author, London, 29 November 1999
12. Interview with the author, London, 1 December 1999
13. Telephone interview with the author, 2 February 2000
14. Ibid
15. Ibid
16. Interview with the author, London, 1 December 1999; for a fuller discussion of the 'new Labourisation' of information during the Kosovo crisis, see Philip Hammond (2000)
17. Interview with the author, London, 18 November 1999
18. Interview with the author, Belfast, 18 October 1999
19. Telephone interview with the author, 2 February 2000
20. Interview with the author, Belfast, 18 October 1999
21. Telephone interview with the author, 2 February 2000

CHAPTER 7: REPORTING THE COLD WAR AND THE NEW WORLD ORDER

1. Interview with the author, London, 29 November 1999
2. Telephone interview with the author, 9 December 1999

3. Submission to the US Congressional Joint Economic Committee; *Daily Telegraph*, 11 November 1989
4. BBC2, Huw Wheldon Lecture by John Simpson, 1993
5. All these press references are dated 2 June 1988
6. Cal McCrystal, 'The World at War', *Independent on Sunday* (Review, pp.39–41), 14 March 1991
7. Hugo Young, 'A Year of No World Order', *Guardian*, 31 December 1992
8. Comment, *Observer*, p.18, 26 December 1993
9. Channel Four, *Critical Eye*, 'Proud Arabs and Texas Oilmen', 1993
10. Channel Four, *Dispatches*, 'The Audit of War', 8 January 1992
11. In a speech at Blaby, 2 February 1991, cited in Gittings (1991, p.22); for a detailed discussion of race and gender in Gulf War rhetoric and imagery, see Enloe (1992) and Farmanfarmaian (1992)
12. BBC2, *Arena*, 'Culture and Imperialism', 1993
13. The *Guardian* alone among the British press argued against using force and quoted a CIA report that sanctions had stopped 97 per cent of Iraqi exports (15 January 1991). And a BBC News item referred to the success of sanctions in wrecking not just Iraq's economy but those of its neighbours, especially Jordan. An American economist estimated that sanctions were having 'more than ten times the impact [than on] economies in past episodes, where sanctions have *succeeded* in achieving their goal' (BBC1, 21.00, 14 January 1991).
14. BBC2, *Assignment*, 'Uncle Sam's Last Stand', 1991
15. Channel Four, *Dispatches*, 'The Audit of War', 8 January 1992
16. M. Fineman, 'The Oil Factor in Somalia', *Los Angeles Times*, 18 January 1993; pp.234–8 in Jensen (1994)
17. Philo and McLaughlin, 'ITN Passes the Tebbit Test', *New Statesman and Society*, 29 January 1993
18. BBC2, *Late Show*, 'Tales from Sarajevo', 1994
19. Ibid
20. Ibid

CHAPTER 8: WAR, OBJECTIVITY AND THE JOURNALISM OF ATTACHMENT

1. Telephone interview with the author, 29 February, 2000
2. Interview with the author, Surrey, 25 October 1999
3. Channel Four, *Babitsky's War*, 2000
4. Telephone interview with the author, 4 February 2000
5. Interview with the author, Belfast, 18 October 1999
6. Telephone interview with the author, 29 February, 2000
7. Interview with the author, London, 29 November 1999
8. Email correspondence with the author, 5 December 1999
9. See for example, *Berlin Correspondent* (1942), *Circle of Deceit* (1981), *Salvador* (1983), *Under Fire* (1983), *The Killing Fields* (1984) and *Welcome to Sarajevo* (1999)
10. 'Courage under fire', *Guardian*, 20 September 1999
11. Telephone interview with the author, 2 November 1999
12. 'Courage under Fire'

13. Telephone interview with the author, 2 November 1999
14. Telephone Interview with the author, 29 February 2000; see also *Guardian*, 26 May 2000
15. Interview with the author, London, 25 October 1999
16. Telephone interview with the author, 9 December 1999
17. Ibid
18. Interview with the author, Belfast, 18 October 1999
19. Interview with the author, London, 27 October 1999
20. Interview with the author, Belfast, 18 October 1999
21. Interview with the author, London, 27 October 1999
22. BBC2, *Late Show*, 'Tales from Sarajevo', 1994

CHAPTER 9: 'SOMETHING MUST BE DONE' JOURNALISM

1. Email correspondence with the author, 5 December 1999
2. 'Shooting the Messenger', *Guardian* 2, 17 September 1993
3. Interview with the author, London, 29 November 1999
4. ibid
5. BBC2, Huw Wheldon Lecture, 1993
6. Gowing is now with BBC World News
7. 'Shooting the Messenger', *Guardian 2*, 17 September 1993; see Lippmann (1992), p.170
8. *Guardian*, 17 September 1993
9. BBC2, *Late Show*, 'Tales from Sarajevo', 1994
10. 'The Kurds Five Years On: TV News' Finest Hour', *New Statesman*, 5 April 1996
11. Telephone interview with the author, 29 February 2000
12. Telephone interview with the author, 4 February 2000
13. Interview with the author, London, 25 October 1999
14. Channel Four, *Dying to Tell the Story*, 1999
15. Interview with the author, London, 27 October 1999
16. Interview the author, Surrey, 25 October 1999; original emphasis
17. Interview with the author, London, 26 October 1999
18. Email correspondence with the author, 5 December 1999
19. Interview with the author, London, 29 November 1999
20. Ibid

CHAPTER 10: CONCLUSION

1. Martin Bell, interview with the author, London, 27 October 1999
2. *Independent*, 13 October 2001
3. 'Sheer Folly' *Media Guardian*, 15 October 2001
4. 'Error Follows Error in BBC Row', *Guardian*, 11 October 2001
5. 'News from the Front Line', Monday Review, the *Independent*, 15 October 2001
6. 'A Public Flooded with Images from Friend and Foe Alike', *New York Times*, 10 October 2001
7. See, for example, John Keegan, 'In this War of Civilisations the West Will Prevail', *Daily Telegraph*, 8 October 2001
8. 'The West Has Won', *Guardian*, 11 October 2001
9. Telephone interview with the author, 29 February 2000

APPENDIX 1: RECOMMENDATIONS TO NEWS ORGANISATIONS FOR JOUNALISTS' SAFETY

1. Richard Tait, 'Unacceptable Danger', IPI Report No. 1, www.freemedia.at/IPIReport1.01

APPENDIX 2: SURVIVING HOSTILE REGIONS

1. IPI: www.freemedia.at/IPIReport1.01

Bibliography

Adams, Valerie (1986) *The Media and the Falklands Campaign* (London: Macmillan)

Ahmad, Eqbal (1992) 'Portent of a New Century', in Bennis and Moushabeck (eds) *Beyond the Storm: A Gulf Crisis Reader* (Edinburgh: Canongate), pp.7–21

Arnett, Peter (1996) 'The Clash of Arms in Exotic Locales', *Media Studies Journal: Journalists in Peril*, Vol.10, No.4, Fall

Aubrey, Crispin (ed.) (1982) *Nukespeak: The Media and the Bomb* (London: Comedia/Minority Press Group)

Aucoin, James L. (2001) 'Epistemic Responsibility and Narrative Theory: The Literary Journalism of Ryszard Kapuscinski', *Journalism*, Vol.2. No.1 April, pp.5–21

Baker, James (1996) 'Report First, Check Later', *Harvard International Journal of Press/Politics*, Vol.1, No.2, pp.3–9

Barnett, Steven et al (2000) *From Callaghan to Kosovo: Changing Trends in British Television News* (London: University of Westminster Press)

Bell, Martin (1993) 'Testament of an Interventionist', *British Journalism Review*, Vol.4, No.4, pp.8–11

Bell, Martin (1995) *In Harm's Way* (London: Hamish Hamilton)

Bell, Martin (1997) 'TV News: How Far Should We Go?', *British Journalism Review*, Vol.8, No.1, pp.7–16

Bell, Martin (1998) 'The Truth is Our Currency', *Harvard International Journal Press/Politics*, Vol.3, No.1, pp.102–9

Bennett, Stephen E. et al (1997) 'American Public Opinion and the Civil War in Bosnia: Attention, Knowledge, and the Media', *Harvard International Journal of Press/Politics*, Vol.2, No.4, pp.87–105

Bjork, Ulf Jonas (1994) 'Latest from the Canadian Revolution: Early War Correspondence in the New York Herald, 1837–1838', *Journalism Quarterly*, Vol.71, No.4, pp. 851–8

Blanchard, Margaret (1992) 'Free Expression and Wartime: Lessons from the Past, Hopes for the Future', *Journalism Quarterly*, Vol.69, No.1, Spring, pp.5–17

Boot, William (1990) 'Wading Around in the Panama Pool', *Columbia Journalism Review*, March/April, pp.18–20

Boot, William (1991) 'The Pool', *Columbia Journalism Review*, May/June, pp.24–7

Borovik, Artyom (1990) *The Hidden War: A Russian Journalist's Account of the Soviet War in Afghanistan* (London: Faber & Faber)

Bourdieu, Pierre (1972) 'Systems of Education and Systems of Thought', in Young, Michael F.D. (ed.) *Knowledge and Control: New Directions for the Sociology of Education*, (London: Collier-Macmillan)

Braestrup, Peter (1983) *Big Story: How the American Press and Television Reported and Interpreted the Crisis of Tet 1968 in Vietnam and Washington* (London: Yale University Press)

Braestrup, Peter (1985) *Battle Lines: Report of the Twentieth Century Fund Task Force on the Military and the Media* (New York: Priority Press)

Brothers, Caroline (1997) *War and Photography: A Cultural History* (London: Routledge)

Brown, Charles H. (1967) *The Correspondents War: Journalists in the Spanish-American War* (New York: Charles Scribner's Sons)

Burchett, Wilfred (1980) *At the Barricades* (London: Quartet)

Burns, John C. (1996) 'The Media as Impartial Observers or Protagonists: Conflict Reporting or Conflict Encouragement in Former Yugolsavia', in Gow, James et al (eds) *Bosnia by Television* (London: BFI), pp.92–100

Burrowes, John (1984) *Frontline Report: A Journalist's Notebook* (Edinburgh: Mainstream)

Bushinsky, Jay (2001) 'Modern Day Gladiators', IPI Report No.1

Cameron, James (1967) *Point of Departure* (London: Oriel Press)

Campbell, Alistair (1999) 'Communications Lessons for NATO, the Military and Media', *Royal United Services Institute Journal*, Vol.144, No.4, pp.31–6

Carey, John (1987) *Faber Book of Reportage* (London: Faber)

Carr, E.H. (1986) *What is History?*, 2nd edition (London: Macmillan)

Carruthers, Susan L. (1995) *Winning Hearts and Minds: British Governments, the Media and Colonial Counterinsurgency, 1944–60* (London: Leicester University Press)

Carruthers, Susan L. (2000) *The Media at War: Communication and Conflict in the Twentieth Century* (London: Macmillan)

Chandler, David (2000) 'Western Intervention and the Disintegration of Yugoslavia', in Hammond, Philip and Edward S. Herman (eds) *Degraded Capability: The Media and the Kosovo Crisis* (London: Pluto Press), pp.19–30

Chang, Wong Ho (1991) 'Images of the Soviet Union in American Newspapers: A Content Analysis of Three Newspapers', in Dennis, Everette E. et al (eds) *Beyond the Cold War: Soviet and American Media Images* (London: Sage), pp.65–83

Chomsky, Noam (1975) 'The Remaking of History', *Ramparts*, August/September

Chomsky, Noam (1989) *Necessary Illusions* (London: Pluto Press)

Chomsky, Noam (1992a) Deterring Democracy (London: Vintage)

Chomsky, Noam (1992b) '"What We Say Goes" – the Middle East in the New World Order', in Peters, Cynthia (ed.) *Collateral Damage: The New World Order at Home and Abroad* (Boston, MA: Southend Press) pp.49–92

Chomsky, Noam (1993) *Year 501: The Conquest Continues* (Boston, MA: Southend Press)

Chomsky, Noam (1994) *World Orders, Old and New* (London: Pluto Press)

Chomsky, Noam (1999) *The New Military Humanism: Lessons From Kosovo* (London: Pluto Press)

Collier, Richard (1989) *The Warcos: The War Correspondents of the Second World War* (London: Weidenfeld and Nicolson)

Crozier, Emmett (1959) *American Reporters on the Western Front, 1914–1918* (New York: Oxford University Press)

Cumings, Bruce (1992) *War and Television* (London: Verso)

Dennis, Everette E. et al (eds) (1991) *Beyond the Cold War: Soviet and American Media Images* (London: Sage)

Derradji, Taoufiq (1996) 'Algerian Journalists – Casualties of a Dirty War', *Media Studies Journal: Journalists in Peril*, Vol.10, No.4, Fall

Dickson, Sandra (1994) 'Understanding Media Bias: The Press and the US Invasion of Panama', *Journalism Quarterly*, Vol.71, No.4, Winter, pp.809–19

Didion, Joan (1983) *Salvador* (London: Chatto & Windus)

Dorman, William A. and Mansour Farhang (1987) *The US Press and Iran: Foreign Policy and the Journalism of Deference* (London: University of California Press)

Dosch-Fleurot, Arno (1931) *Through War to Revolution: Being the Experiences of a Newspaper Correspondent in War and Revolution 1914–1920* (London: Bodley Head)

Dunsmore, Barry (1996) 'The Next War: Live?' *Harvard International Journal Press/Politics*, Vol.1, No.3, pp.3–5

Elwood-Akers, Virginia (1988) *Women War Correspondents in the Vietnam War, 1961–1975* (Methuen, NJ: Scarecrow Press, Inc.)

Enloe, Cynthia (1992) 'The Gendered Gulf', in Peters, Cynthia (ed.) *Collateral Damage: The New World Order at Home and Abroad* (Boston, MA: Southend Press), pp.93–110

Entman, Robert M. and Andrew Rojecki (1993) 'Freezing out the Public: Elite and Media framing of the US Anti-Nuclear Movement', *Political Communication*, Vol.10, No.2, pp.155–73

Ewing, Joseph H. (1991) 'The New Sherman Letters', in Matthews, Lloyd J. (ed.) *Newsmen and National Defense: Is Conflict Inevitable?* (New York: Brassey's), pp.19–29

Farmanfarmaian, Abouali (1992) 'Did You Measure Up?: The Role of Race and Sexuality in the Gulf War', in Peters, Cynthia (ed.) *Collateral Damage: The New World Order at Home and Abroad* (Boston, MA:Southend Press), pp.111–38

Farrar, Martin J. (1998) *News From the Front: War Correspondents on the Western Front 1914–18* (London: Sutton Publishing)

Fialka, John J. (1992) *Hotel Warriors: Covering the Gulf War* (Washington, DC: Woodrow Wilson Center Press)

Fleming, Dan (2001) 'The Kosovo Conflict on the Web: A Case Study', in Fleming, Dan (ed.) *Formations: A 21st Century Media Studies Text Book* (Manchester: Manchester University Press), pp.116–19

Foden, Giles (1999a) 'The First Media War', *Daily Mail & Guardian* (Johannesburg) 7 October

Foden, Giles (1999b) *Ladysmith* (London: Faber & Faber)

Fox, Robert (1988) 'Foreign Bodies' (Part 4), *The Listener*, 9 June, pp.14–15

Franco, Victor (1963) *The Morning After: A French Journalist's Impressions of Cuba Under Castro* (London: Pall Mall Press)

Gellhorn, Martha (1993) *The Face of War* (London: Granta Books)

Gellhorn, Martha (1994) 'The Invasion of Panama', in Granta Books (eds)*The Best of Granta Reportage* (London: Granta Books), pp.269–87

Gerbner, George (1991) 'The Image of Russians in American Media and the "New Epoch" ', in Dennis, Everette E. et al (eds) *Beyond the Cold War: Soviet and American Media Images* (London: Sage), pp.31–5

Gitlin, Todd (1980) *The Whole World is Watching: The Mass Media in the Making and the Unmaking of the New Left* (Berkley, CA: University of California Press)

Gittings, J. (ed.) (1991) *Beyond the Gulf War: The Middle East and the New World Order* (London: CIIR)

Glasgow University Media Group (1976) *Bad News* (London: Routledge & Kegan Paul)

Glasgow University Media Group (1985) *War and Peace News* (Milton Keynes: Open University Press)

Glasser, Theodore L. (1992), 'Objectivity and News Reporting', in Cohen, E. (ed.) *Philosophical Issues in Journalism* (Oxford: Oxford University Press), pp.176–83

Goff, Peter (2000) 'Introduction', in Goff, Peter (ed.)*The Kosovo News and Propaganda War* (Vienna: International Press Institute), pp.13–34

Goodman, Walter (1991) 'Arnett', *Columbia Journalism Review*, May/June, pp.29–31

Goodwin, Jan (1987) *Caught in the Crossfire: A Woman Journalist's Breathtaking Experiences in War-torn Afghanistan* (London: Macdonald)

Gourevitch, Philip (1998) *We Wish To Inform You That Tomorrow We Will Be Killed With Our Families: Stories from Rwanda* (London: Picador)

Gowing, Nik (1995) 'This Reporter Can Never be a Footnote', *British Journalism Review*, Vol.6, No.4, pp.67–71

Gowing, Nik (1996) 'Real-time TV Coverage from War: Does it Make or Break Government Policy?', in Gow, James et al (eds) *Bosnia By Television* (London: BFI), pp.81–91

Gowing, Nik (1997) 'Media Coverage: Help or Hindrance in Conflict Prevention', report to the Carnegie Commission on Preventing Deadly Conflict, New York

Gowing, Nik (1998) 'Dispatches from Disaster Zones: The Reporting of Humanitarian Emergencies', conference paper, *New Challenges and Problems for Information Management in Complex Emergencies*, London, 27–28 May

Halberstam, David (1979) *The Powers That Be* (London: Chatto & Windus)

Halberstam, David (1991) 'Television and the Instant Enemy', in Sifry, Micah L. and Christopher Cerf (eds) *The Gulf War Reader: History Documents, Opinion* (New York: Times Books) pp.385–8

Halliday, Julian et al (1992) 'Framing the Crisis in Eastern Europe', in Raboy, Mark and Bernard Dagenais (eds) *Media, Crisis and Democracy: Mass Communication and the Disruption of Social Order* (London: Sage), pp.63–78

Hallin, Daniel C (1986) *The 'Uncensored War': The Media and Vietnam* (London: University of California Press)

Hallin, Daniel C. and Paolo Mancini (1989) *Friendly Enemies* (Perugia: Perugia Press)

Halloran, Richard (1991) 'Soldiers and Scribblers: A Common Mission', in Matthews, Lloyd J.(ed.) *Newsmen and National Defense: Is Conflict Inevitable?* (New York: Brassey's), pp.39–59

Hammond, Philip (1999) 'Reporting Kosovo: Journalists versus Propaganda', in Goff, Peter (ed.) *The Kosovo News and Propaganda War* (Vienna: International Press Institute), pp.62–7

Hammond, Philip (2000) 'Third Way War: New Labour, the British Media and Kosovo', in Hammond, Philip and Edward S. Herman (eds) *Degraded Capability: The Media and the Kosovo Crisis* (London: Pluto Press), pp.123–31

Hammond, William M. (1991) 'The Army and Public Affairs: A Glance Back', in Matthews, Lloyd J. (ed.) *Newsmen and National Defense: Is Conflict Inevitable?* (NewYork: Brassey's), pp.1–18

Hankinson, Alan (1982) *Man of Wars: William Howard Russell of* The Times (London: Heinemann)

Harris, Robert (1983) *Gotcha! The Media, the Government and the Falklands Crisis* (London: Faber)

Hawkins, Desmond (1985) *War Report: D-Day to VE Day* (London: BBC)

Hedges, Chris (1991) 'The Unilaterals', *Columbia Journalism Review*, May/June, pp.27–9

Herman, Edward S. and David Petersen (2000) 'CNN's Selling NATO's War Globally', in Hammond, Philip and Edward S. Herman (eds) *Degraded Capability: The Media and the Kosovo Crisis* (London: Pluto Press), pp.111–22

Herr, Michael (1978) *Dispatches* (London: Picador)

Hertsgaard, Mark (1988) *On Bended Knee: The Press and the Reagan Presidency* (New York: Schocken Books)

Hickman, Tom (1995) *What Did You Do in the War, Auntie? The BBC at War 1939–45* (London: BBC Books)

Hilsum, Lindsey (1997) 'Crossing the Line to Commitment', in *British Journalism Review*, Vol.8, No.1, pp.29–33

Hindle, Wilfred (ed.) (1939) *Foreign Correspondent: Personal Adventures Abroad in Search of the News by Twelve British Journalists* (London: Harrap & Co.)

Hoffman, Fred S. (1991) 'The Panama Press Pool Deployment: A Critique', in Matthews, Lloyd J. (ed.) *Newsmen and National Defense: Is Conflict Inevitable?* (New York: Brassey's), pp.91–109

Hollowell, John (1977) *Fact and Fiction: the New Journalism and the Non-Ficiton Novel* (Chapel Hill, NC: University of North Carolina Press)

Holme, Christopher (1995) 'The Reporter at Guernica', *British Journalism Review*, Vol.6, No.2, pp.46–51

Hughes, Mark (1992) 'Words at War: Reflections of a Marine Public Affairs Officer in the Persian Gulf', *Government Information Quarterly*, Vol.9, No.4, pp.431–71

Hume, Mick (1997) *Whose War is it Anyway? The Dangers of the Journalism of Attachment* (London: BM Inform Inc.)

Hume, Mick (2000) 'Was LM Bullied into Oblivion?', *British Journalism Review*, Vol.11, No.2, pp. 40–4

Ignatieff, Michael (1995) 'The Seductiveness of Moral Disgust', *Index on Censorhip*, Vol.24, No.5, September/October, pp.22–38

Jensen, C./Project Censored (1994) *Censored: The News that Didn't Make the News and Why* (New York: Four Walls Eight Windows)

Kapuscinksi, Ryszard (1982) *Shah of Shahs* (London: Picador)

Kapuscinksi, Ryszard (1983) *The Emperor* (London: Picador)

Kapuscinksi, Ryszard (2001) *The Shadow of the Sun: My African Life* (London: Allen Lane/The Penguin Press)

Keane, Fergal (1995) *Season of Blood: A Rwandan Journey* (London: Viking)

Keeble, Richard (1999) 'A Balkan Birthday for NATO', *British Journalism Review*, Vol.10, No.2, pp.16–20

Kennedy, Paul (1989) *The Rise and Fall of the Great Powers: Economic Change and Military Conflict from 1500–2000* (London: Fontana)

Kirtley, Jane E. (1992) 'The Eye of the Sandstorm: The Erosion of First Amendment Principles in Wartime', *Government Information Quarterly*, Vol.9, No.4, pp.473–90

Knightley, Phillip (1982) *The First Casualty: The War Correspondent as Hero, Propagandist, and Myth Maker*, 2nd edition (London: Quartet)

Knightley, Phillip (1988) 'Foreign Bodies' (Part 3), *The Listener*, 2 June, pp.12–13

Knightley, Phillip (1995) 'The Cheerleaders of World War II', in *British Journalism Review*, Vol.6, No.2, pp.40–5

Kolbenschlag, George R. (1990) *A Whirlwind Passes: Newspaper Correspondents and the Sioux Indian Disturbances of 1890–91* (Vermillion, SD: University of South Dakota Press)

Laband, John and Ian Knight (1996) *The War Correspondents: The Anglo-Zulu War* (London: Bramley Books)

Lambert, Andrew and Stephen Badsey (1994) *The Crimean War: The War Correspondents* (London: Sutton)

Lambert, Derek (1987) *Just Like the Blitz: A Reporter's Notebook* (London: Hamish Hamilton)

Lande, Nathaniel (1996) *Dispatches from the Front: A History of the American War Correspondent*, (New York: Oxford University Press)

Lawrence, Anthony (1972) *A Foreign Correspondent* (London: Allen and Unwin)

Leslie, Jacques (1995) *The Mark: A War Correspondent's Memoir of Vietnam and Cambodia* (New York: Four Walls Eight Windows)

Lichtenberg, Judith (1996) 'In Defense of Objectivity Revisited', in Curran, James and Martin Gurevitch (eds) *Mass Media and Society*, 2nd edition (London: Edward Arnold)

Lippman, Walter (1992) 'Stereotypes, Public Opinion and the Press', in Cohen, E. (ed.) *Philosophical Issues in Journalism* (Oxford: Oxford University Press), pp.161–75

Livingston, Steven (1997) 'Clarifying the CNN Effect: An Examination of Media Effects According to Type of Military Intervention', Research Paper R-18 (Harvard: Joan Shorenstein Center Press/Politics/Public Policy)

Lukosiunas, Marius A. (1991) 'Enemy, Friend, or Competitor? A Content Analysis of the *Christian Science Monitor* and *Izvestia*', in Dennis, Everette E. et al (eds) *Beyond the Cold War: Soviet and American Media Images* (London: Sage), pp.100–10

MacArthur, J. (1992) *Second Front: Censorship and the Gulf War* (London: University of California Press)

MacGregor, Brent (1997) *Live, Direct and Biased? Making Television News in the Satellite Age* (London: Edward Arnold)

McLaughlin, Greg (1993) 'Coming In from the Cold: British TV Coverage of the East European Revolutions', in Aulich, James and Wilcox (eds) *Europe Without Walls: Art, Posters and Revolution 1989–93* (Manchester: Manchester City Art Galleries), pp.189–99

McLaughlin, Greg (1999) 'Refugees, Migrants and the Fall of the Berlin Wall', in Philo, Greg (ed.) *Message Received* (London: Longman), pp.197–209

McLaughlin, Greg (2001) 'War Reporting at the End of the 20th Century' in Fleming, Dan (ed.) *Formations: A 21st Century Media Studies Text Book* (Manchester: Manchester University Press), pp.116–19

McNair, Brian (1988) *Images of the Enemy* (London: Routledge)

McNair, Brian (1994) *News and Journalism in the UK* (London:Routledge)

McNulty, Mel (1999) 'Media Ethnicisation and the International Response to War and Genocide in Rwanda', in Tim Allen and Jean Seaton (eds) *The Media of Conflict: War Reporting and Representations of Ethnic Violence* (London: Zed Books) pp.268–86

Massing, Michael (1991) 'Another Front', *Columbia Journalism Review*, May/June, pp.23–4

Matthews, Herbert L. (1971) *A World in Revolution: A Newspaperman's Memoir* (New York: Scribner's)

Matthews, Lloyd J. (ed.) (1991) *Newsmen and National Defense: Is Conflict Inevitable?* (New York: Brassey's)

Mercer, Derek, Geoff Mungham and Kevin Williams (1987) *The Fog of War: The Media on the Battlefield* (London: Heinemann)

Mickiewicz, Ellen (1991) 'Images of America', in Dennis, Everette E. et al (eds) *Beyond the Cold War: Soviet and American Media Images* (London: Sage), pp.21–30

Miller, David (1994) *Don't Mention the War: Northern Ireland, Propaganda and the Media* (London: Pluto Press)

Mills, C. Wright (1959) *The Sociological Imagination* (Oxford: Oxford University Press)

Minear, Larry et al (1996) *The News Media, Civil War and Humanitarian Action* (London: Lynne Reiner Publishers)

Misser, Francois and Yves Jaumain (1994) 'Death By Radio', *Index on Censorship*, Vol.23, September/October, pp.72–4

Morrison, David and Howard Tumber (1988) *Journalists at War: The Dynamics of News Reporting During the Falklands War* (London: Sage)

Mowlana, Hamid et al (eds) (1992) *Triumph of the Image: The Media's War in the Persian Gulf* (Oxford: Westview Press)

Nash, William L. (1998) 'The Military and the Media in Bosnia', *Harvard International Journal Press/Politics*, Vol.3. No.4, pp.131–5

Neuman, Johanna (1995) *Lights, Camera, War!* (New York: St Martin's Press)

New Left Review (ed.) (1982) *Exterminism and Cold War* (London: Verso)

Nicholson, Michael (1993) *Natasha's Story* (London: Pan Books)

Page, Charles A. (1898) *Letters of a War Correspondent* (Boston, MA: LC Page & Co.)

Parenti, Michael (1993) *Inventing Reality: The Politics of the News Media*, 2nd edition (New York: St Martin's Press)

Pedelty, Mark (1995) *War Stories: The Culture of the Foreign Correspondent* (London: Routledge)

Perry, William J. (1996) 'The Pentagon and the Press', *Harvard International Journal of Press/Politics*, Vol.1, No.1, pp.121–6

Peters, Cynthia (ed.) (1992) *Collateral Damage: The New World Order at Home and Abroad* (Boston, MA: Southend Press)

Peters Talbott, Shannon (1996) 'Early Chechen Coverage Tests Print Journalists' Independence', *Transition*, 9 August, pp.48–51

Philips Price, Morgan (1997) *Dispatches from the Revolution, Russia 1916–18*, Tania Rose (ed.) (London: Pluto Press)

Philo, Greg and Greg McLaughlin (1995) 'The British Media and the Gulf War', in Philo, Greg (ed.) *The Glasgow Media Group Reader, Vol.2* (London: Routledge), pp.146–56

Pilger, John (2001) *Heroes* (London: Vintage), pp.254–65

Prochnau, William (1995) *Once Upon A Distant War* (New York: Times Books)

Richter, Andrei G. (1991) 'Enemy Turned Partner: A Content Analysis of *Newsweek* and *Novoye Vremya*', in Dennis, Everette E. et al (eds) *Beyond the Cold War: Soviet and American Media Images* (London: Sage), pp.91–9

Roth, Mitchel P. (ed.) (1997) *Historical Dictionary of War Journalism* (London: Greenwood Press)

Rothberg, Robert I. and Thomas G. Weiss (eds) (1996) *From Massacres to Genocide: The Media, Public Policy and Humanitarian Crises* (Cambridge, MA: Brookings/WPF)

Royle, Trevor (1989) *War Report: The War Correspondent's View of Battle from the Crimea to the Falklands* (London: Gratton Books)

Rutland, Peter (1996) 'Russian Television and the Chechen War', *OMRI Analytical Brief*, No.331, 10 September

Sabey, Ruth (1982) 'Disarming the Disarmers', in Aubrey, Crispin (ed.) *Nukespeak: The Media and the Bomb* (London: Comedia/Minority Press Group), pp.55–63

Sarkesian, Sam C. (1991) 'Soldiers, Scholars and the Media', in Matthews, Lloyd J. (ed.) *Newsmen and National Defense: Is Conflict Inevitable?* (New York: Brassey's), pp.61–9.

Schorr, Daniel (1995) 'Ten Days that Shook the White House', in Hiebert, R.E. (ed.) *Impact of Mass Media: Current Issues* (White Plains, NY: Longman), pp.53–7

Schudson, Michael (1978) *Discovering News* (New York: Basic Books)

Sebba, Anne (1994) *Battling For News: The Rise of the Women Reporter* (London: Sceptre)

Shakespeare, Nicholas (1998) 'Martha Gellhorn', *Granta No.62*, Summer, pp.215–35

Shaw, Martin (1996) *Civil Society and Media in Global Crises* (London: Pinter)

Sheehan, Neil (1989) *A Bright Shining Lie: John Paul Vann and America in Vietnam* (New York: Vintage)

Sobel, Richard (1998) 'Portraying American Public Opinion toward the Bosnian Crisis', *Harvard International Journal of Press Politics*, Vol.3, No.2, pp.16–33

Southworth, Herbert R. (1977) *Guernica! Guernica! A Study of Journalism, Diplomacy, Propaganda and History* (Berkeley: University of California Press)

Stenbuck, Jack (1995) *The Typewriter Battalion* (New York: William Morrow & Co. Inc.)

Streckfuss, Richard (1990) 'Objectivity in Journalism: A Search and a Reassessment', *Journalism Quarterly*, Vol.67, No.4, pp.973–83

Sussman, Leonard R. (1991) 'Dying (and Being Killed) on the Job: A Case Study of World Journalists, 1982–1987', *Journalism Quarterly*, Vol.68, No.1/2, Spring/Summer, pp.195–9

Sweeney, Michael S. (1998) ' "Delays and Vexations": Jack London and the Russo-Japanese War', *Journalism & Mass Communications Quarterly*, Vol.75, No.3, Autumn, pp.548–9

Tait, Richard (2001) 'Unacceptable Danger', International Press Institute, Vienna, Report No.1

Teichner, Martha (1996) 'No Sense at All', in *Media Studies Journal: Journalists in Peril*, Vol.10, No.4, Fall

Thompson, Edward (1982) 'Notes on Exterminism, the Last Stage of Civilization', in New Left Review (ed.) *Exterminsim and Cold War* (London: Verso), pp.1–34

Thomson, Alex (1992) *Smokescreen: The Media, the Censors, the Gulf* (Tunbridge Wells: Laburnham and Spellmount)

Tuchman, Gaye (1972) 'Objectivity as Strategic Ritual: An Examination of Newsmen's Notions of Objectivity', *American Journal of Sociology*, Vol.77, No.4, pp.660–70

Utley, Garrick (1998) 'The Shrinking of Foreign News: From Broadcast to Narrowcast', in Foote, Joe S. (ed.) *Live From the Trenches: The Changing Role of the Television News Correspondent* (Carbondale, IL: Southern Illinois University Press), pp.84–93

Vulliamy, Ed (1993) 'This War Has Changed My Life', *British Journalism Review*, Vol.4, No.2, pp.5–11

Wagner, Lydia (1989) *Women War Correspondents of World War II* (New York: Greenwood Press)

Wakefield, Dan (1974) 'The Personal Voice and the Impersonal Eye', in Weber, R. (ed.) *The Reporter As Artist: A Look at the New Journalism Controversy* (New York: Hastings House), pp.39–48

Ward, Stephen J. (1998) 'An Answer to Martin Bell: Objectivity and Attachment in Journalism', *International Journal Press/Politics*, Vol. 3, No.3, Cambridge, MA: MIT Press, pp.121–5

Washburn, Stanley (1982) *On the Russian Front in WWI: Memoirs of an American War Correspondent* (New York: Robert Spellar & Sons)

Weschler, Lawrence (1990) 'The Media's One and Only Freedom Story', in *Columbia Journalism Review*, March/April, pp.25–31

Williams, Kevin (1993) 'The Light at the End of the Tunnel: The Mass Media, Public Opinion and the Vietnam War', in Eldridge, John (ed.) *Getting the Message: News, Truth, Power* (London: Routledge) pp.305–30

Williams, Pete (1995) 'The Pentagon Position on Mass Media', in Hiebert, Ray Eldon (ed.) *Impact of Mass Media: Current Issues*, 3rd edition (White Plains, NY: Longman), pp.327–34

Williams Walsh, Mary (1990) 'Mission: Afghanistan', *Columbia Journalism Review*, January/February, pp.27–36

Wilson, Andrew (1982) 'The Defence Correspondent', in Aubrey, Crispin (ed.) *Nukespeak: The Media and the Bomb* (London: Comedia/Minority Press Group), pp.33–7

Woofinden, Bob (1988) 'Foreign Bodies' (Part 1), *The Listener*, 19 May, pp.14–15

Zassoursky, Yassen N. (1991) 'Changing Images of the Soviet Union and the United States', in Dennis, Everette E. et al (eds) *Beyond the Cold War: Soviet and American Media Images*, (London: Sage), pp.11–20

Index